South Yorkshire's Transport

ISBN 1 898432 33 3

Companion Volumes

Beyond Reality – *The Workington Factory story and the Final Years of Leyland Bus*

In course of preparation

Glasgow's Transport
40 Years buses in Sheffield – *colour album*

For full list of all bus, truck and rail titles from Venture Publications Ltd please send stamped addressed envelope to:

128 Pikes Lane, Glossop, Derbyshire SK13 8EH

Front Cover Illustration

Sheffield is unique in the UK in being able to show the bus and tram industry's respective products for the low-floor market, seen here in Hillsborough on a Supertram Duewag-built articulated unit and a Mainline Wright-bodied Volvo B10L. Behind is Hillsborough Barracks, completed in 1854 and since 1991 renovated for use as a commercial centre. The Supertram service through Hillsborough commenced on 23rd October 1995, the same day as the low-floor bus fleet was introduced on long-established services 13/14.

Photo: John A. Senior

Produced for the Publishers
Venture Publications, Glossop, Derbyshire,
by Mopok Graphics, Glossop SK13 8EH
using computerised origination

The British Bus and Truck Heritage

South Yorkshire's Transport

1974-1995

D Scott Hellewell

Venture *publications*

CONTENTS

PREFACE

Charles Hall's book *Sheffield Transport* took the story of the city's transport from its beginnings up to 1974, when big changes were about to take place. Two events happened on 1st April 1974: firstly the establishment of the South Yorkshire Metropolitan County Council and, secondly, the establishment of South Yorkshire Passenger Transport Executive (SYPTE). Both these events were to have major and dramatic effects on the provision of public transport, both in South Yorkshire and the rest of the country.

This book takes the story from these two events in 1974 up to the present day – a period of 21 years – and thus a time for reflection. Unlike Charles Hall's book this one looks at South Yorkshire, not just Sheffield. Because SYPTE had wider responsibilities than just running buses (important as that was) this book looks at transportation issues, including railways, as well as at bus operations. It looks at the direct operations of SYPTE (inherited from the former municipalities in Doncaster, Rotherham and Sheffield) as well as those of the former National Bus Company (NBC) subsidiaries and those of the independents who were gradually bought up by SYPTE.

The Metropolitan County lasted only for 12 years but during that time had a greater influence than any other on the provision and financing of public transport. Indeed it is arguable that its very success led to its own downfall, and that of the other metropolitan counties and GLC. Through all these vicissitudes SYPTE has continued, although stripped of its bus operating powers by the 1985 Transport Act. Of late, however, it has made its impact through investment in quality interchanges and bus stations and – above all – in South Yorkshire Supertram.

Shortly after the demise of SYCC on 31st March 1986, bus operation was deregulated on 26th October. The operational transition is dealt with in the book. The turmoil that has followed has led to a fascinating scene for the enthusiast, but one of total confusion to the passenger or bystander. Supertram works have added to the scene of confusion but the benefits are now just starting to be felt. Who knows what the future holds for South Yorkshire's transport?. On the national front there are signs of early stirrings that all is not well with public transport in Britain.

This book does not purport to be the official history of either South Yorkshire PTA or PTE. It is a record – hopefully accurate – of the events that have occurred in the provision of public passenger transport in South Yorkshire over the past 21 years. The Author was personally involved in this scene for 12 years from 1974 until 1988. He, therefore, brings to it a direct insight and personal commentary as to the events of that period – and what lay behind them. Not all involved may agree with the interpretation of events.

It is difficult with a book of this nature spanning such a long period not to be over-influenced by the benefit of hindsight. In compiling this book the Author has attempted to avoid falling into this trap. It is for the reader to judge whether he has been successful or not.

Public transport is about the movement of people. In Britain public transport policy has been a political football lacking the continuity found elsewhere in the developed world. During the period covered by this book there have been major social, organisational and political changes all of which have an effect – for good or bad – upon the market for, and operation of, public transport.

Continued overleaf

PREFACE

Continued from previous page

It is the Author's personal experience that the provision of public transport is, essentially, a team effort. This book too, could not have been written without the help of many people. Some have supplied written text, some information for the appendices, others photographs and reminiscences. The Author gratefully acknowledges their assistance.

Particular reference must be made of Simon Coventry, Rex Faulks, Norman Kay, Wilf Kemp, John Nelson, Bill Price and Duncan Roberts who supplied parts of the text. Bob Rowe also supplied parts of the text and helped edit the book. Reference must also be made to Ian Davies, Dennis Eyres, Bill Kirkland, Noel McDonald, Bill Morris, Garry Nolan, George Peach and John Swan who have commented on early drafts of the book.

Others who have helped in various ways include: John Hardey, Ian Hoskisson, John Jordan, Ivor Marshall, Mike Pestereff and Mike Thompson. I am also grateful to Peter Sephton for providing the Foreword.

Whilst the book reflects a team effort, the Author takes full responsibility for the contents, comments and opinions expressed. He hopes that people will find it of interest to read and as a book of reference. The story of South Yorkshire's Transport covers a fascinating period of public transport development and operation in Britain.

D. Scott Hellewell, FCIT, FIMgt
Wakefield

Summer 1996

Scott Hellewell is a former Vice President of the Chartered Institute of Transport and a Fellow of the Institute of Management. He is also a personal member of the International Union of Public Transport (UITP), and has served on both the International Commission on Traffic and Urban Planning and the International Light Rail Commission.

FOREWORD

Post-war public transport in Britain can have a whole range of descriptions applied to it – Cinderella, political football, unwanted orphan, music hall joke. Successive governments have disgracefully ignored the obvious – that Great Britain is too small a space to be swamped by the rising flood of motor vehicles.

The valuable contribution which high quality public transport can make towards improving the quality of life has been ignored in Britain for most of this century.

Nevertheless, in a few parts of the country a handful of visionary local people have tried to swim against the tide. Generally their efforts have eventually been washed away by the action of governments, who believed the motor car, private housing and road construction industries should be encouraged at any price.

South Yorkshire has been one of the outposts in which community life and values are still seen as important. Good public transport has been observed in other parts of the world to be the catalyst which produces a better quality of life for more people.

Children can gain independence at an earlier age where good public transport operates. From that they develop confidence. If the transport is of particularly high quality they also have less propensity to buy a car when old enough. Shared public facilities such as pubs, clubs, libraries, swimming pools and town-centre shopping are maintained at a higher level than in a mainly car dependent society. The elderly also enjoy a higher quality of life where good public transport enables them to retain mobility and continue their interests outside the home.

However, as people become more affluent, they seek a greater level of independence from others. They move out to the suburbs, buy more cars, shop at out of town supermarkets and drive their children to interminable activities by car. Public transport is seen for a period in their lives as unnecessary – required only for the young, poor, elderly and disadvantaged. The post-war years in Britain have seen this kind of life-style portrayed as the one to which all should aspire.

The history books will eventually record this period as one of the wasted opportunities of the 20th century. They will explain that investment in vastly improved public transport would have prevented such a high level of car dependence. This in turn would have reduced the political challenge of restricting the use of cars, a factor only being talked about as this book is published but inevitable in the years to come. By swimming against this tide, South Yorkshire actually achieved low car growth for fifteen years and could have continued indefinitely had the government not intervened.

Continued overleaf

Peter J Sephton BSc, CEng, MIMechE, MCIT
Chairman and Chief Executive
Mainline Group Ltd

Sheffield's Supertram system has to take its turn with other traffic in the on-street sections as seen here. Delays and frustrations are inevitable when road configurations create situations like this.

Continued from previous page

That is why this book by Scott Hellewell is an important oasis in an otherwise fairly barren desert. It records that, for the last 30 years of the 20th century, many people in the southern part of Yorkshire recognised the value of good public transport and tried valiantly to develop it. They were thwarted frequently – sometimes by central government, sometimes by their own inability to see the wood for the trees, sometimes by the sheer cost of it all, and sometimes by factors way beyond their control like the international price of oil. But they kept on trying and are still trying as they approach the end of the 20th century.

Scott Hellewell was an integral part of these efforts for a number of years. In particular he planned the visionary Supertram system for Sheffield and he designed the world's largest fare increase, when a 75% operating subsidy was removed under the controls imposed by Mrs Thatcher's Conservative government in 1985.

Some still regard South Yorkshire's transport aims as the aspirations of the 'loony left'. These people generally live outside the area. Of those who experienced these trials and tribulations at first hand, hardly anyone will criticise the underlying aim – a higher quality of life, through a higher quality of public transport.

You can read about the challenge of achieving this against the climate of the times in these pages. Long after the contributors have gone to that great bus station in the sky, others will judge whether we were all mad to try, or true visionaries!

Peter J Sephton BSc, CEng, MIMechE, MCIT
Chairman and Chief Executive
Mainline Group Ltd

Summer 1995

1 CHANGE and TRANSITION

The original four Passenger Transport Executives (PTEs) were established in 1969, as a result of the Transport Act 1968. A fifth PTE, Greater Glasgow, subsequently known as Strathclyde PTE, was established in 1973. When preparing the legislation which provided for the original PTEs the then Secretary of State for Transport, Barbara Castle, said that the public transport problems of the major conurbations were too pressing to wait for local government re-organisation which was then on the horizon. As a result South and West Yorkshire, or the West Riding as it then was, 'escaped' from being made fifth and sixth PTEs.

The West Riding County Council was the largest local government body outside London and had its base in Wakefield. The County of the West Riding of Yorkshire stretched from the Derbyshire border to near Ripon, and from Sedbergh to York – 50 miles x 50 miles. Within it were contained the cities of Bradford, Leeds, Sheffield and Wakefield and the County Boroughs of Halifax, Huddersfield, Dewsbury, Barnsley, Doncaster and Rotherham. The cities and county boroughs were unitary authorities whereas a two-tier system existed in the West Riding area. With the exception of Barnsley, Dewsbury and Wakefield, all the cities and County Boroughs operated their own bus services. In transportation terms the West Riding County Council was faced with inter-urban problems, whereas the other local authorities were concerned with urban issues. In spite of considerable 'joint-working' the native independence of Yorkshiremen often led to difficulties at the boundaries – a situation that did not seem to occur in SELNEC/Greater Manchester.

In truth the West Riding was two conurbations in one – hence in due time the establishment of the South and West Yorkshire Metropolitan County Councils. One was focused on Sheffield and the other on Leeds – the two principal cities of Yorkshire which had vied with each other for decades. There are numerous stories as to why or how one or two PTEs were not established in the West Riding in 1969: perhaps the area was just too complex, perhaps the problems were not that pressing. Through its Joint Board inheritance, Sheffield operated buses over a wide area reaching as far as Gainsborough, Manchester, Leeds, Buxton and Chesterfield. Although badly affected by the Beeching cuts to the railway network, there had been no history of rail commuting in South Yorkshire; the converse was true in West Yorkshire.

Whilst the original four PTEs were appointing their directors, Sheffield Transport Committee was appointing a new General Manager to succeed the revered Chaceley Humpidge, who had been in that post since 1961. Noel McDonald was appointed to the post in May 1969 from a similar position with Coventry City Transport – then about to be subsumed into West Midlands PTE. With the arrival of the first PTEs Sheffield was the plumb municipal job in England.

Shortly after his arrival, the redoubtable Alderman Sydney Dyson opened Sheffield Transport Department's (STD's) new offices in Exchange Street on 18th November, 1969. STD was at last able to move out of the rabbit warren at Division Street. The new General Manager was pitched into negotiations regarding the dismemberment of the Sheffield Joint Omnibus Committee (SJOC) where he had the title of 'Secretary'. (These JOCs were a feature unique to Yorkshire, the others being based on Halifax, Huddersfield and Todmorden.). Section 29 of the 1968 Act required the British Railways Board (BRB) to dispose of its interests in the JOCs and for these to be transferred to the National Bus Company (NBC), formed to control the major bus-operating companies in England and Wales under Section 24 of the same Act. Noel McDonald felt that the JOCs were a good concept. The relationship had lasted over 40 years with the Railways benefitting from the bus operating expertise of the municipality. NBC did not need that expertise – it already had it. Although a new organisation, NBC inherited its operating companies from the two major groups, British Electric Traction (BET) and Tilling. The latter had been state-owned since 1948 but BET had sold its bus-operating interests in the run up to the 1968 Act.

It is probably worth re-capping the Joint Committee arrangements. In 1928 the four main Railway Companies applied for and obtained from Parliament powers to provide, own and operate motor omnibuses in any district served by the Companies. Powers were also obtained by the Companies to make working arrangements with any Local Authority, owning or operating road vehicles and providing passenger services. Strong opposition was offered by municipalities and as a result protection was given for services established in the local areas.

As a result of these powers the LMS and LNER Railways intimated to Sheffield Corporation their intention to operate motor omnibuses in certain areas under amicable arrangements, but not in competition with the Corporation. The City Council delegated powers to the Tramways and Motors Committee to direct the operation, and the organisation of day to day running, which was to be managed by a General Manager, Deputy General Manager, Chief Engineer, Chief Accountant and Traffic Superintendent. After lengthy discussion proposals developed on the following lines:

Category 'A' Routes. The Omnibus routes which both commenced and finished within the City Boundary – to remain the property of the Sheffield Corporation.

Category 'B' Routes. Services within a defined area, extending varying distances up to 12 miles beyond the City Boundary, a joint operation of the Corporation and the railways.

Category 'C' Routes. Routes extending for longer distances, well beyond the City Boundary, e.g. Manchester, Gainsborough and Bakewell, wholly owned by the railways but operated by the Corporation.

The Railway Companies agreed to purchase at an agreed valuation 50% of the capital value of the vehicles involved in the Category 'B' Routes and the whole of the value of the vehicles in the 'C' Routes together with a sum for goodwill.

The Sheffield Joint Omnibus Committee, which was a partnership between the Corporation, the LMS and LNER, (subsequently the British Railways Board), was set up with half the members appointed by the Corporation and half from the Railways. The Chairman was appointed in alternate years by the Corporation and the Railways. The General Manager of the undertaking was the permanent Secretary of the Joint Committee and the Corporation operated the services as agents for the Railway.

Buses were purchased by the Corporation for the 'A' Services, and jointly by the Corporation and the Railways for the 'B' Services, and by the Railways for the ' C' Services. Operating expenses were charged to the appropriate service on an agreed basis, and traffic receipts went directly to the owner of the Category.

In the event of a failure to reach agreement in the Joint Committee, provision was made for an arbitrator to be appointed and that would be a body such as the (now Chartered) Institute of Transport. At no time during the existence of the Joint Committee did it become necessary to take action under this provision. Four weekly financial statements were prepared for each category and annual accounts which were subject to audit by representatives of the Railway's chief accountants office.

Under the 1968 Transport Act the Railway bus interests were transferred to the National Bus Company, and after insurmountable problems between the two-parties arising from the Corporation's insistence in maintaining its low fares policy, which prevented the Joint Committee from increasing fares, agreement was reached for the Corporation to purchase all the Category 'B' services and certain Category 'C' services. In October 1969 the Sheffield Joint Committee ceased to operate after 40 years service to the local community.

Charles Hall[1] described the situation thus: "After a long period of negotiation it was finally announced in

(1) Sheffield Transport (TPC 1975). See page 157 for all bracketed text references.

October 1969 that an agreement had been reached under which the Joint Committee would cease to operate and that the Corporation would take over the whole of the Category 'B' services and vehicles. So far as the 'C' Category were concerned the Corporation was not so successful – only three routes, those to Ashton Derwent, Snake Inn and Bakewell via Baslow were to be taken over. There was to be joint operation by the Corporation and NBC on routes to Doncaster, Barnsley, Halifax, Upton, Gainsborough and Manchester". The mechanism by which this complex deal was to take place was through a newly established NBC subsidiary – APT – Amalgamated Passenger Transport Ltd (not to be confused with British Rail's APT!). APT was also involved in complex transfers in West Yorkshire involving Todmorden & Halifax JOC's and Hebble Motor Services Ltd – with some ex-Sheffield JOC vehicles passing to Hebble, and thence to Halifax Corporation! In 1981, it became a central engineering organisation for NBC dealing with reclaimed units from withdrawn vehicles.

The Emerging Scene

From 1945 onwards, as new buses and spares became available, and fuel supplies increased, most of the bus operating mileage curtailed during the war was restored. New services were introduced to meet new demands from housing and industrial developments and passenger numbers rose to levels that, in many cases, were much higher than in pre-war days.

Although costs were rising, so were passenger numbers, and increased fares' revenue kept pace with costs at first, but eventually undertakings had to start increasing the fares, even though many of them were reluctant to do so because they had kept them unchanged for 20 years or more. During the period 1949/51 most operators increased charges and from then on there was a steady decline in passenger numbers, as more cars became available and fares continued to increase. Sheffield City Transport's experience was typical: annual passenger journeys fell from 315m to 188m between 1950 and 1970, a reduction of 40%.

To reduce costs operators reduced the amount of service mileage run, to match the declining patronage, but less frequent services were not as attractive to passengers. The vicious circle of increased costs, higher fares, passenger losses and reduced mileage had begun. This process was accelerated by the increasing availability and use of private cars, which not only took away passengers but also caused congestion. Changed social habits, including home television replacing the cinema, reduced the market. Increasingly fewer and fewer services were profitable and the need to cross-subsidise the weaker routes led to disproportionate fare increases on the 'good' routes. This accelerated the loss of passengers who saw cars as a cheaper alternative, as well as being more convenient. Thinking busmen began to realise that if these trends were not checked, buses would be left as 'residual carriers' of the 'have nots' and those who were too young or too old to drive a car.

The growing congestion of vehicles in urban areas did

not lead only to delay for buses, it triggered off one-way traffic schemes, pedestrianised areas and other traffic management arrangements, that usually made buses less attractive, by making routes less direct, and often restricted penetration into the central areas of cities and towns.

Town planners and highway and traffic engineers grew more concerned about the effects of the numbers of vehicles on the road, and the Buchanan Report "Traffic in Towns"[2] in 1962 expressed these concerns in a powerful way. Some possible solutions or easements were suggested for urban areas, and it was apparent that any major improvements would be very costly. The British bus industry began to realise that it could still have an important role in finding solutions to the traffic problems of urban areas and that this would require investment in public transport, with revenue support where justified, and with traffic management schemes that gave priority to the needs of public transport services. Some operators had an ambivalent attitude towards the idea of financial support, seeing it as a subsidy for those who could not run profitably, rather than as a payment for services that gave benefits to other members of the public, as well as their passengers. Within the industry there had always been cross-subsidisation between routes. Perhaps they were just being realistic because, although highway engineers, planners, interested academics and others could identify a changing role for local public transport, it was some time before national and local government were persuaded to find cash to fund it.

In 1964 there was a General Election and a change in Government with the election of the first Wilson administration. In 1966, following Barbara Castle's appointment as Secretary of State for Transport in December 1965, a White Paper "Transport Policy"[3] was published which gave a complete re-think to the nation's transport policy. In the conurbations it proposed the establishment of Conurbation Transport Authorities (CTAs) which would have had wide powers over the planning and operation of public transport, as well as having highways and car parking powers. Following considerable discussion within the 'transportation world' another White Paper "Public Transport & Traffic"[4] was published in 1967. This proposed the establishment of Passenger Transport Authorities (PTAs). These were to be responsible for the provision of public transport services. Gone were the highway and parking powers – not to be resurrected until the establishment of the Metropolitan Counties in 1974.

The proposals of the 1967 White Paper were incorporated into the Transport Bill of the same year, which became the Transport Act of 1968[5]. The PTAs were to be set up as policy-making bodies within their areas and the executive function was to pass to Passenger Transport Executives, the professional bodies which would run the services. This legislation set up the original four PTA/PTEs in SELNEC (later to become Greater Manchester), Tyneside (later to become Tyne & Wear), Merseyside (based on Liverpool) and West Midlands (based on Birmingham). These PTEs were established in 1969, taking over the municipal passenger transport

undertakings in their areas a few months later. By 1974, good progress had been made on integrating bus operations, standardising fares and conditions, improving services, co-ordinating public transport, highway, traffic and land-use, planning and investing in bus and rail infrastructure etc. Elsewhere some bus priorities and traffic management schemes had been introduced, but progress was slow.

Planning of bus and rail services needed to be done on a more comprehensive basis with more concern for connection and interchange between services. There was a need for greater standardisation of fare charges and conditions of travel. Transport planning also needed to have greater regard for highway, traffic and land use planning.

Financial support for public transport by local authorities (including those on which PTAs had precepted) had grown more widespread and had increased from 1m in 1964 to 19m in 1973.

The period between 1969 and 1974, when the South Yorkshire PTE was formed, was a very unsettled period for the Sheffield Transport Department. In addition to the change of general manager, Sheffield changed its political party and that brought changes in the Department's direction, including the transfer of its computer to the City Treasurer and the loss of some financial control. Labour relations had deteriorated during 1968 and the new general manager was faced with negotiating conditions which allowed services to operate in a normal manner. Noel McDonald recalls that 1972/73 was a particularly bad time as he had three main concerns: running STD; winding up the JOC and acting as 'shadow' DG. It was a very demanding period. Sheffield had been in the vanguard of introducing free concessionary travel for the elderly and disabled, but apart from that STD had operated in the traditional way. The Transport Department was beginning to change significantly and its shape was to be completely altered with the introduction of the Passenger Transport Executive. Noel McDonald felt that the concept of PTEs was right. The old days and the old arrangements, which had provided the City with a fine system, were coming to an end and there was a need to follow through into the new legislation.

On 1st April, 1974 the South Yorkshire Passenger Transport Executive (along with its twin, the West Yorkshire Passenger Transport Executive) was born. A product of the Local Government Act, 1972[6], the Executive, based in Sheffield, was to 'secure the provision of a properly integrated and efficient system of public passenger transport to meet the needs of its area' which, in this case was South Yorkshire. The new Executive assumed responsibility for securing the provision of all public transport in its area. It had the option of taking planning and financial responsibility for local train services, both within its area and up to 25 miles beyond the County boundary. It was also responsible for a large amount of direct bus operation.

PTEs absorbed only the municipally owned bus undertaking which were based in their areas; they had no powers to acquire compulsorily any others (which were mainly the operating subsidiaries of the then new, but now defunct, National Bus Company). Under Section 24 there was a requirement for mutual co-operation, and their services were subject to Traffic Commissioner approval. Section 19, which would have enabled the Executives to replace the Traffic Commissioner by taking responsibility for the licensing system, was never implemented. Nevertheless they were required to 'integrate', a stronger term than to 'co-ordinate' as it means to combine into a whole.

The PTEs had three main duties:

1) To operate the existing bus fleets inherited from the former municipalities
2) To make agreements with others for the provision of bus and, possibly, train services.
3) To develop and market the integrated transport system

The South Yorkshire PTE evolved amid the turmoil of a massive re-organisation of local government. The old county boroughs and many of the counties were disbanded and in their place came a two-tier organisation of county and district councils, with different responsibilities and new boundaries, and those counties which embraced the major conurbations were designated metropolitan counties. Section 202 of the 1972 Act decreed that all metropolitan counties should become passenger transport areas and were thereby brought within the scope of the 1968 Act, in that they would have a PTE with all that went with it. South Yorkshire was now a Metropolitan County. The new Executive, therefore, by authority of Section 17, assumed ownership and control of three municipal bus undertakings, owned by the former County Borough Councils (now Metropolitan District Councils) of Sheffield, Rotherham and Doncaster. The fourth former County Borough Council in the new South Yorkshire, Barnsley, did not own a bus undertaking. Services in that area were provided by Yorkshire Traction Ltd., a National Bus subsidiary, and were not directly affected by the municipal upheaval. They will be discussed in Chapter 8.

This was the background with which the new Executive team came together late in 1973, and took over their responsibilities in South Yorkshire on 1st April 1974. Two Directors had come from the other earlier-established PTEs, which they had similarly helped to develop. The question in everyone's mind was whether things would

Although no electrically powered vehicles were transferred to the PTE fleet, each of the constituent municipalities had a long history of association with electric street transport. Sheffield operated electric trams from 1898 until 1960; Doncaster electric trams from 1902 until 1935 and trolleybuses from 1928 until 1963; Rotherham electric trams from 1903 to 1949 and trolleybuses from 1912 to 1965.

carry on as before, but there were doubts on the horizon with a suspicion that the independence of the original PTEs might be challenged by the new metropolitan counties.

All was contained in the Local Government Act, 1972 – a voluminous document with 274 Sections and 30 Schedules. It was Section 202 which had particular relevance – a relatively short section, which on the face of things, was fairly innocuous. The relevant parts of the 1968 Act became applicable, the Executive retained its statutory duty and it was still a body corporate with a Common Seal. A deeper scrutiny, however, revealed a few subtle changes. The passenger transport areas were now the metropolitan counties. The two boundaries were, therefore, coterminous and there was only one political body from which to draw membership of the PTA. The County Council was, in fact, the PTA. This was very different from the previously independent PTAs. For example, there were 30 members on SELNEC PTA (including 4 Ministerial appointees) representing 67 local authorities. As the PTEs would now be under the complete policy control of the County Council, there was the likelihood of a political Transport Committee which might well deliberate on all manner of detail. But not everything appeared in Section 202. It was Schedule 24 which made numerous amendments to the 1968 Act. It was evident that the Minister had surrendered most of his authority to the counties but of particular importance in this context was an addition to the 1968 Act in the form of a new section – Section 15A.

Section 15 of the 1968 Act defined those things for which the Executives were required to obtain Authority approval. They were all broad policy matters such as major re-organisations of services, annual estimates of income and expenditure, proposals to support local railway services and fares revisions. Section 15A went much further than that. The Authorities were now empowered to give directions to the Executives on any matter, including the exercise and performance of their functions and duties, as laid down in Section 9. The Authorities could now also require the Executive to provide any information, be it financial or operational, and to review their organisations with a view to directing changes to 'secure that the Executive's undertaking is organised in the most efficient manner' and the Executive could not make changes without Authority approval. In theory at least, therefore, there was little independence left, even though they were still bodies corporate with their statutory duties unchanged.

It was understandable that life began with some trepidation. The Executive saw itself as an independent body with its defined powers, duties and Common Seal. Its accounts were prepared under Companies Act requirements, and not those of local government. As will be seen in Chapter 5, the trade unions quickly saw the Executive as their employer with whom they would negotiate; they were quite clear on this issue. But the County Council would like to have seen the PTE as just another department. The County Council was not just a small body of politicians, it had ample professional staff and one of its functions was 'traffic and transportation'!

In due course the Chief Executive and the Secretary of the County Council were to become part-time directors of the PTE which produced a curious situation at Board Meetings, with the Director General (to the County Council in one sense another departmental head) in the Chair.

"Ah yes," said the pundits. "We have reached the ideal. For years bus managements have been unable to get the traffic priorities they would like and now they are a part of the same organisation as the highway authority – the way is now clear for the problems to be solved." Hence the metropolitan counties became analogous to the CTA's proposed in the 1966 White Paper 'Transport Policy'. The accuracy of this assessment remained to be seen. More to the point, there was reason to doubt whether the Executive would be left to paddle its own canoe. The Executive's independence was being strongly challenged. This is not to decry the effectiveness of the County Council staff. On the contrary, collectively, they held a wealth of expertise; it was more a case of 'were there too many cooks ...?' The fact that things did get done – and achievements there were over the ensuring 12 years as will be chronicled in the chapters which follow – was due more to the integrity, goodwill and co-operation of all involved in the provision of passenger transport in South Yorkshire at that time, than to the organisational machinery that had been created.

The mention of 12 years in a history of the first 21 years is interesting. This is the period of time that the system was destined to run before another re-organisation loomed. A Local Government Act, 1985 was to come and its effects would be far reaching and devastating. The PTEs survived but with very different responsibilities, but we are now running ahead of ourselves. Suffice to say that just as 1974 was a watershed, so was 1986.

Prior to 1974 the South Yorkshire area had been more dependent on public transport than the rest of the country. The level of incomes was lower than elsewhere. In 1974 the average wage of full-time male employees was 16% below comparable rates in London, and 5% lower even than relatively depressed areas such as Merseyside. For women the comparison was worse. Car ownership was also much lower than nationally and it had been calculated that at least 75% of the population was dependent on public transport.

It has to be remembered that until 1968 bus fares were set at commercial levels and, as has already been commented upon, the declining number of 'good' routes were cross-subsidising an increasing number of 'poor' routes. Furthermore, traffic congestion was increasing, delaying bus services and increasing operating costs. A two-pronged attack was needed: improvements to allow buses to operate efficiently and subsidies to keep fare increases to more reasonable levels. This action to be taken pending investment in some improved forms of public transport and the benefits stemming from developing an integrated network.

In anticipation of the establishment of the metropolitan counties, and of the Structure Plan process, a new method of funding transportation investment was introduced in 1973 – Transport Policies and Programmes (TPP's). The

TPP's included three timescales: one year, five years and 15 years. Effectively it proposed a budget for the first year, a rolling programme of works for the following five years and a long-term review. Unfortunately after a few years the TPP system degenerated into a bid for money and nothing more – but that's another story. The TPP system covered both revenue and capital accounts – the former covering subsidies. Using revenue support to restrain fare increases, and thus stem the loss of passengers, was a somewhat crude approach. It, of course, appealed to politicians because it has immediate electoral benefits, whereas investment inevitably took some time before there was a pay-back. In the meantime, holding down fares in parts of South Yorkshire in the years 1972 to 1974 had proved to be effectively retaining passengers. Fares had not been increased in Doncaster or Sheffield since 1971. This was the background against which the County Council's transport policies were developed.

The section of the South Yorkshire Labour Party's Manifesto referring to public transport and planning was welcomed by the Executive, being consistent with the aims of the 1968 Act, and with the view of many in the industry. This and the manifesto reference to free transport for all being the ultimate aim are dealt with in Chapter 3.

S/R LUTS

The final element in this period of change and transition was the Sheffield & Rotherham Land Use/Transportation Study (S/R LUTS for short)[7]. Consultants – Martin & Vorhees Associates (MVA) – had been commissioned jointly by the West Riding County Council and the Councils of Sheffield & Rotherham, to undertake a land use/ transportation study in 1972.

The S/R LUTS was undertaken by a joint West Riding County Council/Consultant team in the years 1972–1975.

It was one of the last major LUTS funded principally by Central Government. It came towards the end of the period which had run since the war when the car and its infrastructure had been omnipotent – the run-down in public transport was substantial in this period, although subsidy of bus and rail was growing.

However, when the South Yorkshire Metropolitan County Council came into being during the Study, there was a very strong pro-public transport lobby, which was to manifest itself in very high levels of fare subsidy.

The Study was required by Central Government to recommend whether all the major highway construction in the County was either necessary or justified. It was also required to determine whether additional investment in public transport was justified, and if so, to make recommendations as to the most economically efficient investment. The capital budget for the period 1971–1986 was put at £70 – £75m[17].

S/R LUTS was a major study in so far as it incorporated a major data collection exercise and the development of a new transport planning model. A major complication during the study was the massive inflation in the 1972–74 period with annual rates in excess of 25%.

The Study was innovative in a number of ways, particularly in respect of the interface with the public, who were consulted at several stages, the concentration on the environment and on major improvements to the public transport system.

A conventional process of narrowing down, from many ideas to one preferred strategy, was employed. A vast range of highway, public transport and environmental solutions were examined during the course of the Study.

A 'provisional plan' was produced in late 1974 and evaluated by the Study Team, and also by means of a major community involvement programme. The major planks of the Provisional Plan included several new roads, a major investment in rail including a new loop line under the centre of Sheffield (see Chapter 10), a large number of bus priority measures, particularly in the southern corridors, and a number of measures to improve the quality of the environment in residential areas and city centre.

Generally the recommendations of the Provisional Plan were well received. However, a more detailed evaluation of the rail loop suggested it could not really be justified. During the early stages of the study 'Minitram' had been investigated and subsequently dropped, and also a large number of both 'on and off street' tramways had been studied. There was considerable enthusiasm for the tram proposals and very strong lobbying for their formal inclusion in the final recommendations.

The budget allocation (1972 prices) for the Provisional Plan was:

	£m
Bus Improvements	10.8
Traffic Management	3.5
Rail Improvements	19.0
New roads & road improvements	22.0
Remedial measures	2.1
	58.3

The tramways represented a major investment, and within the very limited capital budget (now £55m), could not be justified. However, a number of routes, including those incorporated into Supertram (see Chapter 14), were recommended to be built as soon as money could be made available. In the meantime reservations of rights of way was recommended and accepted by the new County Council.

Sadly many of the public transport and environmental recommendations were not implemented. However, the Passenger Transport Executive continued to support public transport, had put very considerable amounts of money into supporting the railways and, most recently, had invested in the Light Rail System.

The Joint Planning & Transportation Unit (JPTU) took the S/R LUTS model and developed it to cover the north of the County. A Barnsley LUTS had been completed in 1972 and a parallel study was undertaken in Doncaster between 1972 and 1974[17]. This work was to form the foundations for both the County Structure Plan and the PTE's own Development Plan.

2 SOUTH YORKSHIRE COUNTY COUNCIL

Metropolitan Government

The six new Metropolitan County Councils that came into existence on April 1st 1974 had their origins in the Redcliffe-Maud Commission, established in 1966 by the then Labour Government. It reported its findings in 1969 and proposed a two-tier approach for the major conurbations: Liverpool, Manchester and Birmingham but not for the West Riding of Yorkshire. In South Yorkshire the Commission proposed one authority based on Doncaster and one called Sheffield and South Yorkshire, the latter including the County Boroughs of Barnsley, Rotherham and Sheffield, the Urban and Rural Districts of the former WRCC, as well as a chunk of Derbyshire.

One of the members of the Commission, Derek Senior, produced a minority report in which he criticised the discrepancies in the sizes of Metropolitan districts. He also criticised the Commission's proposals for unitary authorities outside the three conurbations mentioned above. This minority report sparked off lively discussion between both local government officers and councillors. This led to the Labour Party suggesting that two-tier government should be adopted for, amongst other places, Leeds, Sheffield and Tyneside.

In February 1970 the Labour government published its White Paper *Local Government Reform*. It proposed five Metropolitan counties: Birmingham, Liverpool, Manchester, the West Riding of Yorkshire and South Hampshire (based on Southampton). In the 1970 election, Edward Heath and the Conservatives replaced Harold Wilson's Labour administration. In turn they produced a White Paper on local government and the idea was mooted for the first time of six Metropolitan Counties: the 'regular three', Merseyside, Greater Manchester and West Midlands, plus Tyneside (from the Labour White Paper) and 'the new two' West and South Yorkshire (8). With a gestation period of this length and complexity, it is amazing that metropolitan counties had such a short life – lasting only twelve years. However, it is also hardly surprising that they were intended to make an impact on the local government scene in general, and on public transport in particular. Perhaps it also throws some light on why South Yorkshire did not become a Passenger Transport Area until 1974.

Metropolitan County Councils were responsible for: strategic planning, highways, passenger transport, consumer protection, police, fire, emergency planning and recreation. Metropolitan District Councils – of which there were four in South Yorkshire: Barnsley, Doncaster, Rotherham and Sheffield – were responsible for: education, social services, housing, local plans, environmental health, libraries, leisure services and rating. It is interesting to note that Shire County Councils had two additional, big-spending functions that their Metropolitan brothers did not have: namely, education and social services.

The New County

Of the six Metropolitan Counties, South Yorkshire was the second largest in size (West Yorkshire being the largest) and the smallest but one in population (Tyne and Wear being the smallest). Accordingly it had the lowest population density (8.3 persons per hectare). Although the image of South Yorkshire was one of 'dark satanic mills' (more accurately coal mines and steelworks), over 70% of it was officially classed as 'countryside', with over 50% of the land in agricultural use[8].

South Yorkshire stretched from the Derbyshire border just south of Sheffield (unchanged by the re-organisation) to a line drawn between Barnsley & Wakefield. It stretched from west of Penistone to Thorne, just short of Goole. It thus included a substantial part of the high Pennine moors; a small part of the Peak District National Park; the Sheaf, Don and Dearne valleys and the flat lands (sometimes marshlands) around Doncaster. Its principal industries were coal (everywhere), steel (concentrated around Rotherham and Sheffield), chemicals (all along the Don Valley) and a whole variety of engineering: cutlery and precision steels in Rotherham and Sheffield and more general engineering elsewhere.

There were four principal towns – each with a very distinct character – Barnsley, Doncaster, Rotherham, and Sheffield. Although Sheffield was by far the largest in population terms and the county's only City, it is probably true to say that Doncaster had the most diffuse economy, and had succeeded better than the others in widening its economic base. It also had the famous railway works – 'The Plant'. In many respects Doncaster was South Yorkshire's 'Coventry'. It looked much more to Leeds and, to a lesser extent York, than to Sheffield, this being largely due to the development of the railway network.

Prior to 1974 there were 33 separate councils in what became South Yorkshire: four County Boroughs (which each became metropolitan districts), twenty Urban Districts and nine Rural Districts. Barnsley MDC had to assimilate thirteen UDCs or RDCs into itself; Doncaster had to encompass nineteen, Rotherham six but Sheffield only two. This goes some way to explaining why so many Sheffield councillors could be 'spared' to go to the County Council, where they were to have such a dramatic effect. It also explains why South Yorkshire County Council had

100 members; the streamlined metropolitan government had reduced the representation of the people.

The first official meeting of the South Yorkshire Metropolitan County Joint Committee (the preparatory body for the future County Council) took place in Sheffield Town Hall on 17th February, 1972[8]. There had, however, been various preparatory or working meetings before that. Two important and mould-making decisions were taken: one political, the other administrative. The political decision was to appoint Alderman Sir Ron Ironmonger as Chairman and Alderman J. S. Crowther as Vice-Chairman of the Joint Committee. Both were men of stature in their localities and both were Leaders of their respective Councils, Sheffield and Rotherham. The second decision was to appoint D. B. Harrison (Town Clerk of Sheffield) and P. J. Butcher (Clerk to the WRCC) as Joint Secretaries.

This first meeting also agreed to establish a number of working parties to collate information and give advice; of relevance in this context were working parties for Transportation, Planning, Highways and Traffic. Having three Working Parties was a surprising decision, having regard to the fact that by the 1970s there were many local authorities with Joint Planning and Transportation Committees or Highways and Planning Committees. It is also of interest to note the title 'transportation' rather than 'transport', when it was clearly going to look at public transport matters, including the municipal inheritance.

In parallel with these arrangements the Labour Party formed working parties related to the policy areas referred to above. They drew their membership from interested party members in the District Labour Parties. These working groups were to lay the framework for the County election manifesto. One of these working parties covered the areas of planning, transportation and industrial development – an interesting grouping, and already showing the broader approach to 'transportation' that was to be adopted in South Yorkshire. Indeed, the final report of this group included the comment that it had hoped to produce '... a sound Socialist basis for the programmes of the new County Council'.[8]

Traffic & Transportation Planning

Because of the importance they attached to these policy documents, the County Labour Party published them to ensure widespread knowledge. In the present context it is only relevant to look in some detail at what was said about Traffic & Transportation Planning. Highlights include:-

- a commitment to the principle that public transport should be regarded both as a social service and an instrument of planning policy
- a regret that the non-municipal transport undertakings were not to be transferred to the new PTE
- an agreement to set up joint consultation arrangements between the County Council and Metropolitan District Councils
- the need to improve the bus service in many of the more rural areas of the County

- free public transport for the elderly, handicapped and disabled as an immediate objective. (This to be regarded as a first step towards the ultimate provision of free public transport for all.)
- the need to examine ways of improving the running times of buses by the provision of bus-only lanes and other priority or exclusivity measures
- great importance was attached to the integration of rail and bus services (and to oppose any further curtailment of rail services catering for South Yorkshire).
- discouragement of the use of private cars in urban centres for commuting (because they choke roads at peak periods and occupy parking spaces throughout the day)
- urgently to review all existing road programmes.

In this can clearly be seen the foundations of the Grand Design which will be considered in the next Chapter. In the meantime we should get back to the organisation and administration of the new County Council itself.

Elections

The elections for the new Council took place on 12th April, 1973. Not surprisingly Labour won South Yorkshire with 82 out of the 100 seats. (Labour also won the other five new Met. Counties and regained control of the Greater London Council (GLC).) There were thirteen Conservatives, four Independents and one Liberal. The election for the new Metropolitan District Councils took place on 10th May and all four South Yorkshire Districts became Labour controlled, although as it turned out their shades of red varied considerably. Sir Ron Ironmonger became the Leader of the new County Council and Tom Baynham (a former Leader of the WRCC) became the Council's first Chairman – a political post, not a civic functionary in the mould of a Lord Mayor[8].

Elections for Committee Chairmanships and other appointments took place on 16th April, 1973. Appointments of interest are: Ken Sampey, ex-Chairman of Doncaster Corporation Transport Committee became Deputy Leader and Deputy Chairman of the Transport Committee. Roy Thwaites became the Labour Whip and Chairman of the County's Transport Committee – both positions having been filled by him in Sheffield. George Henry Moores of Rotherham became Chairman of the Highways Committee, with David Glover of Doncaster as his Deputy. Councillor John Driver and Councillor Charlie Smith were Chairman and Deputy Chairman, respectively, of the Planning Committee. George Henry Moores was Chairman of the Joint Planning and Transportation Sub-Committee.

This Joint Sub-Committee was an interesting arrangement set up to oversee the work of the Joint Planning and Transportation Unit (JPTU) – of which more anon. Officially it was a sub-committee of the three principal committees – highways, planning and transport – but in many respects it acted as a co-ordinating committee above them. Sometimes reports went to the Joint Sub before going to a main Committee, as would be expected with a sub-committee; on other occasions reports went to, or were 'received' by, one of the principal committees before being passed to the Joint Sub. The Joint P & T Sub-Committee consisted of the Chairman and Deputy Chairman of the Highways, Planning and Transport Committees, together with the Leader and Deputy Leader of the County Council and two Councillors from the Opposition.

Each of the three principal committees involved in transport matters formed four Area Sub-Committees – one for each of the Metropolitan Districts. However, in the case of Transport these Sub-Committees were Area Advisory Sub-Committees – a subtly different status reflecting the PTE's independence from the County Council. These Sub-Committees were made up of members from both the County Council and appropriate District Councils.

The full County Council became the Passenger Transport Authority, although it exercised its powers through the Transport Committee which had substantial delegated powers. The Council also had a Policy Committee with Policy Advisory Sub-Committees and a Budget Sub-Committee that dealt with major financial matters involving the PTE. The Policy Committee was the power-house of the Council and the Chief Officers reported to it. The Director General was a member of the Chief Officer's Team, although the Chief Executive had no authority over him.

Later the Council had formed a new Passenger Transport Finance sub-Committee and among the items that the PTE had asked to go on the Agenda for its first meeting in September 1973 was the item – Simplified fares proposal. The same item appeared on many more Agendas before simplified fares were eventually introduced in 1984.

Officers

F. A. (Tony) Mallet was appointed the Chief Executive of the new County Council. P. J. Butcher, who had been Joint Secretary of the interim Joint Committee stayed to become Chief Executive of the West Yorkshire CC. Tony Mallet had been Peter Butcher's deputy in the WRCC at Wakefield. The County Secretary – a new type of post – was filled by John Harris, an ambitious local government officer, who came from Bournemouth, but had previously worked in the UKAEA. David Chynoweth was appointed the County Treasurer – the youngest in the country at the age of 32. He came to South Yorkshire from Essex County Council. All three officials were to feature often in the PTE debates and public transport issues.

Norman Ellis was appointed County Engineer, he had been Deputy County Engineer in the former WRCC. He was skilled both technically – particularly in transportation issues – and with regard to dealing with councillors. He had a great sense of fun. He retired in 1979 to be replaced by John Kirkham. John had been Head of the Direct Works Organisation in Sheffield. From the start the Deputy County Engineer had been Keith Williams who moved to become County Surveyor in West Sussex in 1980. Keith Williams was succeeded as Deputy by Ivor Marshall, the former Chief Engineer Major Works. Fours years later,

when John Kirkham retired, Ivor Marshall became County Engineer – the last person to hold that post.

M. J. (Mike) Thompson was appointed County Planning Officer. Mike had been one of the two Assistant County Planning Officers with the West Riding with responsibilities for urban areas, including transportation and development. He was an extremely able town planner and had a knack of getting on with everyone. Whilst the County Engineer had two deputies, the County Planning Officer had only one, and he headed up the Joint Planning and Transportation Unit (JPTU), to which reference has already been made. P. J. (Peter) Mason filled this post – he had been a Section Engineer in the Forward Planning Group in WRCC where he had worked to Norman Ellis. When Peter Mason left in 1981 to go to Lothian Regional Council as Head of the Roads Department, Bill Morris, previously one of the Chief Engineers, took over as Head of the JPTU. The JPTU was a major innovation. It was staffed by people from the County Engineer's Department and County Planning Department and from SYPTE. Half the PTE's planning establishment (four people) were allocated to the JPTU. They were ably lead by R. J. (Roger) Pickup, who had experience in the WRCC.

Both in concept and in practice the JPTU worked extremely well. As the story of South Yorkshire's transport unfolds it will be realised the generally helpful and constructive influence that Messrs. Ellis, Thompson, Mason and Norman Kay had in the foundation period, and subsequently how Messrs. Kirkham, Thompson, Morris and the Author continued to have throughout the life of the County Council. Excellent working relationships were established with the PTE to mutual benefit. It is no exaggeration to say that the Joint Unit performed in a way that could have served as a model of the kind of co-ordinated transport planning envisaged in the 1968 Transport Act.

Initially County Staff were scattered round premises in Rotherham, Conisbrough, Sheffield and Brierley, as well as in the Regent Street Offices in Barnsley. Council meetings were held in Barnsley Town Hall, which was somewhat cramped, having seats for a 60-member council[8]. In this first period the Labour Party allowed members to be both County & Met. District Councillors – how they had time to do both jobs, when both were newly evolving and requiring considerable commitment, was never clear! Although this should have fostered good relationships and smooth transition, the reverse was true for some reason – particularly in regard to the County Council's relationship with Sheffield and, to a lesser extent, Doncaster.

The County emblem was designed by a 19-year-old graphic design student at Sheffield Polytechnic, Paul Mansell[8]. He produced the white rose with SY initials underneath forming a bud in green. The outline of the rose was in purple. It was the most effective of all the Met. County symbols and was used extensively and was instantly recognisable – far superior to SYPTE's apologia of a symbol – but more of that anon! The County's motto was 'Each shall strive for the benefit of all'. Not only was it nice to have a motto in English, it was both a Christian and

Socialist motto, although not all Socialists are Christians or Christians Socialist!

The real work of the Shadow County Council began in December 1973, with the decisions on the Budget for 1974/75. The initial budget was set at £36.2m with almost £2.5m being set aside for transport subsidy[8]. Before the end of the year a government circular required cuts in expenditure in support of Anthony Barber's mini-budget. Authorities were asked to cut 20% off capital spending and 10% off revenue account. Thus the Council had an early taste of what was to become a way of life – continuous pressure from central government to make budget cuts. The final budget was for £34m on revenue account and £12.8m on capital spending – representing a rate of 17.8p in the pound. The preparation and revision of the budget had highlighted frictions between County and District Councils, as well as the usual Labour v. Conservative arguments. It also marked the start of the Press's obsession with South Yorkshire politics and, particularly, the level of subsidy. Up to this time neither Doncaster nor Rotherham had ever subsidised their transport[8].

The Inaugural Meeting of the County Council took place on 3rd April 1974, at the Town Hall, Barnsley. Arguments raged for much of the year as to the location of County Hall, with Barnsley and Sheffield slogging it out. Eventually Barnsley was confirmed as the County Town with the new offices being occupied in July 1975. The official opening took place on 22nd March 1976. Thereafter, and for a number of years, there was pressure on the SYPTE to relocate its offices from Exchange Street, Sheffield.

There was perpetual tension – and often much argument – between the County Council and the Met. District Councils and vice versa. A particular bone of contention in the transportation field related to highway maintenance where, initially, the Districts did the work on behalf of the County Engineer. Eventually the County withdrew the Agency Agreement, deciding to do all the work itself. This caused much bad blood. Sheffield – who had always felt themselves a cut above everybody else – could not accept playing 'second fiddle' to the County, particularly with the loss of the County Hall. Fortunately, these difficulties did not impinge on SYPTE, although there were other difficulties between the PTE and the County, which are dealt with later in the book.

In 1977 when Councillor Ken Sampey stood down as Deputy Leader of the Council, to become a full-time officer of his Union NACODS, he was replaced by Councillor Roy Thwaites. Councillor Alex Waugh, a strong supporter of the transport policy, replaced Roy Thwaites as Chairman of the Passenger Transport Committee. Harold Butler, a railwayman from Doncaster, became Deputy Chairman.

Unfortunately, Sir Ron Ironmonger suffered a stroke a few months later and had a long stay in hospital. On his return he carried on as Leader until early in 1979 when he stood down as Leader, and became Deputy to Roy Thwaites who replaced him. Sir Ron, an outstanding figure in local politics, had been made a Freeman of the City of Sheffield earlier in the year. It was widely acknowledged that his leadership had been vital to the County Council's success.

The development of the County Council transport policy is dealt with in the next Chapter, and the problems of implementation are covered in Chapter 5. A new Council was elected in May 1977. The Labour Party still retained control with 62 seats – a loss of twenty. There were 31 Conservatives (a gain of eighteen), two Liberals (a gain of one), one Independent and four Ratepayers – a new breed. It is worth noting that Labour lost neighbouring West Yorkshire to the Conservatives. Labour success in South Yorkshire was ascribed largely to the transport policy. Four years later, in 1981, Labour's position was restored with their having 82 seats; Conservatives fourteen, Liberals three and Ratepayers one. This was to be the last Council.

Above: Councillor Alex Waugh (right) and Norman Kay at Midland Road Garage Rotherham, on the occasion of the laying of the foundation stone of the new garage. (E Kay collection)

Councillor Roy Thwaites (standing in front of the centre of the bus), seen here with members of the PTA and PTE, was the first Chairman of South Yorkshire PTA and later leader of South Yorkshire County Council. (E Kay collection)

3 THE GRAND DESIGN

Throughout South Yorkshire Metropolitan County Council's twelve- year life from 1974, its public transport policy was a dominating issue. It is unusual for one issue to be the focus of so much continuing conflict between a local authority and the Government. South Yorkshire County Council's case for higher transport spending than the Government desired was so strongly presented and so well supported by the PTE's successful application of the policy, that other Metropolitan Counties and GLC were encouraged to follow suit from 1981.

Many came to see 'cheap fares' as a policy in itself, whereas it was only one aspect of the Council's transport commitment. It went along with the improvement of bus and rail services, investment in vehicles and facilities, introducing traffic management schemes to help bus movement, and ensuring that general planning and transport planning were co-ordinated. Together they were directed towards meeting the responsibilities the County Council shared with the PTE under the provisions of the 1968 Transport Act. The Council's main reason for supporting low fares was for the transportation benefits this would provide.

The underlying rationale of the Council's transport policy was unassailable. Support for public transport through favourable planning and traffic management measures, and through direct capital or revenue financing, did provide substantial benefits for users and non-users. There was justifiable debate about the scale of assistance, its cost, and in terms of value for money, about the emphasis given to various aspects of the policy. The Council well understood that however attractive public transport became, it could not, on its own, stop the relentless growth in private car usage. But pending the introduction of some acceptable away of restraining the use of cars in urban areas, it made sense to retain and improve an effective and well patronised public transport network. Once passengers have been lost they are difficult to attract back again to public transport.

In 1974 South Yorkshire had a unique set of circumstances that together gave the new County Council an opportunity and confidence to embark on, and sustain a positive, pro-public transport campaign. It was encouraged and assisted by a number of things including:-

1. The Metropolitan County Councils were powerful bodies with a limited range of activities. They were 'strategic authorities' dealing with such things as planning and transportation, as well as the emergency services. The control of the high spending departments – housing,

education, social services – was left with the Metropolitan District Councils.

2. South Yorkshire was designated a Passenger Transport Area which led to the establishment of the PTA and PTE. The PTE had powers of precept on the District Councils, and from 1975/76, transportation was partially funded through the Transport Supplementary Grant (TSG).

3. Confident of being elected, the South Yorkshire Labour Party drew up a programme they intended to follow on election. Labour won 82 seats out of 100.

4. The new Council had a nucleus of capable determined Councillors with previous knowledge of local government, some of them having had Passenger Transport and Planning Committee experience. It had also recruited able and experienced officers, anxious to show how well they could perform in their new roles.

5. The original four PTAs had members nominated by the various County, County Boroughs and District Councils, as well as having independent members appointed by the Secretary of State. From 1974 the PTAs became single authority bodies under directly elected members. It was easier to adopt controversial policies, and possible to hold them in the face of strong opposition from outside. Furthermore the amendments by the 1972 Local Government Act to the 1968 Act effectively led to a loss of independence of the PTEs.

6. The continuing high rate of year-on-year inflation from 1975 onwards accelerated the effects of the Council's fares policy, the annual budget decision to keep fares unchanged being the equivalent of a massive reduction in real terms.

7. There was a smaller proportion of car owners in South Yorkshire than in most of the rest of the country, and bus services were well used.

As will be discussed in the next Chapter, the newly-established PTE had a major task in welding together the three municipal undertakings it had inherited, as well as laying the foundations for future developments. It also had to establish a modus vivendi with both the NBC and BR. Above all it was responsible for the daily operation of around 900 buses carrying about 700,000 passengers per day.

The local NBC subsidiary companies advised the Executive in May 1974 that applications for fare increases would soon be submitted to the Traffic Commissioners. They had increased fares as recently as April that year, but inflation was very high. They wanted to know the

Executive's intentions, particularly on jointly operated sections of route on which NBC had traditionally set fares.

There were many issues on which it was important for the Executive to get policy decisions from the County Council for operational, financial and budgeting reasons. The Council members had held a series of seminars at which there had been extensive discussions of these issues. Whilst some general consensus had emerged there were no firm proposals. Councillor Roy Thwaites, Chairman of the Council's Passenger Transport Committee was also anxious to present a comprehensive policy document to the Council: the intention being that this would also form the basis of the budget for 1974/75.

In September 1974, Councillor Roy Thwaites, Chairman of the County's Transport Committee produced a report *Tomorrow's Transport for South Yorkshire*[9]. A precis of this report forms the basis of much of this Chapter. However, it must be said that much of the work in Roy Thwaites' report came from a PTE report to the Passenger Transport Committee on April 9th, 1974. In that, the hand of Philip Baggaley the PTE's Operations and Marketing Manager can be clearly discerned.

Although the Executive had worked with the Chairman in producing his report for the Council, and had supplied most of the figures, they had considered there were still too many unknown factors for them to be able to say the proposals could all be had for a specific amount of money. For example, NBC did not accept the basis of calculation for concessionary fares. Following extensive discussion with the PTE and consultations with Senior Members, Councillor Thwaites presented his detailed and comprehensive report and proposals to the County Council in September 1974. It would not be an exaggeration to state that Councillor Thwaites' Report was the foundation stone of the County Council's transport policy.

In a separate report, submitted along with it, the Executive made it clear that they were not in disagreement with the policy issues. It was difficult to predict the effect of major changes in fares and concessions because of a lack of reliable passenger statistics for the County as a whole. Discussions with other operators had indicated problems that could arise in calculating compensation payments. Whilst it was possible to evaluate any one of the proposed changes, taken together they had a combined effect which could not be assessed with any reasonable accuracy. In these circumstances the Executive felt it could not afford to make such fundamental policy proposals for an early and concurrent implementation without greater certainty about the financial outcome.

The Role of Public Transport

Identifying that it is the most vulnerable section of the community – the poor, the old, children and the handicapped – that will always be public transport users, public transport policy was aimed at providing a standard that was acceptable and necessary as an alternative to the private car. Good access was identified as a key issue, not only in the strategic sense of land use, town and highway planning, but also in the specific sense of providing access

to centres of activity and population. Routes should be as direct as possible, the road network should meet the needs of public transport. For the foreseeable future buses were seen as providing for the bulk of passenger movements, with frequency and reliability being key issues. Improved standards of vehicles, provision of bus priority measures, introduction of express services and the needs of rural areas were all pointers to the future.

Because of the different policies followed by the three municipalities, and the very different policies pursued by bus companies, there was a need to introduce certain common standards, notably:

– a common, county-wide fares policy, including travel concessions
– co-ordination of all public transport
– a policy for rural transport provision
– investment in buses and staff to provide enhanced frequencies and new routes
– discussions with NBC and private operators with a view to acquiring their services

The manifesto commitment, to establish joint consultation committees for each of the four Metropolitan Districts, was also highlighted. It is worth quoting in full what the document had to say about fares: 'The aim of the County will be to provide free public transport for the elderly, the handicapped and disabled, as an immediate objective. This will be regarded as a first step towards the ultimate provision of free transport for all'. The proposals were to be funded by income from ' ... a realistic fares structure ....' and subsidies. 'Subsidies were now accepted as a proper means of financing public transport, especially in those areas of transport provision with a social content". These included 'keeping fares to an acceptable level'.[9]

Concessionary fares

Concessionary fare schemes were seen as being achieved in two phases: Phase I within each District; Phase II county-wide. Sheffield & Rotherham had similar schemes so it was mainly a question of enhancing them and bringing Doncaster into line to establish commonality, and to introduce such a scheme into Barnsley. Concessionary fares for registered blind people, the mentally and physically handicapped, and scholars living beyond the qualified distance, were to be negotiated by individual District Councils and SYPTE.

The cost of concessionary travel schemes was to be computed using the 'Litherland formula' (known as such following a legal action in the High Court). This calculated the "total charge per pass on the basis of the average number of journeys to be made by each passholder, at a notional fare equivalent to the average cost of conveying one passenger, less 5% for induced travel". For the financial year 1975/76, the cost to the County of providing concessionary fares was put at £2,676,000. This was based upon there being just over 200,000 eligible persons in the County, a take-up rate of 87% and a value 15.14p. It was agreed that this calculation would require updating annually.

Children's fares

Scholars and children's travel concessions also required rationalising. Historically these had been funded by full fare-paying passengers, since they were not accepted as a 'concession' in the same way as those for the elderly were. (This was to come much later, in the 1985 Transport Act, as a result of considerable lobbying by PTAs and local authorities.) As part of the 'Grand Design' it was felt that children's fares should be provided as part of a social service, and paid for out of the rates. Historically, children had been charged half the adult fare; it was now proposed to charge them 2p up to an adult fare of 12p, 4p up to 20p, 6p up to 30p, 8p up to 40p and so on. Computing the cost on the 'Litherland formula' identified it as being £1,890,000. Additionally local education authorities would still be responsible for paying the cost of meeting their statutory travel obligations.

Ordinary Fares

The report set out in considerable detail the traditional method of calculating bus fares in Britain, and the items which influence costs of bus service provision which had, traditionally, been recovered from the fare-box. Fundamentally the bulk of the revenue must be derived from the various fare denominations, where the main weight of traffic is carried. In most of Britain this had led to:

- fare stage points (usually about every ½ mile or every 2 or 3 stops in urban areas)
- fare scales that 'taper', ie the rate-per-mile declines with the greater distance travelled.

These traditional arrangements benefit the passenger, in that they pay only for the journey undertaken (and usually pay at the time of travel), but are complicated to understand, as well as being slow in operation. There was, therefore, pressure to introduce a simplified fares system or even 'flat' fares. The latter have the effect of raising the cost of short distance travel – where the bulk of the passengers are involved – and reducing the cost of longer distance travel, where the passengers are prepared to pay more. There are, of course, a number of operational complications where there is more than one operator on the route, or where regard needs to be paid to different passenger flows or even, on occasion, rail fares.

In 1974, there were wide variations in bus fares throughout the new County of South Yorkshire. These reflected the historical nature of bus service provision, as well as the traffic density of the different areas. Furthermore, the fares of the former municipalities had been under political control and thus had not risen in line with costs. The policy implications of introducing a county-wide fare scale into the present scenario of disparate fares, were considered in great detail in the report. One side effect was that although the PTE had a major influence with two-thirds of the services through its municipal inheritance, on routes joint with other operators, their revenue proportions would be adversely affected as the other partners increased their fares, if the PTE kept theirs constant. Already the Sheffield-Barnsley route share of receipts on a 50:50 basis had dropped to 44:56 in Yorkshire Tractions' favour, following STD's policy of holding fares

A comparison of fare scales in the South Yorkshire area for the principal operators showed that in general

---

PASSENGER TRANSPORT EXECUTIVE FARES SCALE

Based on a comparison with the Fares at the Equivalent Mileage Values with South Yorkshire Passenger Transport Exdecutive Fares up to 12 miles.

Mileage	South Yorks	West Midlands	Tyne & Wear	Merseyside		West Yorks		Strath-clyde	Greater Manchester
				Off-Peak	Peak*	Off-Peak	Peak+		
	p	p	p	p	p	p	p	p	p
0.5	3	12	14	10	10	10	10	13	12
1.0	4	20	14	10	10	20	20	25	23
1.5	5	25	20	18	18	30	30	25	23
2.0	6	32	26	18	18	30	30	45	30
2.5	7	32	32	27	27	40	30	50	30
3.0	8	32	32	27	27	40	30	50	35
3.5	8	40	37	36	36	50	30	50	35
4.0	9	40	37	36	36	50	30	50	46
4.5	9	40	37	36	36	50	30	50	46
5.0	10	40	37	36	36	50	30	55	58
5.5	10	50	37	36	36	60	30	55	58
6.0	11	50	37	36	36	60	30	55	58
6.5	12	50	45	45	36	60	30	55	58
7.0	14	60	45	45	36	60	30	55	70
7.5	14	60	45	45	36	60	30	55	70
9.0	16	70	45	45	36	70	30	60	70
10.5	18	80	58	54	36	70	30	70	80
12.0	20	90	58	54	36	80	30	70	80

* Off-peak – Monday to Friday 0930-1600, 1800 – last bus; Saturday and Sunday all day.
+ Off-peak – Monday to Friday 0930-1500, 1800 – last bus; Saturday and Sunday all day.
(a) Weekly and/or monthly travel card facilities are available except in South Yorkshire
(b) Where PTEs operate outside their own Metropolitan Counties then separate fares scales apply on those services operating into adjacent Shire Counties.

APPROXIMATE DISTRIBUTION OF PASSENGERS ON PTE'S OWN SERVICES BY DISTANCE

(including the children riding the appropriate distances)

Distance	Sheffield %	Rotherham %	Doncaster %
up to 1.0 mile	19.7	32.2	28.0
1 to 2.0	33.2	26.9	42.1
2 to 3.0	20.0	21.0	25.1
3 to 4.0	12.5	11.3 (	(
		(	(
4 to 5.0	6.6	(8.6	(4.8
over 5.0	8.0	(	(
	100.0	100.0	100.0

terms the independent's fare scales were 'in-line' with the relevant major operator. The table above shows the distribution of passengers and clearly identifies the 'big city' effect of Sheffield in comparison with other centres of population in the County. In reality there were seven different fare scales: Sheffield City, Sheffield Outer, Rotherham, Doncaster, Yorkshire Traction, West Riding and East Midlands.

Alternative Fare Methods.

The complexity of traditional bus fare calculation and collection methods will be well known to readers. However, the report went into considerable detail as to the alternatives that were available:

– flat fares
– coarse fares
– rationalised fares.

The effects on the PTE run services of various levels of flat fare were estimated to be:-

Flat Fare	Effect on Revenue £ m	Effect on Adult Passenger Numbers
2p	- 5.3	Loss of small number of those paying 1p in Rotherham and Doncaster
3p	- 2.3	Small loss in Rotherham & Doncaster
4p	- 1.6	Small loss Sheffield, 16% loss Rotherham & Doncaster
5p	Negligible	Loss of large numbers of short distance riders and up to 30% overall in Rotherham and Doncaster
8p	+ 2.4	20% loss in Sheffield, 40% loss in Rotherham, 50% loss in Doncaster

Coarse fares and other simplifications

These were examined in detail but with the existing scales being so finely graduated, having at the lower ends 1p increments for each half mile stage, moving straight to a coarse scale of 5p, 10p, 15p etc., would have had too big an impact. It would also, like the flat fare proposal, have resulted in unacceptably large passenger losses or very

large additional subsidy payments.

Other, less severe, simplifications were considered but in all of them some loss of passengers or payment of higher subsidy would have been involved. In a normal situation, such as where only one scale of fare was involved, this could have been quite acceptable because the expected benefits would more than offset the disadvantages. However, there were several quite different scales in use in the County and it was concluded that it would not be possible both to rationalise the various scales into a common one, and at the same time to reduce the number of fare stages or increase the size of the increments on the scale.

The three principal NBC subsidiaries in South Yorkshire – Yorkshire Traction, West Riding and East Midland – had increased their fares in September 1974. Municipal fare increases had been as follows:

Doncaster – February 1971
Sheffield – August 1971
Rotherham – July 1973

Doncaster had been able to postpone fare increases by using up reserves.

A two-stage approach to fare standardisation was proposed:

Stage 1 – a single basic mileage structure would be adopted, to be regarded as the 'County Scale', and applied initially in Sheffield. There would be an intermediate scale for Rotherham and Doncaster to soften the effects, thus on the PTE's own services the five scales would be reduced to two.

Stage 2 – The Rotherham and Doncaster fares would be brought up to the 'County Scale' as applied in Sheffield in Stage 1.

It should be appreciated that there were conflicting objectives. Whilst both the PTA and PTE wanted to standardise fares, the PTA wanted to hold or reduce fare levels but could not finance this without spending more than the government wanted. For its part the PTE was conscious of its statutory financial duty "to ensure so far as practicable that net revenue account shall not be in deficit". The Executive were also well aware of the pressures on the County's budget.

The new fares came in on 18th January 1975, and had the effect of adding 1p for journeys up to 2 miles, and 2p for journeys between 2 & 5+ miles. NBC fare scales were generally increased by 1p. There were a number of minor concessions to 'soften' these increases, including special fares for hospital visitors and the retention of 2p fares on Sheffield & Doncaster central area services. Early in 1975 the Traffic Commissioners granted an application by the NBC subsidiaries to raise fares by an average of 25%, to take effect from 1st March, 1975. With the approval of the Council the Executive arranged for the increases to be applied only to those existing fares below the level of the Executive's standard scale, and the average increase applied amounted to only 10%. This was the second major step towards county-wide standard fares.

The PTE were keen to simplify the fare structure since this would have assisted in the conversion of services to one-person-operation, as well as simplifying fare-tables, passenger information and marketing. In January 1976 Stage 2 of the fares standardisation was achieved when Rotherham and Doncaster fares went to the 'County Scale' and from then on the fare levels were the same on all SYPTE-operated services in the County.

Standardisation of fares on NBC subsidiaries and the independents took a little longer. However, the PTE's objective of fare simplification was eventually introduced during the lifetime of the County Council even though it did not wish to countenance any fare increases – to balance some fare decreases – so as to have a neutral effect on revenue. Even when it was part of the accepted policy for non-PTE operators in the County to hold fares down to the new standard level, some members of the Council found it difficult to agree that these operators should be compensated. This was because in the past they had regarded all non-municipal operators as competitors.

Transport Policies & Programmes (TPP).

The introduction of the new local government structure in April 1974 also saw the introduction that year of new arrangements for planning and financing transport. Brief reference was made in Chapter 1 to the TPP system which was designed to assist in the implementation of Structure Plan proposals and had three timescales: 1 year, 5 years and 10 years. The timetable required the TPP to be submitted to the Department of Environment/Department of Transport in July for the following financial year, with decisions being received from London in the December. It was, therefore, a continuous process; implementing Year 1, whilst preparing Year 2. The revenue support for 1974/75 was £3.4m. Additionally £1m had been earmarked for improvements to levels and standards of service, and £500,000 towards the standardisation of wage levels between the PTE's previously separate undertakings. At that stage no rural bus grant was being received. It was also a period of high inflation so that every 1% increase in inflation added approximately £200,000 to the revenue support required. In their application the County Council were, essentially, buying time whilst they reviewed the situation. Early information was already coming through, as to the beneficial effects that holding down fares was having on passenger carryings, as evidenced in Sheffield and Doncaster. There were also clear signs that the costs of motoring were increasing greater than the rate of inflation.

Service Development

There was a popular misconception that the South Yorkshire policy was one of 'cheap fares' only, and it is hoped to dispel this half-truth. The over-riding requirement was to improve service reliability. This was to be achieved by: staff recruitment, improved vehicle maintenance and the introduction of more

bus priorities. This phase was to be followed by a programme of service development which will be dealt with more fully in Chapter 6. However, it is appropriate here to identify the main areas and principles behind it. Three main types of service improvement were seen:-

    (1) Increasing the number of peak period vehicles
    (2) Increasing off-peak frequencies
    (3) Introducing new facilities

The first group of improvements were aimed at reducing overcrowding in the peak, and the inability to get on the first bus, even on frequent services. The second group sought to address those off-peak services that were sufficiently busy to justify increased frequencies. New facilities were aimed at: rural parts of the County, limited stop peak journeys, orbital services (stemming from the S/R LUTS Study) and City Centre services as well as services for new housing developments. The report (9) noted that 'The available funds for improvements should be spread equitably over the County in accordance with the differing needs of the various communities and this implies support in some cases for NBC and even independent operators'.

Whilst spreading resources 'equitably over the county' was a good socialist principle, it failed to reflect needs and the difference in starting data. Historically Sheffield had had a higher level of service provision and thus it would be impossible for any of the other three Districts to catch up. This was particularly relevant to the Dearne Valley towns which had suffered considerable loss of employment, and which relied principally on YTC for their services.

In highlighting areas for improvement the report[9] commented: 'In certain cases where roads may not be suitable for normal bus operation, it may be necessary to use small buses, which are not economical in terms of wages costs'. It should be remembered that this comment was made in September 1974 – nearly 10 years before the 'minibus revolution'. It is also interesting to note that no thought was given to different rates of pay for small buses, since the only differential pay was between crew and one-person-operated buses.

Mechanical Resources

Vehicles

It will be appreciated readily that increasing peak period frequencies and introducing new services would require more buses – thus the fleet would need to expand. These increases, together with increased off-peak period frequencies, would lead to substantial increases in vehicle mileage, and hence a greater call on maintenance resources. New buses were not readily available at that time and those already on order were overdue, so that maintenance requirements of the existing fleet were increasing. Early policy decisions were required as to the placing of orders for new buses and/or a programme of re-certifying old buses.

Garages

At the time of the establishment of the PTE, Sheffield had only four running garages: Leadmill, East Bank, Greenland

and Herries, together with Central Works at Queens Road, for maintenance, overhaul and painting. There was one garage each at Doncaster and Rotherham. The whole of the Sheffield fleet could not be housed under cover at night, and this was considered unsatisfactory from a maintenance point of view. It certainly required fitters to spend time 'shunting' buses to get those requiring to be worked upon. Maintenance facilities were inadequate because the pits had been built for narrower and shorter buses. There was spare capacity at Doncaster and Rotherham, partly because of earlier fleet reductions. Markers were, therefore, being put down for substantial capital expenditure on vehicles and garages.

Manpower Resources

The additional services and vehicles referred to above, together with the additional maintenance commitments, were going to require additional staff. In these days it is difficult to comprehend, but in the early 1970s the bus industry in general, and Sheffield District in particular, were experiencing difficulty in operating the then existing level of service, let alone contemplating the increase now being proposed. The Report[9] comments: 'the whole manpower policy will of necessity revolve around the ability to recruit and maintain the right calibre of employee in all categories, and it is recognised that this will not be easy in the highly competitive market which prevails at present '.

Reference was made to the problems of consolidating three separate undertakings into one with regard to pay rates, bonus schemes, conditions of service, working practices, etc, etc. Naturally, this lead to requests for harmonisation across the three Districts. The Trade Unions were also seeking to set up local negotiating machinery, similar to that which exists in other PTEs.

Financial effect

The financial effect on the year 1975/76 of the policy decisions contained in the 'Grand Design' were estimated to be as follows:-

	£m (1974)
Total income (excluding SYCC payments)	11,585
Total expenditure (including payments to other operators)	20,909
DEFICIT	9,324

The deficit was made up as follows:-

	£m (1974)
Elderly persons travel concessions	2,676
Children's reduced fares	1,890
TPP programme (service development and resource provision)	4,758
	9,324

This was equated to 2½p in every pound of rateable value (pre Poll or Council Tax days) for the Labour Party to fulfil their manifesto pledge to South Yorkshire.

Caution

As indicated at the beginning of this Chapter, the report[9] on the 'Grand Design' was greatly influenced by the Chairman of the PTA – Councillor Roy Thwaites. The Executive's own report to the same Committee commented: 'In general terms the PTE will welcome the decisions called for ..... So whilst the PTE have reservations about the report, they are not so much on policy issues .....'. Understandably the Executive were cautious, being concerned about the practicalities of bringing about these changes and were naturally well aware of their financial duties under the Transport Act 1968.

Also the Members' desires, as set out by Roy Thwaites, often had scant regard to 'custom-and practice', particularly in dealing with other operators. (This is surprising having regard to the history of the Sheffield JOC or was it perhaps because of it?) The PTA did not want to take any action that would bolster the NBC subsidiaries or private operators, since it was their policy to acquire them. There was an inconsistency of policy in the PTA preventing the PTE submitting 'in-line' fare applications with the decision to extend control to all bus services in the County. In the County's eyes the control of bus services meant purchasing the NBC subsidiaries and independent operators. Paying subsidies to them for keeping their fares from increasing, and paying for travel concessions, was not considered a satisfactory alternative.

The cautious reaction of the PTE to the 'Grand Design' related to that concerns regarding service reliability which was still not satisfactory, the vehicle situation was still critical and staff recruitment was difficult. The Executive did not want to accept commitments that it felt unable to deliver.

Furthermore, the NBC had not accepted the basis of calculating the value of the concessionary fare proposals. There was high inflation and the Trade Unions were pressing for increased wages, as well as standardisation of wages and conditions across the PTE. YTC had also submitted a claim for Rural Bus Grant of some £50,000 for 1974. An appendix to the Executive's Report hints at future problems. If NBC and independent operators were to be asked to peg their fares, the increase in fares foregone would have to be made up by the PTE in order to implement the County's policy. Since these operators accounted for 30% of bus operation, considerable grant would be required merely to 'hold' the situation whilst going nowhere towards the rationalisation or standardisation of fares.

The 'Grand Design' was nothing less than that. However, as will be seen in Chapter 5, its achievement was going to pose challenges to both the County Council and the Executive. The County were keen to honour their manifesto commitments, the Executive had resource problems, there was continuing high inflation, and the government was calling for reduced transport spending.

4 SOUTH YORKSHIRE PTE

The Story of the South Yorkshire Passenger Transport Executive (SYPTE) falls into two parts. The first part covers the period from 1974 to 1986, when it was both the major bus operator in the area, as well as being the body responsible for planning and developing an integrated public transport system for the County. The second part of the story covers the period from 1986 to the present day. Following the implementation of the 1985 Transport Act, the PTE lost its bus operating powers and became the agency for securing the provision of public transport, for supporting the local rail service and for developing the public transport infrastructure.

PART 1 1973 – 1986

The legislation establishing the PTE was quite clear that whilst policy was to be the responsibility of the PTA, together with approving their Budget and appointing the Directors, the PTE itself was an independent corporate body responsible for the implementation of the PTA's policies. Furthermore, all the assets were vested in the PTE. This was legislation passed by the Labour (Wilson) Government in 1968 and so it would not be unreasonable to assume that it would be supported by Labour controlled County Councils.

The original four PTEs, established four years earlier in 1969, had shown their independence and were making great strides along the lines that Barbara Castle had hoped. Certainly two of them – SELNEC and Tyneside – had 'men of vision' as referred to in the White Paper.[3] It was not surprising, therefore, that SYPTE intended to show its independence from the start. The County Council members, as well as certain County Officers, would have preferred the PTE to be a full County Department, with Directors as Chief Officers and the County owning all the assets.

Sheffield Transport Department was, at the time, one of the largest municipal operations in Britain, had an outstanding reputation and a reasonable degree of independence – its offices were separate from the Town Hall and it produced its own accounts. The General Manager, Noel McDonald, had established a good working relationship with the City Council, particularly the Transport Committee and its Chairman, Councillor Roy Thwaites, and Sir Ron Ironmonger, Leader of the Council. Thus when these Councillors were translated to the new County they already knew the views of their 'shadow' DG. With two of the four Directors coming from SELNEC PTE – Norman Kay and Len Trueman – this re-inforced the view of the PTE's statutory position of independence where compliance with statutory duties required it.

The Organisation of SYPTE.

Under the Local Government Act 1972 each Metropolitan County became a Passenger Transport Area and the County Council became the Passenger Transport Authority (PTA). The concept of PTAs, already well established in five conurbations, was thus extended to South and West Yorkshire.

The Passenger Transport Executive had been formed with extensive powers, and the responsibility for developing an integrated and efficient passenger transport system. In doing this it was required to follow the broad policy objectives determined for it by the Authority (the County Council). The Executive and National Bus Company subsidiaries, the latter running 27% of local bus services, had a statutory duty to co-operate in re-organising services. Under Section 20 of the 1968 Act the Executive had a special duty to examine, and keep under permanent review, all of the local railway services, with a view to integrating services within their area.

A Memorandum from the Department of Transport to the new Passenger Transport Authorities in South and West Yorkshire described the roles of the two bodies in some detail, emphasising that, unlike the departments of the Council, the Executive was not just an operating agency, but was a separate statutory body with commercial remits, which owned the system it operated. But it also made clear that the Authority had to decide the broad lines of policy the Executive must follow, and were given specific powers to give directions and to make grants to the Executive, and also to require the Executive to provide information or to review their organisation. The Executive was required to obtain the Authority's approval for major financial or service re-organisational matters.

Even before the 1972 Act[6] was implemented the new Councils and Chief Executives had protested through the Association of Metropolitan Authorities (AMA) about the separate status of the Executives. They said it was just an accident of timing that because the first Passenger Transport Areas had been set up before the creation of Metropolitan Counties, the Authorities and Executives were separate organisations. The AMA said the 1972 Act should have remedied this, and made the PTE's Council Departments. This did not augur well for the new relationship between the Executive and the County Council. As the new regulations stood it was apparent that the two bodies would have to co-operate fully, working closely together with the aim of integrating public transport in the area, as required by the 1968 Transport Act. In drafting the legislation the Minister would have taken into account the fact that in the fields of highways, planning, consumer protection, fire services, etc., County or District Councils were the only authorities carrying out those functions. Public transport was, however, provided by the PTE and a number of operators, National Bus; British Rail and independent private operators. In addition the operating part of the Executive's function was of a commercial nature and had to have regard to market factors.

The new Metropolitan County Members and their officers were anxious about the autonomy conferred on the Executive. The former Doncaster, Rotherham and Sheffield municipal bus undertakings had a history of successful operation throughout most of the County. They had been owned and controlled by the local Councils and some former members of the Transport Committees had been appointed to the County Council. As the Passenger Transport Authority, the County Council had important public transport policy responsibilities to discharge. It was apprehensive about having to rely on the Executive, considered by the Council as an unelected group of professionals, working at 'arms' length' to implement them. The fact that the Council intended to make a large financial commitment to public transport increased its concern.

For their part the PTE Directors and Officers had a paramount concern to organise the PTE so it could carry out the statutory duties in the most effective way. They also had some anxieties about whether their responsibilities under the Transport Act might conflict with those under the Companies Act, and wanted to build up a good working relationship with the Authority. The Minister's guidance memorandum had stated "It should be remembered that, unlike the departments of the Council, the Executive is not just an operating agency, but is a separate statutory body with commercial remits, which owns the system it operates". The Minister had also explained that the division of responsibilities was to protect the Authority from being distracted by day to day detail, and allow it to concentrate on important issues of policy.

The legislation required the Executive to consist of a Director General and no less than two, or more than eight other Directors to be appointed by the Authority, and the following appointments had been made:-

> Director General
> Director of Finance & Administration
> Director of Industrial Relations
> Director of Operations and Planning
> Director of Engineering

The functions were largely self-selecting: Operations and Planning were the raison d'tre of PTE's, engineering provided the essential technical back-up, and finance to control the annual budgets and financial accounts of the business, in due course likely to involve substantial payments to third parties. The only 'optional' function was Industrial Relations, but having regard to his experience in Coventry and in Sheffield, Noel McDonald was sure that this was an essential function, particularly in view of the man power-intensive nature of the industry.

The First Executive

Noel McDonald, the General Manager of Sheffield Transport Department, who had been Acting Director General in a shadow role, was confirmed as the first DG of SYPTE. He was well-versed in joint working, and had served in eight municipal transport undertakings over a period of 40 years. When he came to Sheffield in 1969, as General Manager, he was also Secretary of the Joint Omnibus Committee which administered the Railway interest in the bus operation. All this experience stood him in good stead to be South Yorkshire's first Director General.

In retrospect it is interesting to read an interview that Noel McDonald gave to the "Sheffield Telegraph" in September 1972. In this he comments: "Today's transport managers ...... are doing a holding job. These are interim years with old policies threadbare and new ones not yet shaped ..... The (public transport) industry has developed a kind of separateness ..... in future I think we shall become more a part of the corporate whole".

Both these comments were to become reality in South Yorkshire, but after Noel had left. At the end of the article Noel is quoted as saying: "Perhaps the most important thing I have learnt from my point-of-view is that public transport here (Sheffield) plays a bigger part in the life of the city than anywhere else I have been".

The position of 'shadow' DG was a particularly lonely one since he had not yet any colleagues with whom he could discuss things. From time-to-time, and in retrospect, Noel McDonald and Tom Lord (the first Director General of West Yorkshire PTE and former General Manager of Leeds City Transport) would compare notes on their proposals, arrangements and problems and find much in common. Although he was 58 at the time, the Authority wanted Noel McDonald to become the first DG and see the smooth transition from the three municipalities to SYPTE. He agreed to do this for two years and then to review the position.

It is difficult to discern Sheffield's attitude to SYCC. It appeared to be one of support provided they 'controlled' it – and the headquarters was in Sheffield. There was considerable variance between both members and officers of the two authorities. Once established the County wanted to control the PTE, including employing the staff and buying the buses. The separate identity of the PTE had to be pointed out repeatedly.

Dennis Eyres, the Deputy General Manager and Chief Accountant of the Sheffield undertaking, was appointed the PTE's Director of Finance and Administration. Clearly the imprint of Sheffield was going to be felt very strongly on the new PTE, although not quite as strongly as some may have expected at the time. Dennis was a Certified Accountant by profession and had spent most of his life in the bus industry. Initially he had been with the British Electric Traction (BET) group, and had spent some time with them in Sussex and the West Indies. He joined STD in 1955 and rose to the position of Deputy General Manager in 1961. Dennis presented a stern exterior but, underneath, he was always concerned with welfare matters and saw STD very much as a 'family'. He did not suffer fools gladly and detested what he saw as outside interference.

Two of the newcomers both came 'across the Pennines' from SELNEC PTE. Of the original four PTEs it is fair to say that SELNEC had made the greatest impact on the conurbation public transport scene. It had shown a progressive attitude to the 'new' role of public transport, as described in the first Chapter, and a refreshing open-mindedness of approach to what had become a very conservative industry. Having said that, some of SELNEC's achievements were, at that stage, only skin deep.

H.N.(Norman) Kay was appointed Director of Operations and Planning for SYPTE. Prior to the formation of SELNEC PTE Norman had been General Manager at Bury. He was appointed Divisional Manager (South) and Associate Director for the Southern Division of SELNEC PTE, based upon Stockport. After about three years he was translated to the same position in the Central Division. Norman Kay was a municipal busman to his finger tips, with very wide experience, and a person who quickly saw the new challenges and opportunities offered by the 1968 Act and the PTE's.

The second ex-SELNEC person was L.J. Trueman, who became the Director of Industrial Relations. To say 'Len' was a character was a gross understatement. Those who had known him in Manchester City Transport Department (MCTD) days, where he had been Chief Cashier, knew him as 'Joe'. Those, like the Author, who only met him in SELNEC, knew him as 'Len'. He was a 'big man' in every way and a person with wide interests outside transport. He had welded SELNEC together on the staff and personnel side and that was clearly why he was appointed to the top IR job in SYPTE.

The third director to join was Eric Kay – no relation to Norman, although both were Lancastrians. Eric was a Leyland-trained mechanical engineer who had spent his life in the bus industry. Following training he joined Manchester City Transport as a Technical Assistant before going to Blackpool as Chief Engineer, and where he got his experience with trams. Immediately prior to coming to SYPTE he had been General Manager and Engineer at Brighton Corporation Transport. Here he had done pioneering work with one-man operation of conventional double deckers and split step-entrance to ease boarding for the less mobile passenger.

The Directors took up their appointments before the official starting date for the Executive on 1st April 1974. They held their first meeting on 19th October, 1973 and in December 1973 they approved a provisional establishment of officers, and shortly afterwards made the appointments of Chief Officers, mostly from staff transferred. An Executive Secretary was not appointed until some weeks later. This was to be T.D.I. (Ian) Hoskisson, who came from Kesteven County Council, where he had been Assistant County Clerk. Ian was a qualified Solicitor and had received his Local Government training with the West Riding County Council at Wakefield. Key posts were filled quickly, with other posts being added later as the need for them was proven. This approach led to some of the job descriptions beginning to overlap, the main problem being between district and functional management.

Ian Hoskisson, PTE Secretary (SYPTE)

Sheffield had been one of the Country's biggest municipal transport undertakings and, unlike many of the others, had carried out its own accountancy work. The Accounting section was transferred to the Executive's Central Establishment along with Senior Engineers, Traffic Officers and Administrative staff, who had been responsible for policy making in their sections. In Rotherham and Doncaster the Management structure was left largely intact, although there were changes in job titles and specifications. In Sheffield the Central Works was transferred to the Central engineering function. In all three operating units District Managers were appointed, (in place of General Managers),

The original five PTE directors. From left to right - Norman Kay, Len Trueman, Noel McDonald, Dennis Eyres and Eric Kay. (E Kay collection)

without deputies, responsible for day-to-day operation and supervision of Executive-owned bus services in their District. They were also responsible for assisting the Executive in liaison with the Area Advisory Sub-Committees, County and District Council Offices concerned with education, housing, highway planning, traffic management and bus shelters. The District Managers were also to represent the PTE on day-to-day matters in liaising with other operators, major employers, parish councils, etc.

Having identified the functions and filled the posts, there remained the question of the District Managers. Although now titled a 'District', Sheffield was still a major operation with some 750-odd buses and K. E. (Ken) Griffiths, the GM of Rotherham, was appointed. However, Ken hinted from time-to-time that he had expected to be appointed a Director and, as an engineer, he was always quick to criticise the Engineering function's failings which surfaced on occasions. Having failed to get the Director of Operations and Planning position at SYPTE, R. R. (Bob) Davies, the GM at Doncaster, had accepted the position of Operations Manager with WYPTE, subsequently becoming Director of Operations and Planning on John Rostron's retirement (which was not long in coming). R.A. (Ron) Beale, Deputy GM at Doncaster had been appointed Acting GM, following Bob Davies' departure. He was appointed District Manager for SYPTE. Ken Griffith's place at Rotherham was taken by Sydney Bloor who had been his Traffic Superintendent previously.

The original three District Managers, from left to right, Ron Beale, Ken Griffiths and Sydney Bloor. *(E Kay collection)*

In addition to these immediate concerns related to their bus operation, the Executive had to give consideration to their wider responsibilities under the '68 Act, namely:-
- provision of services by other bus operators
- relationships with British Rail
- liaison with the County Council on planning and finance matters
- involvement with the County Council in their Corporate Management through the Programme Area Team (PAT) activities

Transportation planning was itself going through a period of flux with the introduction of the TPP arrangements described earlier. The County Structure Plan was going to be a major item, as was liaison with the Metropolitan districts, in the production of Local Plans. The S/R LUTS Study (also referred to previously) was drawing to a close and would provide input to these plans, as well as the Executive's own Development Plan, to be produced in due course. The County had established the JPTU and this required both staff and a great deal of management time from the PTE.

Early in 1973 a South Yorkshire Passenger Transport Working Party had produced comprehensive reports, following a review of the financial, industrial relations and engineering aspects of the three municipal undertakings, Doncaster, Rotherham and Sheffield, together with a survey of all services operated within the Area, including those of other operators. With this basic information, together with more recent operating results, consolidated revenue estimates for the three undertakings were prepared in October 1973, for the year ending 31st March 1975. This showed an estimated shortfall of £3,425,000. The Capital account showed estimated expenditure of £2,375,000 for the same period.

Immediate problems

The platform staff shortages in Sheffield had been causing the cancellation of a number of peak period buses daily, as well as many journeys on Friday and Saturday evenings. Because this had gone on for so long the engineering section had become accustomed to providing fewer buses than were required for a full turn-out. When the platform staff shortages were overcome and the full schedule of duties could be covered, this disclosed a serious engineering deficiency (largely caused by the late delivery of new buses), which was difficult to correct. The Executive's senior engineering function had been helping out the District staff and the Director of Engineering proposed, as a way of ensuring similar problems did not arise in future, that the engineering work should be removed from the control of the District Management, and should be controlled centrally. It is surprising that such an issue should surface at this stage, since one would have thought that it would have been considered earlier. To run the Executive's operations on a functional basis, cutting out the general management at district level, would then have been an option. The Executive decided that on balance they would prefer the existing structure to remain, and it was not acceptable to them for Engineering to be centralised on its own. It was agreed that the job descriptions of District Managers should be clarified to acknowledge the organisational changes that had been made since they were first appointed. For the first couple of years the Chief Officers and District Managers attended Executive meetings only on rare occasions. These officers did have regular meetings of their own, and one of their main tasks was to examine and comment on the 28 days revenue and expenditure figures as they were produced.

Former Sheffield Daimler Fleetline 223 and Leyland National 4 showing the very first SY logo and light coffee livery.
(Martin Llewellyn)

Alternative organisations

As in any transport re-organisation the key thing is to ensure that bus services continued to run despite the organisational upheavals. (The passenger should not notice any difference – although the keen enthusiast might notice a change in the legal lettering!) In considering the organisational alternatives, the existence of four Metropolitan Districts, each with an Area Advisory Sub-Committee, had to be taken into account. However, there were a number of alternative organisational arrangements open to the Executive including a Divisional Structure e.g. North and South or Hallam & Don, or a garage-based structure. In the event a District structure was adopted. This perpetrated the imbalance of 'big' Sheffield relative to the other two Districts, but had the benefit or avoiding any further changes to Sheffield and the ensuing increase in workload. For more obvious reasons the grafting onto STD (only recently shorn of its JOC responsibilities) of the Planning and Marketing functions, together with an enhanced financial capability and thus creating a centralised PTE (Greater Sheffield Transport, in effect) was probably a non-starter. It is arguable that the SYPTE organisation fell between two stools, neither building upon the previous excellent STD organisation, nor making a complete break to handle future challenges.

Fares

The whole question of the need to rationalise fares and conditions across the County and then to develop an all-embracing fares policy, including concessionary fares, was dealt with extensively in the previous Chapter. A very great deal of management time and effort was needed to evaluate the operational and financial implications of the numerous options considered and to consult on these.

New Livery

When the Executive decided to adopt a standard colour scheme for the South Yorkshire fleet to create a new recognisable corporate image, they felt they had several constraints, although some other PTEs had clearly felt less inhibited. To obviate complaints of partisanship they

wanted to avoid any of the three liveries in which the buses from Doncaster, Rotherham and Sheffield had been painted. National Bus Companies in the area already used red or green, so the choice was limited. It is not clear how the 'coffee and cream' livery came about – it is said that a Director's wife had suggested "try coffee and cream" and when a bus had been painted in that colour scheme it certainly met the criterion of not looking like any other buses! But how characterless it looked in comparison with the attractive livery of the Sheffield fleet, or indeed the modern image adopted so recently by Doncaster Corporation. In the absence of any alternative suggestions the Executive liked better, they settled for the nondescript "coffee and cream".

Although buses in their new colours drew some unkind comments from members of the public, and had been referred to at a County Council meeting where it was agreed, quite rightly, that this was not a matter for Council policy, but one for the Executive to decide, there was no doubt that they had succeeded in drawing attention to the new Organisation. However, the Executive Members demonstrated that they were not entirely colour blind, as some had suggested, by declining a proposal from the County Council's Publicity Sub-Committee that the new livery should include two strips running round the buses in the Council's newly adopted colours of green and purple. The PTE adopted a slanting, stylized 'SY' symbol which became known as the 'flying duck', with South Yorkshire Transport being written in a remote place on the bus skirt. Adoption of the County's symbol would have been much better, but would have led to a loss of 'separateness' and, to be fair, the buses were owned by the Executive.

Relationships with the County Council

Relations with the County Council were regularly discussed at early meetings of the Executive. The Director General had said his aim was to co-operate as fully as possible with the County Council, and at the same time to preserve the independence of the Executive, where compliance with statutory duties required it. The Board were agreed that this was a reasonable way to proceed. The Executive did not want Council Officers or Members to become involved in day-to-day management matters, such as industrial relations and negotiations on pay and conditions, the physical operation of services, engineering, or financial matters where the PTE had clear responsibility. However, in joint activities concerning responsibilities shared with the Council, the PTE intended to take part enthusiastically.

The Council's Chief Executive was invited to one meeting and said the County Council had already decided there would be no separate Passenger Transport Authority and that the County Council would act in that capacity, just as it did as the Highway Authority. The Chairman of the County Council would be, technically, the Chairman of the Passenger Transport Authority. Councillor Roy Thwaites was Chairman of the Passenger Transport Committee, which would advise the County Council in its capacity as the Authority.

The Policy Committee was the power house of the Council and the Chief Officers' Team reported to it. The Director General was a member of the Chief Officers' Team, but the Council's Chief Executive did not have authority over the Director General. The Director General could not be required to attend meetings of the Council's Passenger Transport Committee, but it was hoped that he would do so.

The County Council wanted the PTE to submit its annual estimates in a form approved by the County Treasurer, but the Director of Finance considered some of the requirements encroached on the duties of the Executive. The County Council had power to appoint Auditors for the PTE, and there was a choice between private auditors or the District Auditor. The Executive had a preference for outside auditors because they could be a source of specialist advice on matters concerning Companies Act responsibilities of the PTE. In the event the District Auditor was appointed. Appointment of Internal Auditors was a matter for the Executive to decide. The County Treasurer would have preferred the work to be done by the Council's own team, but the Executive took the view that Internal Audit was an essential part of its management structure and decided to employ its own. All these issues took up a great deal of management time.

Particularly to those Directors with experience of the earlier PTA/PTE organisations it appeared that the County Council's approach had been to set up arrangements that would put the PTE as close to being in the position of a Council Department as the legislation would permit. Had it been realised how strong was to be the County Council's commitment to public transport, and that it would overshadow the rest of their activities, the Council's point-of-view would have been better understood.

There had already been proposals for the PTE head office, located initially in Sheffield, to be located at County Council Headquarters in Barnsley. It was suggested that the Director of Operations and Planning and his planning staff should move first and the rest would follow when accommodation was available. Such an arrangement was impracticable. The PTE welcomed the establishment of the proposed JPTU, and agreed to contribute some staff. It also saw the merit in the Director of Operations and Planning being a member of the Council's Corporate Planning Group. Co-ordinated planning was one of the things PTEs had been set up to achieve. However, the general invitation for other Directors or Officers to join in various Council inter-departmental working groups was declined. Individual requests to join would be considered on their merits. From the Council's joint services the Executive agreed to use the Estates Surveyor, the Architectural Services and the Legal Section for litigation, instead of using outside professional services.

It should be noted that even the original PTEs were experiencing difficulties at this time with the establishment of the new Metropolitan County Councils. The transition from SELNEC PTA to Greater Manchester PTA was marked by changed attitudes of both members and Council Officers. Elected members and their officers were used to monthly meetings with decisions being taken by the Council. PTAs were not established in that way. The PTAs, including the new Counties, had all the controls they needed. They appointed the DG and, in conjunction with him, the other Directors, they established the policies to be followed and they approved the PTE's budget. What more could they want? To some hands-on control meant dealing with the minutiae of operation. This was difficult for a large municipality – it was impossible for a PTE, but some members could not accept this and some County Officers did not go out of their way to dissuade them. Of course, some County Officers were jealous of the PTE's 'power' as they saw it. In mitigation, it had to be remembered that a great deal had to be done in a short time, both by and at the County, as well as by and at the PTE. "Everything was new and everybody was learning" as Noel McDonald said in retrospect.

The New Director General

In the Spring of 1976 Noel McDonald retired as Director General and was succeeded by Norman Kay, the Director of Operations and Planning. The Executive decided not to appoint a successor to the Director of Operations & Planning's position but, instead, to create a new post entitled "Controller of Operations and Planning". A Controller was a hybrid position – less than a Director but higher than a Chief Officer – but it carried full functional responsibility for the Operations and Planning Department. It did not have the corporate responsibility of a Director.

It is interesting to quote the new Director General's thoughts of this period:

"There were several reasons for the proposal. Executive Boards exercising a collective management, as required by the legislation, had worked satisfactorily for the original PTEs, where the PTA was made up of members appointed by their Councils, rather than directly elected representatives, as was now the case. However, two year's experience of the new situation showed that collective management did not provide the best kind of interface with a County Council with a unified policy. The PTE was not like a large public company answerable to shareholders. The main contract was with the Council through a strongly supported Chairman of Committee, who was also determined, extremely able, and had a great interest in and knowledge of public transport. He was entitled to be properly informed about the Executive's activities, and it was important for the Executive to present a unified view from a single source so that the Chairman did not have to be referred to different spokesmen. There had been a tendency for Directors to keep functions in separate compartments. Those directors and officers who met Council Members at meetings had to be able to answer questions about main activities. Council members were entitled to information about how their policies were being implemented and where the financial support had been increasing despite Government opposition. We had to be able to assure them that the Executive were in complete control of projects and activities. For these reasons I thought a non-functional approach was needed at Executive level".

"SYCC's bus operations were no bigger than those of several municipal operations in the past, and in terms of passenger numbers no greater than Sheffield Transport had been 20 – 30 years earlier. These all had general managers not a collective management. I was aware of the PTE's other important duties in addition to bus operations, the main ones being concerned with co-ordination of other public transport operations and with co-ordinated planning and long-term planning, so plainly something more than just a General Manager was required. However, we had to proceed from the existing position and reducing the number of directors was a logical first step. My opinion at the time was that we should aim for the minimum of D.G. + two others".

It is surprising that after only two years the Executive structure was found to be wanting, just as the relationships between Head Office and the Districts had required re-definition. When establishing a new organisation it is inevitable that it will be necessary to make some 'adjustments' to correct parts that are not working as had been anticipated. When devising a new organisation one tries to devise the most logical structure for the job in hand – and to put to one side any thoughts about the people to fill the posts. It is at a later stage that one tries to match job and people specifications. It is people that make organisations work. Whilst it is true that people can make a deficient organisation work, it is also true that a good organisation can perform sub-optimally on account of

personalities within that organisation.

As has been indicated previously the original SYPTE organisation followed the logical pattern, adopted by the earlier PTEs, of having a DG and four functional Directors; one for each of the main functions. Most functions were dual. e.g. Operations and Planning and thus each Director had answering to him two Chief Officers. These Chief Officers (and indeed the District Managers) were experienced and respected persons within the industry. The 'total' formed the management team. When the Director of Operations & Planning's post became vacant in West Yorkshire (following John Rostron's retirement) it was filled by elevating Bob Davies. In SELNEC PTE, which was forever having management consultants in and re-organising, the idea of non-functional directors never surfaced. It is true that they created the first 'Controller's' position when they appointed Jack Thompson as Controller of Integrated Operation. Subsequently a series of 'Executive' posts were created e.g. Personnel Executive. Gradually, and over time, County Officers became non-executive directors of PTEs. Non-functional directors became unique to SYPTE.

At both director and chief officer level (and the subsequent intermediate level of Controller) it becomes increasingly difficult to find time to 'think' and to consider strategic issues. The more so when the County policies demanded so much change (all positive) over such a short timescale. It is a truism that delegation is a management skill and from this stems also the management of one's time. Some people are skilled in this, others less so. (The Author would put himself in the second category! – and indeed is on record as saying "I operated by day and planned by night".)

It also has to be remembered during this period that, however it is expressed, there was friction between the Executive and certain County Officers. The AMA was on record as wishing the PTEs to become County Departments, with DGs having Chief Officer status. Specifically, in South Yorkshire's case, there was a County Council resolution to the effect of it appointing County Officers as PTE Directors. The Head of a major function could be appointed by the Executive if he was not a Director. All these and other issues were to influence the future structure and working of the SYPTE.

Thus the position of 'Controller' was introduced into SYPTE. The first such position was that of Controller of Operations and Planning and the Author was appointed to this new position, taking up the post in September 1976. He had been involved in PTE's from the very start, having originally joined SELNEC PTE in November, 1969 as 'Planner'. He had been involved with all its bus priority, integration and railway issues, and was a keen proponent of integration. The Controller of Operations and Planning was supported by two Chief Officers P.D. (Philip) Baggaley as Operations and Marketing Manager and R.W. (Rex) Faulks as Chief Planning Officer.

The next change came in 1978 when Dennis Eyres retired. As has been mentioned there was pressure to appoint the County Treasurer as the new Director of

Finance, but the Executive considered such a dual role impractical and unacceptable. Dennis's successor was A.F. (Alex) Ritchie who came to SYPTE from the County Treasurer's Department of Oxfordshire County Council. Alex's post was entitled 'Chief Finance Officer' since the title of Financial Controller had been used to describe the No.2 in the Finance Department – a post held throughout the life of the Executive by M.N. (Mike) Pestereff.

Shortly after Alec Ritchie's appointment there followed two other Controller appointments in quick succession. First in order of taking up the post with SYPTE was W. (Bill) Kirkland who joined the bus industry in SELNEC, where he was the Chief Engineer of the Central Division, based on Hyde Road Works. Bill joined SYPTE from Greater Glasgow PTE. The other appointment was that of I.P. (Ian) Smith, to the position of Controller of Manpower Services. Ian came from a similar post in West Yorkshire PTE. Prior to that he had spent his life in the coal mining industry.

Each of the four functions was now headed by a Controller and thus the Director of Engineering, Eric Kay and Director of Industrial Relations, had their functional titles removed so that they both became Directors, with no functional responsibilities. This 'team'; Director General, two Directors, four Controllers and Secretary, Ian Hoskisson, was to continue for a year-or-two unchanged. The Director General had achieved his objective of 'DG + two others'.

The Executive Board did not welcome the idea of appointing County Officers as directors, believing that it would create divided loyalties, and would not be good for PTE staff morale. An alternative way of achieving what the Senior Council Members said they wanted, by involving their Officers in a Committee of the Executive (County/PTE Policy Co-ordination Committee) was proposed by the PTE. This idea had the support of the Chairman of the Passenger Transport Committee, and at one time looked to have the possibility of succeeding, but industrial action by some PTE staff on the day of the local council elections made the Council members doubt the PTE staff's commitment to the success of their policies. Following this the Council decided to appoint the County Chief

Executive and the County Treasurer to be non-executive Directors of the PTE. Thus Tony Mallett and David Chynoweth joined the Executive. When Tony Mallett retired his place was taken by John Harris who was his successor as Chief Executive. When David Chynoweth left to become Director of Finance for Lothian Regional Council he was succeeded by R.C. (Bob) Johnson, who joined the Executive as a non-Executive Director.

In 1978 further development in County/PTE arrangements came with the establishment of the 'Transport Panel'. This enabled policy discussions to take place between the Chairman, Deputy Chairman and Senior Members, County Council Officers and the Executive. It provided an excellent forum for informed debate and assisted greatly in implementing policies and prioritising matters.

The Executive's internal organisation was also revised in 1978, whereby there was an Executive Board and Management Committee (later changed to Management Board) arrangement. As the then DG commented, "Perhaps not an ideal arrangement and not one that might have been chosen had we started with a clean sheet. However, it could be claimed that it worked satisfactorily, which is what matters". The Management Board was the main forum for deciding how to set about and to deal with the basic work of the enterprise. It also kept directors and chief officers in touch with what was going on in all parts of the undertaking.

Among the Management Boards' main activities were the construction and approval of corporate and financial plans and budgets; the monitoring of financial budgets through the 4-weekly comparison statements, considering and approving where necessary, building and other projects and monitoring these projects, receiving and commenting on the Operations and Planning Controller's monthly meeting minutes; and receiving and dealing with reports on engineering activities and industrial relations matters. A great deal of attention was given to day-to-day service performance standards, vital in an industry whose success depended on how well it was judged to be satisfying the diverse needs of its customers. The aim was to maintain a proper balance between ongoing day-to-day operations and planning for the future. Other main business was that concerned with other organisations – the County Council on major policy, financial and planning matters, other bus operators and British Rail, District Councils, Government Departments, Trades Unions, other PTE's and national bodies concerned in the industry.

The 1968 Act had laid down specific responsibilities for the PTE and these were well understood. The County Council had invested their credibility and a great deal of finance in a policy of support for public transport. The PTE employees

From left to right, Ian Smith, who joined the PTE in 1979 and became Director General in 1984, Eric Kay, Director and Bill Kirkland, Controller of Engineering and Property Services from 1979. *(E Kay collection)*

This page, top, middle and foot:

It is 1975 and changes to the fleet are becoming apparent. Alexander bodied Leopard 55 still carries the experimental logo, whilst former Rotherham Daimler 1145 is operating in Doncaster, repainted into PTE livery but without logo. ECW bodied Daimler Fleetline 784 from the first batch of vehicles delivered following the formation of the PTE is pursued by a standard Sheffield Atlantean, 319, from the last batch of vehicles delivered to the Transport Department, and still in original colours.

(Mike Fowler)

This page, top, middle and foot:

In Doncaster a small batch of Metro-Scanias has entered service and 502 carries the new County Council crest, a short lived arrangement. Also in Doncaster native Fleetline 1104 still carries Corporation colours: only the fleet number has been altered, whilst another ECW bodied Fleetline 806 travels out of town along Cleveland Street – the photographers' original caption states "notice the absence of traffic!"

(Mike Fowler)

knew that they had to show that public transport could deliver the benefits promised within the budgets approved, and the organisation shared in the commitment to achieving this, even if it did not always agree on the best ways of doing so. There was machinery for consultation with unions' representatives at local and central level. As required by the 1968 Act a joint policy statement was published by the PTE and PTA in April 1976, and in due course, the PTE produced its Development Plan describing its proposals for the future of the passenger transport system.

In 1980 the AMA called on the Department of the Environment to abolish PTEs as separate organisations. They had never been happy about the autonomy of the Executives and alleged they (the Councils) did not have control over PTE spending. Some time later the DOE agreed to set up a Working Party, which the PTEs were not asked to join. The AMA case consisted of generalisations and a few specific complaints about particular Executives. The Civil Servants did not seem to have much enthusiasm for the AMA proposals and the report of the Working Party did not persuade the Minister to abolish PTEs.

The next change took place when Len Trueman retired in 1980. The post of Director was advertised, both internally and externally, and all four Controllers applied for it. There was intense but friendly competition, since it was felt that the person who was appointed was likely to become the next Director General, although Norman Kay's retirement was still some way off. In the event Ian Smith was appointed to be the new Director. Not long after his appointment he became 'Commercial' Director and Eric Kay became Technical Director. Once again the issue of functional/non-functional directors arose, since it was not clear whether they were still considered to be non-functional directors.

Ian Smith's former position of Controller of Manpower Services was advertised and W. (Wilf) Kemp was appointed, taking up his post in 1980. Wilf was a 'Rotherham lad' but had spent much of his career away from South Yorkshire whilst working for the Wellworthy Group. Wilf had considerable experience in personnel management, particularly in the engineering industry. The Executive now consisted of a Director General (Norman Kay), a Technical Director (Eric Kay), a Commercial Director (Ian Smith) and two non-Executive Directors, Tony Mallett and David Chynoweth; it met monthly. The Director General, Executive (non-functional) Directors and four Controllers met fortnightly as the Management Board. Ian Hoskisson was the Secretary to both the Executive and Management Board. This was the line up until Eric Kay retired in 1983. When Eric retired, the post of Technical Director was duly advertised and many thought that Bill Kirkland would be appointed to the post. This was not to be. A.E. (Albert) Booth was appointed, to the consternation of both SYPTE and the bus industry at large. Albert had been the Labour MP for Barrow-in-Furness for a long time, losing his seat at the 1983 General Election. How or why he was appointed to the post was never clear, although as a former Shadow Minister of Transport it was felt that

he might assist on forthcoming legislative issues. It would be wrong to describe Albert as 'a fish-out-of-water' since he tried hard to master becoming a professional, but inevitably he always saw Political solutions to problems rather than technical ones. It was the old story of 'cobblers sticking to lasts'.

Norman Kay retired in July 1984, after over 40 years in the business and about the time of the publication of the White Paper 'Buses' which was to so change the industry he had served. As conjectured by the Controllers earlier, Ian Smith was appointed Director General to succeed Norman Kay. By this time it was now clear that there were to be fundamental changes to the bus industry in general and to Metropolitan government. Without wishing to jump into the next Chapter, the on-going battles between central government and South Yorkshire County Council were not going to be won. Indeed, the Metropolitan Counties themselves would be fighting for their very survival, as would be the bus industry as it had been known for 50 years. With these challenges in mind the Executive, still headed by Norman Kay, decided to appoint Scott Hellewell as Controller of Executive Planning and Development, charged with preparing the PTE for the changes and challenges ahead. He handed over his operating responsibilities to R. G. (Bob) Rowe who became Controller of Operations.

The vacancy of Commercial Director created by Ian Smith's elevation was filled, following interview, by P. J. (Peter) Sephton. Peter, a Chartered Mechanical Engineer by training, had had a number of engineering and management jobs in the bus industry. Before his appointment to South Yorkshire he had been General Manager of Plymouth City Bus – the new style adopted by Peter for the former Plymouth City Transport. Peter was an able manager, with an innate marketing flair.

The final line-up of the SYPTE Management Board was:-

Director General	: Ian Smith
Commercial Director	: Peter Sephton
Technical Director	: Albert Booth
Controller of Executive Planning and Development	: Scott Hellewell
Chief Finance Officer	: Alex Ritchie
Controller of Engineering and Property Services	: Bill Kirkland
Controller of Manpower Services	: Wilf Kemp
Controller of Operations	: Bob Rowe
Secretary	: Ian Hoskisson

This team continued until the end of 1985 when the changes brought about by legislation started to take effect and are dealt with in Chapter 11.

Underneath the Management Board were a number of Chief Officers. An early appointment, and a person who had been invaluable to Noel McDonald in the run-up to the PTE, and thereafter a founding stalwart, was Philip Baggaley. He had spent his entire life with Sheffield Transport and had the position of Traffic Superintendent, before becoming the PTE's Operations and Marketing Manager. His untimely death in harness left an enormous

Philip Baggaley, the PTE's Operations and Marketing Manager from 1974 until 1980. (SYPTE)

He was followed, as Traffic Manager, by Bob Rowe. (SYPTE)

gap, both professionally and personally. Philip was well-loved and well-respected everywhere – a veritable fountain of knowledge. With Philip's death the job was retitled Traffic Manager – a more appropriate description. Bob Rowe, who arrived from City of Nottingham Transport, was appointed Traffic Manager in 1980 and held the post until 1984, when he was made Controller of Operations. Within a year he was seconded to the District Manager's post in Sheffield, to cover for Ken Griffith's regrettable abscence due to illness. In turn Ted Reid was brought across from Doncaster where he was Traffic Suipertintendent. This situation continued for almost a year until Ken's retirement when J.I. (Ian) Davies became the permanent District Manager for Sheffield. Ian arrived from Tyne & Wear PTE, although he had spent a considerable time working for GMPTE and its predecessors.

A. E. (Ted) Bale was the Executive's first Chief Engineer; he had held a similar post in Sheffield Transport Department (STD). When he retired he was succeeded by R.A. (Bob) Stewart who had previously been the Executive's Research and Development Engineer. Bob held this post for the rest of the PTE's existence. Arthur Fairclough was the first Personnel Manager for the PTE, having previously been the Industrial Relations Officer in Sheffield. Rex Faulks was appointed Chief Planning Officer and brought a wealth of expertise. He came from a similar position in West Midlands PTE. On his retirement his replacement – Phil Haywood – also came from WMPTE.

Mike Pestereff was the Financial Controller – but with Chief Officer status – again throughout the life of the Executive's operation. Mike had come across from SELNEC at the very beginning of SYPTE.

It is for the reader to draw his or her own conclusions as to the underlying reasons for some of the events that took place over the period covered in this Chapter. The test must surely be "Did the organisation work in implementing the County Council's policies?". To this there is only one answer and that is a clear and unequivocal 'YES'. The SYPTE's 'team'; Executive Directors, Controllers, Secretary, Chief Officers and District Managers was very effective in implementing the 'Grand Design' as will be apparent as the story unfolds through the rest of the book. There is, however, little doubt that the reduction in the number of directors and the creation of 'Controllers' meant that a number of able people did not achieve the director status of which they were capable or realised it later than might otherwise have been the case.

PART 2 1986 – 1995

Under Section 59 of the Transport Act 1985 the PTEs had to transfer their bus operating assets to separate companies with the objective of sale on to the commercial market – thus ending 90 years of public ownership of local transport in Sheffield. Under Section 60 the powers of the PTE to co-ordinate the operation of different bus operators was removed. The PTE's role continued to be to secure the provision of public transport but this time through the tendering process, where bus services could not be provided on a commercial basis. Its Section 20 responsibilities in relation to local rail services continued, as did its responsibilities for developing and marketing a public transport network. However, the scenario in which it worked was now totally changed with the deregulation of buses, the fragmentation and sale of NBC subsidiaries and, in due course, the disposal of South Yorkshire Transport (SYT) Ltd, its erstwhile operating arm.

The 1985 Act received the Royal Assent in October that year, and the story of this period is told more fully in Chapter 11. The ensuing re-organisation is dealt with in Chapter 12. Suffice it to say the responsibilities of the 'new' PTE were: concessionary fares, tendered bus services, local train services, developing new transport systems and infrastructure, responsibilities for bus station and interchanges, bus stops and shelters as well as any marketing and publicity for public transport in their area. There was, therefore, a substantial workload even if somewhat fragmented. There was, however, a limited amount of money for all these items and the PTE's ability to precept in the previous Metropolitan District had been replaced by a billing arrangement. This was a complex and less secure source of funding.

The 'combined' PTE continued to function until 28th February 1986, although shadow appointments were being made during this period. However, from that date the operating arm (South Yorkshire Transport Ltd) and the 'residual' PTE split, so that there could be no conflict of interest between the two sides. This was essential from the

PTE's viewpoint if other operators were to feel that they were all competing on an equal footing for tendered bus services. SYT Ltd moved out of Exchange Street to offices at Meadowhall.

Deregulation came early for several PTE staff in February 1986. They were the team co-opted from all three Districts to prepare the commercial network to be operated at 'D' day, and to carry out the massive task of registering each service with the Traffic Commissioner. Unlike many other PTEs, South Yorkshire decided to keep the network intact, rather than reducing frequencies or chopping off parts of routes. Continuity and reliability were to be bywords. This was thought to be beneficial, in that services like the 52, which had operated since tram days between Handsworth and Crookes, continued to operate between Handsworth and Crookes, rather than between Lodge Moor and Wybourn.

Hundreds of forms registering the services were completed, luckily using computer technology to reduce the pen work. However, each Registration had to be accompanied by a map showing details of the route. This was a most time-consuming process. At the end of the exercise there was no doubt, amongst the staff involved, of the roads which had bus services along them!

Within the PTE, the newly-appointed Co-ordination Officers set to work assessing the commercial intention of each operator, and the producing tender specifications which provided services or journeys to plug the gaps. Almost all the non-commercial services were re-instated under tender. The tender specifications were duly sent out and operators started work on pricing up the PTE's requests.

The Director General of the 'residual' PTE continued to be Ian Smith, with Alex Ritchie becoming the Director of Finance. Albert Booth moved from being Technical Director to become the Director of Planning. Ian Hoskisson continued as Secretary. In carrying out their duties, referred to above, the Executive had to ensure that they did not inhibit competition in the provision of bus services. In due course Albert Booth resigned from the PTE and Phil Haywood was appointed Director of Planning. Ian Smith continued as Director General until mid-1988.

The fourth – and current – Director General of South Yorkshire PTE is J.H.M. (Jim) Russell – who took up the post in July 1988. Jim had a background in aviation: initially with the RAF, then 6 years with the Royal Aircraft Establishment before joining British European Airways (BEA, as it then was) in 1968. He introduced Europe's first 'Shuttle' operation before going into marketing. At the merger of BOAC and BEA in 1977 Jim continued his career in marketing and general management. In all respects Jim was completely different to his three predecessors and has lead a team which has 'notched up' a number of successes: Meadowhall Interchange, Sheffield Interchange, support for additional and new rail services and, above all, Supertram. The foundations for many of these schemes were laid in SYCC and the 'original' SYPTE days – such is the gestation period for these projects, but to bring them to fruition is a major achievement.

The present PTE Directors, left to right, Phil Haywood, Jim Russell and Alex Ritchie. *(SYPTE)*

A feature of the new PTE were presentations to retiring employees; many faces to be found still with the PTE and/or Mainline are present in this photograph. *(SYPTE)*

5   IMPLEMENTING THE POLICY

From the earliest days, even when the South Yorkshire County Council was in embryo, it was clear that transport and transportation issues were going to feature very prominently. Transport was seen as a social and economic planning tool, not a service to be provided for profit. Such policies were founded in the mainstream of post-war Labour Party thinking. The South Yorkshire County Council could, therefore, have reasonably expected strong support for these policies from the Labour Party nationally, from the Government of the day (there were Labour administrations until March 1979) and from the Trade Union movement. In fact, the opposite was to be true as will be shown in this Chapter.

GOVERNMENT & THE COUNTY COUNCIL

The Metropolitan Counties had been conceived in the heady days of Structure Planning, which were to be funded through the TPP system. But immediately they were set up – even still in 'shadow' form – guidance from government was for funds to be cut back. This situation continued and worsened throughout the period, as will be discussed in this Chapter. The twelve-year life of the County Council spanned four governments at Westminster, under three very different Prime Ministers:

1974 – 1976	Labour	(Harold Wilson, Prime Minister)
1976 – 1979	Labour	(Jim Callaghan, Prime Minister)
1979 – 1983	Conservative	(Margaret Thatcher, Prime Minister)
1983 – 1987	Conservative	(Margaret Thatcher, Prime Minister)

The Budgetary Process

The Executive's Annual Revenue and Capital Budgets, which were co-ordinated with those of the Council, went through a long and arduous process. Starting each year with information produced for the annual TPP submission to the Minister, the next stage was a better defined version for the Council's Corporate and Financial Plan. Along with this the PTE would determine what it would need to do in the following year to continue improving services, make necessary asset replacement and comply with the Council's proposals. Meanwhile, the current year's operations were being monitored against what had been projected earlier and in the light of variations in trends, and of changes in estimates of inflation for the coming year, the PTE's working estimates were produced. It was not easy to reflect changes in trends or other influencing factors occurring in the second half of the year. All the

items in it were scrutinised and questioned, and additions and deletions made as the timetable for completion of capital projects had to be amended. This was sometimes necessary because of variable progress on building work, but the largest changes were caused by late delivery of vehicles. The Minister's decisions on Transport Supplementary Grant (TSG) and Rate Support Grant (RSG) often had a large and last-minute effect, and were usually made in mid-December. In the light of these grants and advice from the Policy Committee the estimates went through the Council procedure for final approval and a decision on the rate precept. Every year the PTE budget was more tightly drawn and more strictly monitored, the whole process being much more rigorous than when bus operators met all their costs out of passenger's fares. With such a large amount of the revenue coming from the rates the spotlight was clearly on the PTE.

Having started out with a determination to provide revenue support to hold fares down it was very difficult for members to face having to make a decision to increase fares in their first year. There were compelling reasons why it was necessary for them to do so: the limited funds available to the Council for its first year's budget; the Government's stated need to restrict the finance available for the new TSG, due to start in April 1975; and also the higher than expected increase in inflation during the year. It was also necessary to standardise the different fare scales charged within the County, as has been discussed previously. The Council was committed to introducing free travel for all elderly residents and to reducing children's fares and these two items would be very costly.

The decision to increase fares at that time was a measure of the robustness of the Council's transport policy. Being prepared to let fares increase to a level that could be seen as a fair and reasonable basis at which they could be contained in future, demonstrated that the Council saw fare levels as only one element in a wider transportation strategy. The decision to commit extra funds to the improvement of services at a time of such financial stringency was further support for this view.

Holding fares steady

From the beginning of 1976, when the rationalised fares scheme and standard concessions for children and the elderly had been established, the fares remained unchanged until 1984: the effect on fares of high rates of inflation made this the equivalent of large reductions in real terms.

The County Council stuck with such tenacity to their decision to keep fares unchanged in the face of strong disapproval from the Labour Government until 1979, and then outright hostility by the succeeding Conservative Government, that South Yorkshire became virtually synonymous with 'cheap fares'. The news media found the County to be a ready and continuing source of articles and good headlines.

In September 1975 two Directors attended an important meeting of the County Council's Budget Sub-Committee. Before introducing his report on the Capital Programme and Revenue Estimates for 1976/77, the County Treasurer reported on recent Government Circulars about counter-inflation measures. These had said that Government spending on transport would be 10% less in the coming year and recommended that fares be increased to off-set this. There was also a warning that deductions could be made from RSG and TSG if Government advice was not followed.

The Treasurer said that implementing the advice in the Circulars could lead to a virtual standstill Budget. He asked:-

1) Should the advice in the Circulars be accepted?
2) Should the current policy of revenue support be re-considered?
3) What level of precept should be aimed at in 1976/77?

There was a reminder about previous Government advice proposing that levels of fares support included in the TPP, and that TSG should be reduced by 50% in real terms between 1975/76 and 1978/79. Now that policy had hardened and less cash was to be made available through RSG. The Government had said that fares increases should go beyond what was need to recoup inflation and the real level of fares subsidies should be reduced by additional fares increases.

The Report on TSG for 1976/77 referred to the original grant of £11m to the PTE which represented approximately 24% of the net requirements of the County. The Council Members were told in the Report that without fares increases the transport budget would rise to £16m in 1976/77 (£17m if payments were made to British Rail). The alternative, if Government advice was followed, was a fares increase to bring in 38% extra revenue leaving a precept of £10m (£11m with British Rail).

These disturbing reports by the County Treasurer were noted, and the next item was the Passenger Transport Committee's request for a supplementary estimate of £385,000 for the extension of OAP Concessions and increased fares support to NBC. The Treasurer warned that such supplementary estimates for fare support could become an open-ended commitment. It was for these reasons that there was a reluctance to make agreements with either NBC or BR. The PTE representatives were asked if this extra sum could be met out of the Executive's budget. When told that it could not, the Sub-Committee erupted, its members apparently having been told (incorrectly) that this would be possible. County Officers and Members complained that the PTE had not been reporting budget variations. Even though the Executive

members were able to quote reports to Committees that covered all the budget adjustments made by the PTE, the Councillors, prompted by the Council Officers, clearly felt they should have greater control over PTE budgets and spending. The apparent problem, due in the first place to a misunderstanding, led to several meetings between the Executive Board and senior Council Members and officers and to some revised budget procedures.

Reference has already been made to the Metropolitan County Council's view that the PTE's should be Council Departments and not separate organisations. Part of SYCC's problem was in being a very powerful and effective body, which did not seem to have enough responsibilities to justify having 100 members. Also it was even then, devoting a quarter of its spending to public transport policies and, as some local authorities had directly run public transport services in the past, the PTE seemed to them a natural target for takeover. But in taking this view SYCC and the other counties were ignoring the fact that the Transport Act had separated the setting of overall policies away from the day-to-day control of planning and operation of services, which was to be in professional hands. Parliament had decided it would be more effective that way.

It would be wrong to give an impression that these conflicts led to a lack of co-operation or to generally poor working relationships. Both organisations shared a common purpose, worked well together, and produced good results. The Executive and its employees had a commitment to the success of the County's policies. The Council members and their staffs had a very strong interest in the success of the PTE's activities, but there were times when this interest manifested itself in strange ways.

Because of the Council's acute financial crisis every meeting of the Executive Board at that time gave consideration to the current year's budget and that for 1976/77. Budget control procedures were becoming a major corporate activity. The Executive members knew that it was a commonly held view that revenue support payments 'leaked away' into higher costs and inefficiencies. They were determined that the Council's transport policies would not be left open to criticism because of any financial or technical deficiencies of the PTE.

When the dire warnings contained in the Government circulars, and the advice of the County Treasurer had been digested, the County Labour Party held a special meeting in October 1975, to decide its policy for the following year. They were not short of advice: the press, local and national, were telling them there was no way to avoid increasing fares, and national politicians of both parties mostly said the same. The Government advice, that fares should increase beyond what was needed to keep up with inflation, was backed up by threats that grants could be withheld if the advice was not followed. The County Council saw this as an attack on local government and what hurt most was the fact that it was being made by a Labour Government. Reluctantly the Leader of the County Council, Sir Ron Ironmonger, supported a move to increase fares, but only to a level that was well below what the Government had asked for. When the County Labour Party debated this issue the meeting went on for four hours and local politicians who were present have described it as the most important landmark in the Council's history. Following this debate, which the Leader lost, Sir Ron swung his full authority behind the Policy. The ultimate decision to retain the policy, and keep fares unchanged, was a surprise to many, and most of those who took part in the debate must have been relieved that after weeks of agonising the die had been cast. They were going to keep their policy, even if this meant clashing head-on with the Government.[8]

Having made their decision the Council Members defended it firmly in the face of strong opposition from the Government and elsewhere. Senior Members met criticism with reasoned transportation, planning, social and environmental arguments which refuted the arguments of those who claimed that SYCC was so obsessed with cheap fares that it failed to give proper attention to other transport policies. Sir Ron countered by criticising the Government thus:

"On the one hand they are urging us to make it a semi-public service, but on the other they are saying it must be a viable undertaking, but you obviously cannot have both. One hopes that the Government will decide soon which course they really want to take".[8]

That statement sums up neatly Britain's public transport policy dilemma for the last 50 years. The Minister of Transport responded to the decision by cutting the amount available to SYCC in Transport Supplementary Grant by over 30%.

Year 1976/77.

After the efforts and traumas of the early years 1976/77 was a good year for SYPTE.

- 95 new double-deck buses were received, but this number included only seven of the order placed by Sheffield Transport in 1971. Significant progress was made in vehicle research as will be described in Chapter 7.
- The County Council approved the Executive's proposal to enter into an agreement with British Railways to commence on 1st April 1977, covering three local rail services. Under its terms the PTE was to specify the quantity and quality of service to be operated and the fares to be charged and make good to British Railways any deficit incurred (see Chapter 10).
- Additional service improvements were made. The Executive's buses carried an increased number of passengers, and revenue from passengers on PTE and other operators' buses was buoyant. These successful operations were confirming the effectiveness of the Council's Transport Polices, especially when compared with falling passenger numbers elsewhere.
- Because of higher passenger income, the success of the Government's prices and incomes policy in containing inflation together with the effect of deferring the starting date of the operating agreement with British Rail, the amount of grant required by the PTE was

much less than the amount provided in the budget.
- A check on claims for compensation for applying elderly persons concessions disclosed a large overpayment to one operator (showing the difficulties in calculating such payments). It was suggested by the operator that repayment should not be made as this would only bring forward the date when further general fares subvention would be required. The Executive said this would transfer part of the cost of fare subvention to the elderly persons concessionary scheme and could not be permitted. Subsidy payments ought to be correctly identified.
- The Executive set up a Working Party to consider a system of route costing, which would be effective in a situation where a substantial proportion of income is derived from sources other than fares. This would also assist in the formation of claims for TSG under the Transport Policies and Programmes procedure. The County Treasurer supplied a member for the Working Party.

Budgets for 1977/78

Preparation of the Budget Estimates for 1977/78 was again a long process. After the Executive had gone through its own rigorous process and produced the minimum budget required to keep services operating, the Council asked for an estimate of the effects of saving a further £500,000. The PTE was asked to identify services that could be cut with a minimum effect on passengers, and NBC subsidiaries were asked to identify what savings they could make, if required to do so.

In the normal course of bus operations service variations are made to meet changes in demand, e.g. old schools being replaced by new ones on different routes, housing developments, industrial developments and employment changes. Modest reductions can often be made without causing much inconvenience, and the savings permit some improvements to be made elsewhere, without requiring any additional resources – 'teeming and ladling'. Such minor changes have very little impact on the budget and with passenger numbers still increasing the Executive would really be needing more mileage, rather than less. To achieve a saving of £500,000 by service cuts would cause great inconvenience and the County Council and the Executive would need to consider whether this would conflict with their duties under the Transport Act.

The Executive carried out the exercise, although Senior Members had said they would be reluctant to make cuts in service in order to retain the fares policy. It would, of course, have made nonsense of the County's transport policy if fares were held down but not enough buses were run to carry the passengers. In the event no reductions were made, fares remained unchanged, and the rates precept had a large increase.

The Council were particularly concerned about this Budget for 1977/78 because the Transport Minister had announced there would be no grant for South Yorkshire in that year, which meant that any extra costs would have to be met by the Rates precept. It was also County Council election year and polling would take place soon after the increased rates precept was announced. In their 1977 election campaign the Labour Group emphasised strongly that they had kept their promises on transport. Although they lost 20 seats they still had a majority on the Council with 62 out of 100 seats. Only two other counties had been retained under Labour control and the party had done badly throughout the country. It was an accepted view that Labour had done better in South Yorkshire because of the transport policies.

One way or another the County Council was able to approve the provision each year of extra funds for service improvement and also to finance the purchase of small local operators when they decided they wished to sell. This was in addition to holding fares at the 1976 level.

Under a Conservative Government (1979)

It had been a pleasant surprise when, after the change of Government, the Conservative Transport Minister announced a transport grant of up to £10m for SYCC for 1979/80. Shortly afterwards though, the Government decided to limit rate support grant to a level that would allow local government only 13% extra to cover inflation, which was forecast, in 1982, to be 20%. SYCC's decision to keep fares unchanged was contrasted with that of West Yorkshire where a fares increase of 24% was approved.

The Council's campaign against Government spending restrictions gained some support, and became part of a wider one for local government to be able to decide its own spending policies. The Labour Party in 1979 wanted to take the South Yorkshire scheme as a basis for a national transport strategy. After its spokesmen had been to South Yorkshire to study operations at first hand, they urged the Labour Party National Executive to adopt the low fares and high public subsidy approach in fighting the proposed new Transport Bill.

In 1980 the County Council precept rose to more than 50p in the £1, representing total spending of more than £100m by the County. There was a threat of legal action by Sheffield Chamber of Commerce. The Rates Curb Consortium and the Sheffield Ratepayers Association had collected a large number of signatures on petitions calling for the County Council to reduce expenditure. Various ratepayers' groups, the Chamber of Commerce, Sir Keith Joseph and the Rotherham Advertiser were among those who were complaining about the effect of cheap fares on rates and indirectly, some claimed, on employment. SYCC Officers produced figures to show South Yorkshire ratepayers paid 13 per cent less than the national average.[8]

At an Association of District Council's Conference, Roy Thwaites had gained support for South Yorkshire's policies and he told delegates it was a pity the Government had not treated SYCC as pioneers. In fact Ministry of Transport Officers had not been unsympathetic to the South Yorkshire situation. In 1980 Mrs. J. Bridgeman of the Department of Transport and some of her colleagues had visited the PTE, and had discussed at length the Council's policies; how these had been translated by the PTE into service improvements; developments and plans for the future and the results being obtained and progress made. Also considered were the effects on congestion and freedom of vehicular movement. Arrangements had been made to prepare for them a reference document containing a description of the County Council policies for passenger transport, together with significant details of the Executive's operations and plans. At that time, when the other Counties and GLC were still following more conventional transport support policies than SYCC, there might have been a possibility of SYCC being treated as a special case. It would, of course, have required some concession from the Government, which was always unlikely. However, when some of the other counties and GLC began to reduce fares and increase support, in defiance of the Government, there was no longer any hope of special treatment.

In 1981 the newly elected Metropolitan County Councils and GLC were quickly off the mark in announcing fares reductions, in the GLC case cuts averaging 25% in London Transport fares. The Government must have been shocked by the implications for its public spending guide-lines. The subsidy to make up the lost revenue would require supplementary rate demands to be sent out in all the London Boroughs. The London Borough of Bromley challenged GLC in the courts.[12]

A new dimension had been added to SYCC's problems. Earlier threats of legal action in South Yorkshire had not been pursued: now it looked as if the Council could be affected by a legal decision taken elsewhere, and without them being able to defend their position. The London Borough of Bromley were challenging GLC; Solihull District Council were challenging West Midlands County Council and Great Universal Stores were challenging Merseyside County Council.[8]

Government Ministers, concerned that they had been unable to curb high spending Councils, announced that a Bill was to be introduced that would require a Council to hold a referendum of its ratepayers if it proposed to exceed the spending limit set for it. SYCC were in the forefront of protesters and had a great deal of support locally and nationally. The referendum proposal was not pursued.

The Bromley judgement

The PTE Budget Estimates for 1982/83 were ready to go to the Passenger Transport Committee for approval when the judgment of the House of Lords in the Bromley Case became known. The GLC and London Transport Executive were ruled to have acted illegally in reducing fares. Although GLC and LTE were governed by the Transport (London) Act 1969, whereas the Transport Act 1968 applied to SYCC and the PTE, the wording of the two Acts was similar in many respects.

In South Yorkshire it had always been believed that it was lawful for the County Council to make grants of any amount they considered appropriate, and for the PTE to accept such grants. The decision in the London case cast doubt on this belief and the County Council and the PTE separately sought the advice of eminent Queen's Counsel.

On the 13th January 1982 the Executive Board considered the Opinion of Mr. M.J.Spence QC, which was that, in the light of the decision of the House of Lords, the Executive's present course of action was unlawful. He said the Executive were obliged to act in a business-like manner in the setting of fares. The income level should be sought from fares to the extent that a prudent businessman would raise income from fares. Although the maximum amount should be raised from fares, this meant they would be optimum fares, as too big an increase on a single occasion could be counter-productive. Thus fares could be raised gradually over a period, but not too long a period. Counsel had also advised that the County Council had been in breach of its fiduciary duty to the ratepayers, which required a balance to be struck between the ratepayers and the farepayers. (Mr. Mallet, a non-executive member of the Board and SYCC Chief Executive, advised that a similar opinion was likely to be received from Sir Frank Layfield QC, who was being consulted by SYCC.)

Mr. Spence had also advised that the position of other operators who received revenue support in South Yorkshire was different to that of the PTE, because the 1968 Transport Act requirements for NBC differed from those for PTEs. NBC could lawfully accept payments from the Executive for holding down fares (so also, presumably, could the private operators who were not restricted by the legislation. Having run their businesses successfully for years they were no doubt prudent businessmen, although having no legal obligation to act as such).

At a special meeting of the Executive Board on 21st January 1982, several points were raised for further consideration by Counsel. Estimates of yield from various levels of fares were considered, along with estimates for passenger loss. Work was being done on the identification of unremunerative services, for which the County Council were entitled to make payments under a different section of the Act. 'Unremunerative' in this context meant routes which would still be unprofitable even with the maximum amount of revenue raised in fares.

At the Executive Board meeting it was resolved:-

1. To increase adult fares by an average of 75%.
2. That a further increase be made during the year and in the light of the effects of the first increase, to be at a level that would give the optimum yield.
3. Children's fares to be doubled.
4. A flat fare of 5p to be charged to adults and children on the Sheffield City Clipper and Doncaster Inner Circle Services.
5. That proposals should be prepared for increases that would provide a degree of simplification of fares scales.
6. That NBC should be advised, in confidence, of proposals 1 to 3.
7. BR should be asked to increase fares on local services by 75%.
8. The Executive Draft Estimates to be finalised, taking these proposals into account.
9. A joint report should be prepared with the Chief

Executive and the County Treasurer on the legal position arising from the Bromley judgment, and seeking formal approval of the County Council to the initial fares increases.

The controversial PTE Revenue Budget Estimates for 1982/83 were presented to the Budget Sub-Committee of the County Council on 12th February 1982, and although the main recommendations for increased fares had been predicted in discussions with members, and in the written advice that had been circulated to Senior Members following the receipt of legal advice on the implications of the Bromley case, it must have appeared stark and uncompromising. Members of the Sub-Committee had many questions and reservations on the report, and comments on the legal situation.

A highly charged meeting

They remitted the Estimates to the Policy Advisory Sub-Committee A (the Labour Group) three days later. The scene at that meeting was a highly charged one. with approximately 80 members of the Labour Group ranged rounded three sides of the Council Chamber. There was a buzz of conversation, but it was not the usual light banter, and there was an atmosphere of drama and confrontation. The Council Leader called on the Council Chief Executive, who outlined the legal position on the transport policy, and referred to Counsel's advice from Sir Frank Layfield QC, summaries of which had been sent to Councillors.

The Joint Report of the Chief Executive, County Treasurer and the Passenger Transport Executive was presented. The Director General prefaced his remarks by saying the Executive had been committed to the implementation of the Council's transport policies, and had worked hard to ensure the success of the fares policy. The Executive got no pleasure from having to put forward this report which included the above-mentioned points. The Chief Executive had explained why the legal position had changed because of the Bromley case. Some of the comments had been put forward in an unsympathetic way, because the document may have had to form the basis of a defence in the event of an action being taken against the Executive.

The frequency and scale of future increases would depend on experience with the first ones. It was difficult to assess how many passengers would be lost because of the higher fares. There was no experience of such a large increase from such a low base, and after fares had been unchanged for 6 or 7 years.

It was estimated that the yield from these increases, and from a further increase in adult fares later in the year, would be just under £13m. There would be some service reductions depending on the rate of passenger loss. This could be offset by a certain amount of service development which members had been anxious to introduce.

Although papers from the meeting had been sent to Members of the Sub-Committee in advance of the meeting, and there had been regular speculation in the press since the Bromley case, it was still a shock to be given the blunt advice that the only option open to them was to reverse their policy and authorise a large increase in fares and a reduction in services.

The atmosphere built up as details of the proposals were read out. The Council Members had spent 8 years or more holding off the Government's efforts to force a change of policy, and in the process gaining support and encouraging imitators. Now it was all going to end because the PTE were influenced by a legal decision made elsewhere, and without the Council being able to defend their position.

Discussion on the report went on for several hours and, no doubt because of the dismay and frustration of Members, the comments made to Officers and the PTE were acrimonious and heated. Some Members did not seem to have thought that the PTE with its staff of 5,000 or so, who had worked hard to plan and develop successful services, and many Council Officers were themselves not happy at the prospect of the services being cut back. At one point the Council Leader intervened to tell the Members, in effect, "Don't shoot the messengers – they are only telling us what the legal position requires".

The detailed proposals and their predicted effects were queried. This was understandable, because there was no experience of similar changes on which to base the calculation. It was also hard for Members to accept the reason why, if the first increase had a high yield, this would be a good reason for the next increase to be applied more quickly.

Some members were reluctant to accept the opinions of Counsel, drawing attention to differences in the legislation governing SYCC compared to that for GLC, and to other differences in the circumstances. They pointed out that SYCC had never reduced fares or called for a supplementary precept as GLC had done. However, Counsel had been told of these differences in their instructions and had taken them into account in arriving at their opinions.

The need for legal opinions on the positions of the County Council or the PTE was queried. "Wouldn't it have been better to carry on until challenged?" the Chief Executive was asked. He answered that if proper advice had not been obtained when the legal position became uncertain, the Council Member, their Officers and the PTE could have been held to be acting unlawfully. The Council Officers had, in fact, worked very hard during the years of pioneering policy to ensure that the Council had been protected legally. The meeting was adjourned and re-convened two days later when there were further questions.

The County Treasurer made a presentation about the implications of decisions on the fares proposals for the Council's overall budget, and answered questions. Finally it was decided that further legal advice should be sought, but with the deadline for fixing the rate only two weeks away, there was not much time.

A Telex message does not normally have the same dramatic impact as a messenger leaping from a steaming horse and rushing in with despatches, but the Telex message to the PTE that arrived on the 18th February, 1982 had the same effect. It announced that in a reserved judgment delivered on the previous day, Mr. Justice Woolf had ruled that Merseyside County Council had not acted illegally in deciding to cut bus fares by 10% and to levy a supplementary rate to pay for it. This new judgment was based on the 1968 Transport Act which also applied to SYCC. It gave the County Council renewed faith that their policies would survive after all.

When the Budget was considered by the Transport Committee a week later, Members were disappointed to hear that the PTE were still waiting for Mr. Spence, QC to review his opinion. Also an appeal against the Merseyside decision was expected. The PTE were not, at that time, able to withdraw or change the recommendation, but further advice from Counsel could make it possible to delay making a decision on increasing fares.

Holding the line (March 1982)

No decision was taken on the Budget and a further Passenger Transport Committee Meeting was arranged for 2nd March 1982. Before that meeting all Members of the Council had received copies of opinions from Mr. Glover, QC and Mr. Schiemann, QC who had been opposing Counsel in the Merseyside case. They had advised that the Council would be safe in making a decision not to increase fares provided they could show that in making that decision regard had been given to their duty to the ratepayers. They would have to show they had considered both the advantages and disadvantages.

A report from the PTE was also circulated stating that in the light of new advice from Mr. Spence, QC they were not recommending at that stage fares should be increased. Unless the Council required them to make an immediate increase in fares, the PTE would not do so. Two alternative budgets, one with a fares increase and one without, were presented to the appropriate Committees on 2nd March. Along with them was a Joint Report of Council Chief Officers and the PTE. This Review, over 100 pages long, set out the origin, history, benefits, disadvantages, effects, legal implications, government guide-lines, cost and all other information that Members would need when making the decision whether or not to increase fares. The Passenger Transport Committee's decision not to increase fares was endorsed by the other Committees and the Council.

No policy for massive support of public transport can survive for long if it does not ensure the provision of adequate capital funds for renewal and development, and in South Yorkshire the Council had always recognised this. Undertakings originally transferred to the PTE had been gradually reducing in size before then, and the uncertainties of local government re-organisation had led to an almost complete cessation of any capital investment, except for some bus replacement. Gradually an adequate programme of replacement and extension of buildings and facilities was drawn up by the Executive. Orders for new and improved vehicles kept pace with needs. One of the Council's major achievements was its commitment to ensuring the Executive was able to finance this programme.

Service improvements including special services for disabled persons were provided. The Executive had been in the forefront in planning services of this kind. These matters are considered further in the Chapters 6 & 7.

Despite uncertainty about Council funding for the following year and the Government's proposals for new legislation, 1982/3 had been a successful operating year for the Executive. Services had improved in all four Districts, and more passengers travelled. A reduction in work journeys, caused by unemployment in the steel manufacturing and general engineering industries, was offset by extra journeys taken for other purposes. There had been a big reduction in collision accidents.

The trend of higher revenue continued in 1983/84, and also in that year measures previously taken by the Executive to cut costs began to succeed. Because of these variations, together with some favourable extraordinary items, the Executive operated well within its reduced budget and was also able to introduce further service developments.

Nineteen eighty three was a year of major changes in procedures for determining the level of public transport spending by County Councils. The Transport Act 1983 required the PTEs to prepare annually, for the County Councils, plans containing proposals for three years. The plans had to show:-

1. The general level of services to be provided.
2. The general level and structure of fares to be charged.
3. The benefits to potential users.

The plans had to be accompanied by estimates of:-

1. The cost of providing the services and facilities.
2. The level of demand for them.
3. The benefits to potential users.

The Secretary of State was given authority to set a guide-line for the amount of revenue support that could be paid by Metropolitan County Councils to PTE's from 1984/85 onwards. Payments up to the guide-line level were to be protected from any legal action. Surprisingly it did not appear to proscribe payments above the guide-line, and provided SYCC members could satisfy their fiduciary duty again, their policy seemed able to continue.

There had been rumours of further legislation to come that would transform bus operations, and also suggestions that the future of Metropolitan County Councils and the GLC could be challenged. However, the local Labour Group were beginning to feel more confident about the outcome of the next General Election, and hoped any decisions about the future of the Council would be taken by a more friendly Government.

Until then the Council had been considering its future actions, and making decisions without any doubts about its own future. Whatever change either the Government or a successful legal challenge might require in the policies for public transport, the Council had assumed it would be in place to make them. At that time it is unlikely Council Members, or their Officers, thought there was a serious possibility of the Met Counties disappearing after only nine years: major changes in local government structures were not made so frequently. A reduction in the number of Members had been suggested and would have caused no

surprise, although no doubt it would have been resisted. It could have led to savings, and one often got the impression that the chain of Sub-Committees and Committees was partly designed to find Members something to do.

The Executive's responsibilities

Meanwhile, the Executive had begun to look again at their responsibilities. They had accepted revenue support as being essential to maintain an adequate service of local public transport in urban areas. The amount of revenue support was a political decision based on the Council's assessment of the total user/non-user benefits, and the cost to the ratepayers. The operator's reservations were that the revenue support policy should not:-

- affect the PTE's ability to meet statutory duties
- prevent the provision and replacement of assets
- expose the PTE to a large and sudden change in fares policy, that could not be phased in over a period, that could cause hardship to passengers and to employees, and could lead to assets and facilities being surplus to requirements

It was not at that time clear that a major sudden change was inevitable, but if the worst did happen then a prudent operator would have to tell the Council that a prudent businessman would start immediately to move in stages towards the ultimate situation, rather than hanging on to the bitter end.

There was a requirement, on both the PTA and PTE, to provide a great deal of information to the Secretary of State to enable him to determine the protected level of expenditure (PEL) that he considered necessary for the needs of the area. The figure given for 1984/85 was £43m.

In consultation with the County the PTE had evaluated five Options, ranging from continuation of the existing fares levels to meeting the Minister's guide-lines in the first year. Having examined the implications of the options the Executive had decided that the Minister's guide-line was unacceptable, and that they could not support the option aiming to meet it in the first year. They sent the plan to the Council and proposed that only the other four options should be considered. A copy of the plan was sent to the Minister as required by the Act.

The Council considered the plan and decided to accept the option based on a continuation of the current fares. They sent a statement to the Minister advising him of their decision. The Minister's reply was critical of both the Council and the Executive for not accepting the guide-lines and he reduced the protected spending level to £37m. The reduced PEL led to the production of a sixth option, and some variations of the others. After the Council had considered them all, together with other information, they resolved to continue with the policy of no change in fares.

Looked at in retrospect the whole complex exercise required by the Government seemed to be a complete waste of time, since it achieved nothing. The County Council did not change its pro-public transport policy and the Government failed to persuade the County Council of the error of its way. Perhaps it was all an exercise to pave the way for the rate-capping and abolition debates that were to follow.

Another Government White Paper *Rates – Proposals for Rates Limitation etc.* (that led to rate-capping) made it apparent that one way or another the Government would reduce the transport spending of SYCC, even if the County Council survived. When that occurred the amount of revenue support available to the PTE (or its successor) would be severely and quickly cut. The effects on passengers and staff of such an immediate change could be dramatic.

At the Executive's Board meeting held on 3rd January, 1984 this problem was discussed when the draft Estimates, which took into account the six options to be considered by the Council were being approved. It was agreed that an informal meeting should be held with leading members of the County Council, in order to make them aware of the Executive's concern that a decision not to increase fares in 1984/85 and subsequent years, might lead to an excessive level of increase in one of the following years, with a consequent disastrous effect on the number of passengers carried, and which could have been mitigated by introducing more modest fare increases starting in 1984/85.

Also during the year the Executive pressed members for a decision on fares simplification. Retaining the old scales, with 1p increments and starting at a minimum fare of 3p, was restricting the ability to speed up services and to make economies through increased OPO. It was also holding back the marketing of services, in particular the introduction of pre-paid and bulk sales of tickets. When a scale of 5p, 10p, 15p , 20p etc was finally introduced in March 1984, it was long overdue.

SYPTE lagged behind other bus operators in the conversion of services to one-person operation (OPO), This not only reduced costs of service provision, it helped operate services reliably in times of high employment and staff shortages. Heavily loaded services – of which there were many in South Yorkshire – and finely graded fare scales made OPO conversion much more difficult. A number of experiments had been tried with such things as two-stream loading, in an attempt to reduce stop dwell times. The key factor was to simplify the fare structure. This could have been accompanied by setting up off-bus ticket schemes, the use of multi-journey tickets and, possibly, ceasing to give change.

Evaluation of Free Travel

From time to time the Executive would be asked for an up-to-date estimate of the cost of running the service without charging fares (still the Council's ultimate aim). With inflation the cost of collecting fares was coming closer to equalling the amount of fares collected, so it seemed a logical next step.

In May 1982 the Executive's Planning Section made a comprehensive review of the 22 situations world-wide where free fares had been applied. Often these 'experiments' had been of very limited scope and duration. Measured and published facts were also hard to obtain. At the time it had been estimated that if the SYCC policy continued

unchanged and that inflation also continued at the same rate, the cost of collecting fares would equal fare revenue by 1987/88. The County Council model predicted a 6.4% increase in bus passengers, if free fares were introduced. However, there were many imponderables: at what time periods and at what parts of the network would increases in passengers occur? It was most unlikely that they would be spread evenly.

There had been pressure to give the elderly free travel all day, Monday-to-Friday, but this had been resisted before 0930 because of the overloading that would occur. As a result there were queues at bus stops at 0930. Free travel was considered likely to increase the resources required. There would also be problems in collecting passenger journey information for monitoring and planning purposes. Fares would be lost as a marketing aid.

The Executive needed to look at the possibility of bringing in free travel in stages, either at certain periods of the day or week, or for certain classes of passenger. One good target would be the times of day when there was surplus capacity and when eliminating or reducing the fares handling would have created a potential for saving eg:

- free travel before 0700 and after 1900
- free travel on Sundays and Bank Holidays
- free travel outside Monday to Friday peaks
- free travel for children – outside peaks
  – all day

There seemed to be a good case for retaining some fares at certain times, e.g. peak periods, to avoid an excessive increase in costs.

In these exercises the Executive had only been looking at the possible operational effects of free fares and not at whether the Council's aim to introduce them was justified by transportation, economic or social benefits. There was no denying that cheap fares had retained many passengers who would otherwise have ceased to use public transport. Car usage was less in South Yorkshire than most other places and congestion in Sheffield was less than in any urban area of comparable size. Spending on roads had been less than elsewhere, and the number of annual bus journeys per head of population was probably the highest in the country. The Council would have to be satisfied that these benefits would be improved by going to free transport, and that the improvement would be great enough to justify the extra costs. Could they get more transportation or environmental benefits by spending the money in some other way?

Over the past two years the Council had deliberated carefully the cost and benefits of their policy, but they had looked at the benefits already achieved in a general way, and not looked at specific benefits or any selective use of fares. To a large extent this was because there had been little research in this country on the effects of high public transport subsidy, low bus fares and high levels of bus service.

The Executive had started to look at ways of measuring

the social benefits of services to help in deciding priorities between service proposals and had involved the Council's JTPU in its studies. This had led on to the requirement to measure a wider range of benefits for social cost/benefit assessment purposes. The PTE and the Council had commissioned Dr. Phil Goodwin of the Oxford University Transport Studies Unit to carry out a study into the effects of the South Yorkshire policy.[13] The Department of Transport and the TRRL also commissioned Sheffield University to carry out a parallel project. There was close liaison between the two studies. They showed that an apparently stable market showing slight growth had an underlying market structure that was quite volatile. In addition to the transportation and environmental reasons for the Council's support of cheap fares, they also wished to help poorer sections of the community and in particular, elderly persons and children.

THE COUNTY COUNCIL

Power Groups

The County Council structure and organisation was dealt with in Chapter 2. Most, if not all, members of the Labour Group were themselves active trade unionists, for example the Chairman of the Passenger Transport Committee (Alex Waugh) was a member of the T & GWU. Thus whilst there were formal structures that could be shown on organisation charts, there were also many 'dotted lines'. This could, and should, have led to a 'lubricating of the machine', but it practice it had the opposite effect and made the Executive's management role extremely difficult at times.

This situation was not helped by the external pressures being placed upon the County Council, as described earlier in the Chapter. The Executive's objective was to implement the County's policies. The PTE had prepared annual budgets for this, based on its professional assessment of what could reasonably be expected and achieved. When met by unreasonable demands from the work force it sought to negotiate arrangements which the Executive felt reasonable, and on which it could recommend the County to accept as being within the budget. In this respect the Executive were 'protecting' the Council members from the PTE's workforce and Trade Unions.

However, in the eyes of the Trade Unions, the Executive were screwing down their pay and conditions in order for the County to achieve its policies. They often claimed that they were paying for the county's policies through their wages and conditions. This was manifestly untrue, since these improved throughout the period. Furthermore, the County's policies were, uniquely, increasing employment all the time because of the expansionist and service development policies. The Executive were, therefore, the 'meat in the sandwich' – they protected the elected members on the one hand, and the workforce on the other, from face-to-face confrontation that would have been bloody. It is impossible to overstress the debilitating effect this had on management effort over this period. How much more

could have been achieved had there been a 'meeting of minds'.

The background to and the development of the 'Grand Design' was described in Chapter 3. Although SY County Council always had a Socialist majority it was made up of two distinct groups: 'the men of toil' and the 'academics'. The former came from the traditional background of the area's heavy industries: coal, steel and railways. The 'acas' (as they were nicknamed) came from the schools, university and colleges. From time-to-time there was lively banter between them but, by-and-large, they worked well together with the academics helping the others by articulating economic and social justification in support of the County's policies.

Another feature of the Labour Party in South Yorkshire was the various shades across the county. The Sheffield representatives were mostly of a bright red hue (with notable exceptions) whereas those from Barnsley were more pink. Their colleagues in Doncaster had a strong 'blue rinse' and those in Rotherham (with the odd exception) were also well to the right of the Party. With such large majorities the Labour members often created their own (internal) opposition.

The Opposition on the County Council consisted of Conservatives, Liberals, Independents and Ratepayers, although these last two groups often overlapped and had similar objectives. One or two individual Conservative members were extremely good in representing the transport interests of their constituents (even privately supporting the County policies) but otherwise they were a badly-informed and ill-prepared opposition, whom it was difficult to take seriously at times. With one exception, reasoned arguments were not put forward by the opposition.

INDUSTRIAL RELATIONS

When writing in 1995 about industrial relations matters in the 1970s and 1980s, it is difficult to convey to readers the atmosphere pervading in those times. Full employment, the unsocial hours required of public transport employees, Trade Union power both locally and nationally, and government policies, were dominating factors of life.

The establishment of the initial PTEs had shown that the unification of the previously separate conditions and cultures led to adopting the highest common factor for pay and conditions, and the lowest common denominator for output. In South Yorkshire's case this was compounded by occurring at a time of high inflation and a pro-public transport policy.

Historically municipal pay had been determined by the National Joint Council for the Road Passenger Transport Industry (NJIC). One section dealt with platform staff, the other with the engineering/garage side. Company bus operators had their own National Council for the Omnibus Industry (NCOI). Under the auspices of the NJIC representatives of the municipal bus employers (the Federation of Municipal Transport Employers (FMTE)) and the trade unions met to negotiate wages and conditions. The FMTE were advised by the appropriate committees of the Municipal Passenger Transport Association (MPTA). Each municipal undertaking, regardless of size, had an equal vote in deciding the policies to be followed by the employer's side in the NJIC negotiations. The majority of undertakings were small or medium sized and thus had different problems – at least in scale – compared to the large city operators. The smaller operators tended to out-vote the bigger operators.

As a palliative the NJIC made a provision for local agreement of extra payments for increased productivity. However, with inflation being so high productivity payments were not sufficient to enable some large city employers to retain enough staff and thus service reliability deteriorated. Some undertakings, starting with Coventry, but eventually including Manchester and most of the big cities, left the NJIC and reached settlements over-and-above those negotiated by the NJIC. Sheffield remained loyal to the NJIC and after the formation of the original PTEs was the largest municipal operator then extant and thus settlements applicable in Sheffield were highly influenced by the smaller operators.

The keyword during this period was 'productivity'. There was a growing tendency to look at every change or development in working arrangements/practices for something that could be called productivity. In turn any associated payments affected differentials between workers and/or locations. Both management and workforce were looking for productivity but for different reasons: management with a view to reducing cost; the workforce with a view to increasing their pay.

When the first PTEs were established in 1969 they withdrew from the NJIC and individually established their own negotiating and avoidance of disputes procedures. Len Trueman (Joe to many of his earlier friends as mentioned earlier) had been the Number Two to the charismatic Ernest Armstrong in SELNEC PTE, and had done most of the background work in establishing pay and conditions in that PTE. SELNEC PTE brought together eleven former municipal operators ranging in size from twelve to 1200 vehicles. Very good relationships existed between the Trade Unions and management in the SELNEC area, prior to the establishment of SELNEC, and these were built upon by Len Trueman. When appointed to be the Director of Industrial Relations in SYPTE, Len seemed to assume that would be the starting point for establishing SYPTE-wide pay and conditions. The South Yorkshire area in general, and the Sheffield area in particular, did not have a history of good industrial relations and the bus industry was no exception.

Over a period Len Trueman negotiated on behalf of the Executive a Pay, Conditions and Avoidance of Disputes Procedure for all staff in SYPTE – Official staff, platform staff and craftsmen/engineering staff. The procedure reflected the management structure in SYPTE as well as the Trade Union organisation. Apart from pay and overall conditions, eg hours of work or holiday arrangements, changes to working arrangements and practices were initiated at the District level. Where there were inter-District or inter-company operations these were co-ordinated by the Head Office function. Unfortunately if agreement could not be reached two things occurred. Firstly, the 'status quo' had to be continued and, secondly, a 'Failure to Agree' was recorded. The procedure then involved, on the Operating side, the Traffic Manager and Personnel Manager at Head Office. If the dispute was not agreed here it went to the next/final level of Director/Controller. It is arguable that the new IR structures were more, not less institutionalised than previously. These structures had IR specialists taking the lead in operation or technical negotiating to the chagrin of the professionals in these areas. There were also too many people involved in many of the negotiations – often 20+ around a table. However, it must be recognised that these procedures were similar to those elsewhere in other PTEs.

In PTE negotiations, where there were representatives from several garages or Districts, none of them wanted to accept a perceived disadvantage for his location, however much it might benefit another location or the PTE as a whole, e.g. refusals to accept transfers of vehicles and/or staff, particularly when this could have avoided loss of service mileage. With hindsight it does seem that issues that should have been settled in one location or District escalated because of a Failure to Agree or appeals against decisions. In many cases the decision taken at the higher level went against local management and this was an encouragement for the Unions to take issues beyond their originating level. Sometimes this was because Management had not learnt to use the new structure, leading to claims of lack of consultation etc, by the Unions, or because items were allowed to go to the next level with insufficient thought having been given about the possible outcome at that level. Sometimes District management seemed reluctant to discuss items with line management or IR staff at Head Office before reaching a decision, concerned perhaps that they might be thought to be 'passing the buck', or losing status.

Management Structure

The PTE organisation, dealt with in Chapter 4, basically worked well with considerable esprit-de-corps in achieving such a pro-public transport policy. From time-to-time there were the usual tensions Centre v. District but these were nearly always resolved amicably. There was, however, little interchange of staff between Head Office and Central Works and the Districts or vice versa.

From time immemorial public transport had been arranged on a hierarchical basis reflecting, in part, the fact that many of the staff were away from their depot for a long time with only their conscientiousness and timetable to discipline them. Transport has always required a fair degree of self-discipline. Municipal transport also tended to have a departmental structure and this was continued by the PTEs except for the introduction of some geographic structure. The alternatives available to South Yorkshire and the organisation established have been dealt with earlier. SYPTE adopted a formal Departmental structure on pyramidical lines with clear lines of responsibility and reporting. This was well understood by the staff and the

PTA. It complemented the structures of other operators, including NBC and BR and the local authorities with whom the PTE had to work.

Organisationally the PTE was characterised by:

- well defined authority hierarchy
- specified work roles based on four functions; operations, engineering, personnel, finance.
- the need to consolidate the previous municipal operations and to coordinate these with other bus operators and the railways, and to market a County-wide public transport network
- rigid adherence to and dependence upon formal rules, procedures and agreements and controls
- change, generated by consensus
- established career paths and training opportunities

In practice strategic decisions were made by the Executive and Senior Management. Major decisions derived through extensive committee discussion after political consultation and approval where necessary.

The hierarchy featured numerous managerial and specialist levels between Directors/Controllers and direct operatives. This, combined with the high level of central control and extensive Trade Union involvement, may have generated a feeling amongst junior management, particularly garage and workshop-based staff, that they played no part in the decision-making process. The exercise of individual initiatives by staff who had extensive knowledge of and enthusiasm for bus operations was encouraged through consultations and a suggestions scheme.

Training

Right from the outset the Executive had placed training as being of major importance. There was a regular intake of apprentices in the engineering grades and a continuous workload in training platform staff reflecting the need to recruit to cover retirements, those leaving for other jobs and service expansion. In spite of this NALGO refused to accept a graduate training scheme unless all staff came from within the organisation – rather than half from inside and half new recruits. The T & GWU refused one-day 'refresher courses' which sought to improve driver's inter-personal skills and driving techniques on the basis that they were professionals and did not need the improvements!

In 1983/84, for example, the Executive's training and educations scheme providing for further education and day release enabled 160 employees to further their qualifications and technical abilities. There were induction courses for official staff, specialist courses in supervisor/management training, training workshops for supervisors and engineering senior managers, an engineering apprentice training programme, and courses for adult craftsmen. During the year 150 conductors, 224 crew drivers and 114 OPO drivers were trained. The high standard of driver training was reflected in the success rate of drivers entered in the National Safe Driving Awards Scheme, and in the continued reduction year by year in the number of collision accidents in which the Executive's vehicles were involved.

Trade Unions

Employees at all levels throughout the organisation were members of, and represented by, Trade Unions through 'closed shop' agreements. The principal divisions were:

Platform Staff	: T & GWU
Engineering Staff	: AUEW
Administrative & Management	: NALGO

Formal procedural and substantive agreements covered employment terms and conditions, relationships, negotiating rights, working practices, procedures for consultation – and a machinery for the negotiation and the avoidance of disputes.

The system shaped by the history and the development of the PTE consisted of large numbers of representatives – many employed on full-time trade union duties – and numerous committees. The consequence was constant inter-action between the Executive's Industrial Relations specialists, local management and Trade Union representatives.

The structure was much more institutionalised than it had been in pre-PTE days. The industrial relations features of the representative system were characterised by:

- tightly defined agreements – limiting the exercise of discretion or initiative by Managers.
- high levels of demarcation.
- restrictions on resource transfer between locations.
- inefficient scheduling agreements and working practices.
- excessive consultation and negotiation required to enact changes from 'status quo'.

The principal union in the bus industry was (and is) the Transport & General Workers Union (T & GWU). Under the leadership of Jack Jones the T & G had made a policy decision that the interpretation and implementation of union policy was a matter for individual branches (the lowest level of the union structure). The branches were grouped into Districts and the Districts grouped into Regions. Each tier had its own Committee and officers – District & Regional Offices for Road Passenger Transport being full-time paid officials. The four Sheffield Garages of SYPTE constituted one Branch. There were separate Branches for Rotherham & Doncaster, the latter including some membership from the independent operators. This arrangement made it very difficult even for the T & G to impose any overall policy, even if it desired to do so.

Each of the four Sheffield garages – East Bank, Greenland, Herries and Leadmill – had very different attitudes, with Greenland and Leadmill taking a positive view on most things, and generally being more co-operative. However, all jealously guarded their position and all disliked Halfway (when Booth & Fisher came in). The District Managers had their work cut out in dealing with their respective T & G representatives, and service developments were implemented only following long-drawn out negotiations. There was no love lost on the union side between Doncaster, Rotherham & Sheffield, although common cause would often be made by Doncaster, Rotherham and Halfway against Sheffield.

It should be remembered that when the PTE was set up it did not start with a clean sheet of paper, so far as pay and conditions were concerned. History and precedent has a lot to do with attitudes on both sides. Management responsibilities changed overnight in 1974, between 31st March and 1st April, but the public expected – and got – the same bus services. Pressures were always on to meet service. The historical background of the bus industry IR arrangements have been referred to, and Industrial Relations in Sheffield Transport had not been good for some time. They were better in Rotherham and Doncaster and quite reasonable at Yorkshire Traction and Booth & Fisher – all 'unionised' organisations.

Pay Negotiations

The first SYPTE pay claims were the subject of hard bargaining as was to be expected, but why an overtime ban needed to be imposed by Sheffield platform staff for over 2 weeks (plus a complete stoppage on General Election day, 10th October 1974) was beyond understanding. One reason may have been because the negotiations went on so long: the employees were impatient to take advantage of the new situation. They knew the Council were being pressed by the Government on expenditure, and were anxious to get a settlement before legislation stopped the Council from supporting public transport in the way proposed. The Trade Union did not know if the Executive would be able to implement and maintain the Council's policies. At the same time they had some suspicions about the consolidated pay offer being made by the PTE. They were determined to get the maximum price for any benefits given up. There was a real fear by the Unions that the brave new policies of the County Council would be carried on the backs of their members.

For their part the Executive knew that a substantial payment was necessary. Recruitment and retention of staff was prerequisite for successfully performing their duties. At the same time they wanted to take the opportunity, provided by a large settlement, of rationalising the pay structure and setting up the framework for improved productivity. The new consolidated rate offered would produce the highest guaranteed basic weekly-rate of any busmen at the time, but it also involved some reduction in penalty payments. Overall though, it was a very good offer and the PTE had hoped for an earlier settlement. When the Union threatened industrial action they possibly thought concern for the effect on County policies would put pressure on the PTE to settle quickly. The PTE hoped the men would stop short of industrial action because it was not in their own long-term interests. When threats of industrial action are made, but do not have the immediate effect desired, they are rarely cancelled, because events acquire a momentum that cannot be stopped quickly. The overtime

ban and day's strike caused widespread cancellation of service – no-one benefitted.

With the County's policies fully in line with those of the Labour Party nationally and the Trade Union movement generally, especially the T&GWU, positive management/union relationships would have been expected, even if negotiations were tough. In fact trade union attitudes, particularly the T&GWU, were completely unsympathetic and negative. Indeed, it would not have been surprising if one or two individuals had a 'hidden agenda'. Examples of procrastination and opposition to progress, when compared with the situation post-deregulation, are so legion that it is difficult to be rational about the numerous incidents that come to mind.

Some Industrial Relations Issues

It had been the practice in Sheffield for 'no value' tickets to be issued to elderly persons using their passes to travel free, so that the number of such journeys could be counted and charged for. With the extended issue of the passes more tickets would be required and the Sheffield platform staff objected, because this would take up more time. Rotherham and Doncaster staff had not previously issued tickets to passholders. In 1975 it had been agreed that in future the tickets should only be issued on two sample weeks in Sheffield, and that this should also apply in Rotherham and Doncaster. Each time the sample weeks came round there was difficulty in persuading staff to issue the tickets, even though this was the only way the Executive had of ensuring it received the correct payment for the passes, and that the County's payments were justified.

The demand for (and agreement to payment of, it might be added) plusages for the diversions caused by the closure of the Moor in Sheffield; the opposition to the extension of services from Bridge Street to Pond Street, to meet the County's aspirations; the 'easing of schedules' of the late 1970s; the greed that resulted in the pioneering experiments with articulated buses ceasing in 1981; the threatened strikes over issues like the size of chip portions in the canteens; the strike over the occupation of Greyfriars car park in Doncaster; the refusal to use Almex ticket machines in Sheffield; and the general opposition to the extension of one-man operation, tend to look Canute-like.

Other embittered rounds of industrial action took place concerning pay negotiations when in 1984 one-day stoppages occurred resulting, one evening, in the market traders (very concerned at their lost business) parking their vans in a circle around Leadmill garage to prevent buses moving in and out.

Notwithstanding these problems, very extensive staff consultations took place in SYPTE and as an example all its modern buses were built with a specially designed cab layout, agreed with the driver's representatives after experimentally being tested in service. This layout was first seen on the Voith-fitted Atlantean AN68 buses – again a product of the PTE assessing its needs carefully, then specifying its exact requirements.

Perhaps the most controversial of the industrial relations issues that were tackled within the PTE, was that surrounding the use of articulated buses (the Bendis). A future for this kind of vehicle was foreseen as passenger numbers were rising, and after experimenting with various foreign chassis a delivery of five MAN and five Leyland artics duly appeared. These were operated successfully on the Sheffield Clipper service – a city centre distributor. Unfortunately, a long-term agreement on pay rates could not be reached. However, a couple of years later the deadlock was broken and an agreement for artics was concluded. The artics are considered further in Chapter 7.

Bound up in the Bendi agreement was a whole productivity package that facilitated an acceleration of OPO conversion. The reasons for these complex packages related – in part – to the restraining national policies on pay and productivity of the period. The only way of giving pay awards greater than inflation was to show they were earned by productivity increases. The Trade Unions found it hard to accept these principles – promulgated by a Labour Government!

A perpetual problem in South Yorkshire was that of assaults and vandalism. Assaults, mainly on staff, were a serious and increasing problem, being particularly bad in the Sheffield District. All PTE buses had radios and alarms. All incidents were investigated by the management and trade unions together, and the Police gave the maximum amount of assistance they could. In spite of this the platform staff, at the garage affected by the latest incident, felt that 'they had to teach the public a lesson' and curtail or withdraw services. They knew that the management was doing everything possible to contain the problem and their over-reaction was unjustified. Vandalism and graffiti was a problem both in Sheffield and Doncaster – mainly slashed seats and felt pen work. This made the vehicles (even new ones) unpleasant to travel on and cost the Executive £1m a year at its peak. To combat both these problems SYPTE pioneered the use of CCTV cameras in buses.

It would be easy to suggest that the only contribution of the Trade Unions during this period was a negative one. Throughout the PTE's activities there was a general feeling of commitment to the policies of the PTA/PTE and there were many very conscientious staff. Big efforts were made to keep services running satisfactorily, particularly when weather and traffic conditions were bad. Why then, in spite of this, were changes in working practices so hard to achieve? There is no simple or single answer to the question.

Culture

SYPTE embodied many sub-cultures, together with differing employee aspirations and objectives. This was a major influential factor, occasioned by the merging of employment hierarchies – previously independent of each other – into one organisation. All retained their distinct individuality, parochialism and deep self interest. In part this reflected the independent attitude of Yorkshiremen, in part the 'small town' attitudes of Sheffielders, and in part the historical hostility to Sheffield. The over-riding culture features of the PTE grew, however, from its

responsibilities set out in the 1968 Act and to deliver 'The Grand Design'. A more positive statement of support for, and confidence in, public transport could not have been made, but it brought with it extensive political influences.

Public transport was seen as a public service by the 1968 Transport Act. This Act followed two major White Papers and reflected the world-wide view of the need to integrate public transport modes, as well as the integration with land use planning. Many of these features were in the public domain and all were, to some extent, bureaucratic. The bus industry had been regulated since 1930. Looking back from the deregulated/privatised '90s it all looks very strange. In those days it was accepted – as it is in the rest of the developed world today – that public transport's competitor is the private car, not another bus or train as applies today in Britain.

Based upon a monopoly position in the provision of bus services and deficit funded by the County Council, the culture developed in the absence of any competing alternative to the provision of PTE services. Competition existed in the form of the private car. Cost effectiveness was very important and the control of costs and monitoring of revenue to budget were undertaken assiduously, as has been described previously. However, there were other issues to which attention had to be paid, eg:

– meeting service requirements
– providing the most extensive network of services to meet the perceived needs of the community
– job creation and security
– safety and a high sense of social responsibility
– avoiding conflict through consensus management
– encouraging Trade Union participation

The Thatcher government came to power in March 1979, and enacted a number of Trade Union laws in the early 1980s. Over the next few years, through legislation and industrial disputes – notably the miners' strike – and increasing unemployment, the industrial relations scene would change completely. Part of this was caused by the preparations for privatisation and deregulation. Ironically SYPTE's successors to the bus operation were able to achieve all the negative things generated by the 1985 Act (service cuts, garage closures, redundancies, etc.), more easily than the same managers had ever been able to achieve positive developments under the pro-public transport policies of South Yorkshire County Council!

INHERITANCE

The most important single job of a PTE was to operate the bus services inherited from the former municipal operators in its area. This usually meant that, at a stroke, the PTE became the largest operator in the area and this was certainly the case in South Yorkshire. The proportion of bus mileage was:

South Yorkshire PTE	:	67%
NBC Subsidiaries	:	27%
Independent operators	:	6%

The operations of the NBC subsidiaries will be dealt with in Chapter 8 and those of the independents in Chapter 9. This Chapter covers the period from 1974 until 1986 (when the PTE's lost their operating powers). The organisational gestation of SYPTE was dealt with in Chapter 4.

On April 1st 1974 South Yorkshire PTE inherited the former municipal transport operations of Doncaster, Rotherham and Sheffield. The priority was for this to be a 'seamless' transition to be accomplished smoothly. Before going on to consider how the PTE welded these operations into a corporate whole, and then developed them in line with passenger requirements and County Council policies, it is appropriate to reflect upon the scene in April 1974.

DONCASTER

On 11th December 1973 Doncaster Transport issued a souvenir timetable for the 1973/74 period. Municipal operations had begun in 1902 with trams which operated until 1935. The first trolleybuses were introduced in 1928 and were progressively developed. Trolleybus withdrawals began in 1956 and were completed in 1963. Motor buses were first operated in 1922. The Chairman of the Transport Committee was Councillor Ken Sampey, JP. who went on to be a key figure in the new South Yorkshire County Council as was described earlier. The style 'Doncaster Transport' had been introduced in 1972 by Bob Davies the last General Manager of the Undertaking. The overall colour was red with a wide purple band, parallelled by two thin white bands. These passed above the windscreen, swept down vertically behind the driver's cab and then ran around the body under the lower deck windows. 'Doncaster Transport' was written in white Helvetica letters above the rear wheel arch together with a stylised 'DT'. The overall effect was startling, particularly after the drab maroon with a single cream line between decks of the previous regime. It is interested to note that the livery style – but not the colours (!) – was adopted by neighbouring West Yorkshire PTE (although subsequently they dropped it in favour of a simpler application of their Verona green and buttermilk).

Routes & Services

Doncaster Transport operated 31 services, sixteen on their own licence and fifteen jointly with other operators. Most services were radial in nature operating from the town centre to the County Borough boundary, or to the numerous mining villages lying outside – the latter types of services tended to be the joint ones. The only major 'trunk' service was that to Rotherham and Sheffield via Conisbrough, operated jointly with Rotherham Corporation and Sheffield Transport Department.

Doncaster had pioneered the operation of midibuses to 'open up' access to new housing developments such as that in West Bessacar (later numbered 171), when three Seddons entered service late in 1972. From 3rd December 1973 two further Seddon midibuses, this time with extra luggage space, entered service on the Inner Circle. One unusual feature of Doncaster Transport was that for many years route numbers were not displayed, although Bob Davies re-introduced them in the year before the PTE was formed.

One of the Doncaster Seddons used on the Inner Circle.
(Mike Fowler)

Service frequencies were high: typically the old trolleybus routes to Balby, Beckett Road and Wheatley Hills operated a six-minute frequency on weekdays. Most other 'town' routes operated at ten minute intervals. The longer distance joint routes had frequencies of twelve-fifteen minutes. Doncaster Transport also operated some unusual frequencies, such as 9, 13, 27 or 40 minutes! There was one cross-town service: Clay Lane to Weston Road.

Terminal points

Although there were two bus stations in Doncaster the Corporation only ran nine services from the North one and five services from the South one. They had numerous on-street stands at:

St. Sepulchre Gate	:	2 services
By the Arndale Centre	:	3 services
Cleveland Street	:	1 service
Duke Street	:	4 services
Danum (Co-op) Store	:	2 services
Christ Church	:	4 services

The independents' own operations, and those joint with the corporation going eastwards, were concentrated on Christ Church. The NBC subsidiaries, Yorkshire Traction and East Midlands, used the South Bus Station. YTC also used the North one along with West Riding and South Yorkshire Road Transport, an independent operator whose name was apt to cause confusion after SYPTE came into existence, as described more fully in Chapter 9, there were twelve independent operators serving the Doncaster area.

ROTHERHAM

In Rotherham there were some 57 services and Rotherham Corporation Transport Department (RCTD) was licensed on them all – with the exception of what became X91 – either as sole or joint operator. RCTD was sole operator on 27 services of which seven were colliery services. RCTD had ten services joint with Yorkshire Traction, three joint with East Midland and eight with Sheffield Transport. As referred to previously RCTD shared the operation of the Sheffield-Rotherham-Doncaster route with Doncaster Transport & Sheffield Transport Department. It shared the operation of an hourly express service from Mexborough through Rotherham to Sheffield with both YTC and STD. RCTD was an initial participant in the White Rose Group of services focused on the M1 motorway. They operated on the X35; Mexborough-Rotherham-Leeds and the X36 Mexborough-Rotherham-Barnsley-Leeds.

As with Doncaster, most routes were radial, linking the town centre to its suburbs and housing estates, as well as with the adjacent Dearne Valley towns or Barnsley, Sheffield and Chesterfield. An exception was the busy and complex Kimberworth Park, Wingfield, Rockingham and Greasborough group of services. Frequencies on most of the 'town' routes were fifteen minutes, although some of the longer distance ones had 30 minute frequencies. Rotherham, too, had a penchant for odd frequencies: eight, 24 and 40 minutes were common. Of the joint and out-of-town services the Rawmarsh Circular, operated with YTC, ran a ten minute frequency throughout the day. Most of the other routes were hourly, although there was often a half-hourly service at the inner end. All services operated out of the Bus Station, with the exception of five services which operated from College Street and four services which operated from Effingham Street. As will be appreciated RCTD operated on, or was jointly licensed on, all services in the Borough with the exception of Dearneways hourly express service between Thurnscoe and Sheffield.

SHEFFIELD

At the beginning of SYPTE, Sheffield Transport were operating some 91 services on their own licences, 49 of which were services serving the City itself. Twenty-five of these were radial services, mostly operating from Central Bus Station (CBS) although there were seven services operating from Bridge Street Bus Station. Those City routes terminating in CBS tended to come from the post-war housing estates: Jordanthorpe, Herdings, etc as well as places like Mosborough or Stocksbridge. The 60 was an unusual route terminating in the bus station (from 1979), then having major picking up points at Midland Station, Flat Street, Fitzalan Square before going up High Street and West Street to the Royal Hallamshire Hospital or Crimicar Lane. This was one of the busiest city services.

There were also 24 cross-city services, which were mostly focused on High Street and then went either down Leopold Street towards the Moor, or up West Street. In the other direction they went down Commercial Street or into Haymarket/Waingate where they were joined by the other group of cross-town services, which went along Flat Street and passed CBS. All cross-town services were intensive in their operation, running peak frequencies of five, six or seven-and-a half minutes, and had a variety of timing

Former Sheffield AEC Swift 27 on the City Clipper before the days of Articulated buses. *(E Kay collection)*

points in the City Centre. There were some 24 services which could loosely be described as 'B' services (using the old JOC definition) ie longer distance radial services. There were six long distance (mainly former 'C' category) services. STD also ran a number of other services including nine circular services and three miscellaneous services, including the City Clipper (Service 500). Fifteen night services were also run and a great many works and school services.

STD was also involved in 13 joint routes with other operators, as follows:

Chesterfield Transport	:	11, 12, 512
East Midland/Lincolnshire	:	85
East Midland	:	99
North Western	:	272
Yorkshire Traction	:	265, 270, 271
Rotherham Corporation	] :	277/278
Doncaster Transport	] :	

STD was also a founder member of the White Rose Group of motorway express services, being involved on the X31 and X32 services linking Sheffield and Leeds. X31 was the short-lived, non-stop, direct service.

Initial consolidation

From the foregoing it will be appreciated that there was considerable scope for rationalising agreements and simplifying operating matters, not only between the three former municipal undertakings now all under the SYPTE umbrella, but also with NBC subsidiaries and independent operators. However, it takes a considerable amount of time and negotiations to resolve these matters and to evaluate the financial consequences of such changes. Nevertheless, over the next few years agreements would be negotiated with NBC subsidiaries and some independents, whilst other independents would be acquired and consolidated into SYPTE.

However the immediate job on 1st April 1974 was to ensure that the Doncaster, Rotherham and Sheffield Districts of the PTE (as they had now become) turned out the requisite level of service, that cash was collected from fares, the wages were paid and that the normal day-to-day operations continued. One of the benefits of adopting a District structure was that there was minimal change to Doncaster and Rotherham and only small change to Sheffield. Both Doncaster and Rotherham were single garage units. At Doncaster the offices were also at the garage, although this was not then the case in Rotherham.

Although by this time Sheffield was down to four garages, they relied on the Central Works at Queens Road for all their major engineering requirements. This had been transferred to the Executive's Central Engineering function which required altered working arrangements between the District Management, the four garages and the Executive's engineers. Partly for this reason, partly because Sheffield was the location of the PTE's Head Office, and partly because of the size and importance of the City, the Executive's operations in Sheffield were always going to be in the spotlight. Sometimes the operational problems of Sheffield – particularly shortage of vehicles for service, and shortage of staff – would take up a disproportionate amount of the Executive's time.

ORGANISATION

The PTE inherited three well run municipal undertakings, and generally speaking, as far as the operations department was concerned, left these as they were, but under the control of a District Manager, who in turn was assisted by a District Engineer, District Traffic Superintendent, District Personnel Officer and Cashier reporting to him. Above this was placed a central Operations and Planning Department, located at Head Office in Exchange Street, Sheffield. Initially the Department was headed by a Director, Norman Kay. However, on his elevation to DG in 1976, the post was re-designated Controller, and the post was filled by the Author, who held the position until 1984. This structure was more or less replicated for Engineering, Industrial Relations and Finance Departments, with Controllers taking functional responsibility as Directors retired. The creation of the post of Controller led to the establishment of a Management Board upon which Directors and Controllers sat, and to which the District Managers reported. Thus the District Manager, who was responsible for all functions under his control, reported to a collective – the Management Board. This structure was not dissimilar to the other PTEs of the time (although the internal arrangements were different (see Chapter 4)).

Such a situation was not entirely conducive to good management, particularly when the District Managers received, on occasions, conflicting requests from Directors/ Controllers. The relationship of District Managers to the Management Board was further clouded after the first private operator acquisition, when instead of the operation being placed under a District Manager, it was controlled by an Operations Manager who reported directly to the Board! One way of resolving the problem would have been for the District Managers to report through the Controller of Operations and Planning, who gave a monthly Departmental Report to the Management Board, following his own monthly Departmental meeting. This option was never pursued. Conversely, the Engineering Department was always seeking to centralise activities and would like to have got rid of the District Structure. These differences reflected personal preferences as much as the problems facing bus operation.

Area Advisory Sub-Committees

The Passenger Transport Authority resolved early on to establish sub-committees for each of the four districts to comment upon and deal with transport matters which affected their particular area, where local knowledge was useful. A District Manager would regularly liaise with the respective Chairmen of their Passenger Transport Area Advisory Sub-Committee. These Committees would meet on alternative monthls to consider matters of business referred to it by residents in the area, or by the PTA itself.

These Committees were made up of elected members drawn from both the County Transport Committee and the local District Council. The Chairman came from the County. They were a forum through which ideas, requests, petitions or complaints could be aired in the public arena concerning the provision of transport in the area. Because public transport was so heavily used and relied upon by so many people, hardly a meeting would go by without there being requests for extra services or routes to be diverted to serve housing developments. Whilst in some respects these could be nice problems to have, there were not limitless resources available, despite the size of the overall subsidies and considerable care had always to be taken in dealing with these matters to ensure that the people coming forward did not feel aggrieved if their aspirations could not be immediately met.

Originally the County Council Members appointed to the Area Advisory Sub-Committees were drawn from the area concerned. This ensured an awareness of local knowledge and issues in the Sub-Committee deliberations. However, in about 1980 there was a change when the County representatives were drawn from anywhere and thus did not necessarily know the area for the sub-committee on which they were serving. From the PTE's angle this meant producing very detailed reports and maps explaining exactly what the issue was. For the Members it meant site visits for everything, even the most minor bus stop alteration. Initially the system worked well but it became increasingly cumbersome, so that by the mid 1980s there could be seven different Committees, Sub-Committees or Groups involved between the Executive and the County Council. The bureaucracy was becoming excessive. It was just another issue that disappeared with the demise of Metropolitan Councils and bus deregulation.

It was as a result of bringing forward requests for extra services that SYPTE's original "Nipper" network was conceived. The idea was to provide small buses penetrating deep into housing areas and running mainly in the daytime with personalised drivers. Whilst it was not realised at the time, the concept, indeed the very name, would shortly be introduced up and down the country. At the time of SYPTE's foray into this operation it was thought that Bristol LHs had to be used as the only small bus available that was capable of withstanding the rigours of public service vehicle operation. These little buses were drafted in second-hand and were unique in the fleet in having synchromesh gear boxes, as opposed to the semi or fully automatic gearboxes which were normal in the fleet at that time.

These in turn led to the specification of the Dennis Dominos (as also used by GMPTE) whilst the industry elsewhere started its rapid move towards van-based minibuses and high frequency operations. A lot was learned, however, by the Nipper operations; in particular, the importance of customer care – a terminology unheard of at the time. By selecting and training specific drivers the routes were an immediate success and at Skye Edge, for example, the local community would regularly bestow presents on Eric (their driver) and even laid on a party for him on his retirement.

EARLY PRIORITIES

Having ensured a satisfactory transition of its own direct operations, there were a number of priorities for the Executive's Operations & Planning Department. These included the need to:

- establish a Corporate Identity
- rationalise fares
- develop a route re-numbering scheme
- produce composite timetables and route maps

There was also a need, of course, to monitor the daily performance of SYPTE's operations, continuously at District level, and weekly at Director/Controller level and monthly at the Executive/Management Team level. The standardisation of operational equipment, including ticket machines, and the introduction of vehicle radios, were also important matters. Development of bus specifications with Engineering Colleagues (see Chapter 7) and of bus priority, traffic management and low bridge issues were all matters to be developed with the PTE's Planning staff, the JPTU and the County Planning and Engineering Departments. Many of the subjects needed discussing with the Area Advisory Sub-Committees and/or the main Passenger Transport Committee.

Fares Policy

The development of the corporate identity and fares policy has been dealt with at length in Chapter 4. However, it is relevant in this chapter to explain how the implementation was carried out, as far as other operators were concerned. Initially, at least, the first step was to bring all the PTE's services on to the same scale, which became known as 'the County scale'. This had occurred by 1976, but because the independent operators' scales tended

Former London Country Bristol LH, TPJ 64S, now 1052 in the PTE fleet, at Brampton on Rotherham District's Nipper operation.
(Mike Greenwood)

to be lower than the PTE's scale, it was not generally until 1977 that the difficulties began to arise. Had inflation not been running at up to 20% during the mid-1970s, it is possible that this situation would not have developed then. The PTE had already dealt with the NBC fare scales, by opposing the first general increase applied for by the subsidiaries, following the establishment of its policy, and fairly quickly the matter was resolved by a formula of compensatory payments. A joint committee existed between the PTE and the NBC in which it was possible to resolve most issues.

The way forward with the independent operators was not so simple, however, as the County Council was not prepared, at this time, to make a general grant to the operators if they were below the County scale. Specific grants were paid for operators to accept the OAP's and children's concessions. They were, of course, free to sell out to the PTE on the other hand – a classic case of stick and carrot – but even then not all operators were convinced. With the financial pressures on the PTE's budget, and the reluctance of many independents to sell their business at the price the PTE were prepared to pay (many independents had an inflated view of the value of their businesses), it was apparent that an Operating Agreement was required between the parties. However, again the PTE, on behalf of the County Council, was not allowed to enter into such agreements, unless the business concerned indicated its willingness to sell at some stage in the future, or at least give the PTE first refusal.

Derbyshire Services

Historically Sheffield operations included an extensive network of services in Derbyshire. Derbyshire County Council's transport policy was more supportive than most of the Shire Counties. Their general aim was to subsidise only when the maximum revenue had been obtained from fares, and for a period subsidy payments were confined to rural routes. There was pressure for increased payments to SYPTE. A problem occurring on all the routes crossing the South Yorkshire County boundary, but which affected the boundary with Derbyshire more than the others, was that caused by the jump from low fares inside, to the higher ones outside. To reduce the problem the fares scales was 'smoothed out' by making some of the fares just outside the SYCC boundary lower than they normally would have been. This became known as the 'ripple effect'. SYCC met the cost of the loss of revenue.

Leopard 65 operating along a disused railway trackbed on a Park and Ride service operated on contract to Derbyshire County Council in an attempt to relieve traffic congestion associated with the popular Bakewell Show. *(Mike Greenwood)*

Route Re-numbering

All busmen know not to re-number routes since this causes a disproportionate amount of aggravation. But, if a comprehensive public transport network is to be developed with its associated publicity, passenger information and enquiry facilities, it is essential that there is no duplication of service numbers if public confusion is to be avoided. The route re-numbering scheme was devised by Philip Baggaley and the principles are set out below:-

1. Sheffield routes would, in the main, remain unchanged (since they were by far the largest number).
2. Rotherham routes would have '100' added, most falling in the 100-140 series.
3. Doncaster would have '160' added up to 199. The un-numbered Inner Circle became service 160. One exception was the Clay Lane-Weston Road (DCT's '8') which became 158/9.

Metrobus 1948 in Fastline livery leaving Bakewell on one of the services into Derbyshire. *(Mike Greenwood)*

4. Sheffield-based services operating outside the district and cross PTE-District services were numbered in the 200 series.
5. Barnsley District services – mainly operated by YTC – were numbered in the 300 series.
6. School services particularly in Barnsley, and certain out-of-County services in Doncaster (mainly operated by West Riding or South Yorkshire Transport) were numbered in the 400 series.
7. The Sheffield City Clipper retained the number '500', but the series 501upwards was used for private contracts and colliery services.
8. Night services were allocated in the 900 series.
9. Express services were given the prefix 'X', as already established for the X5, X6, X48 etc. services and for the White Rose Group, the only exception being the Limited Stop Sheffield-Chesterfield service which retained 512.

The number 700 was given to the 'Early Bird' service, when it was introduced. This was basically an early-morning variation for commuters on the all-day 'City Clipper', which was aimed at the shopper's market. The 700 series was also used for Sheffield Works Services which had previously been numbered in the 100 series. The 800 series was not used until the special routes for passengers with disabilities were introduced later, as part of the Service Development programme. Certain East Midland services were not re-numbered: 3, 85 & 99 in Sheffield; 10 & 19 in Rotherham and 18, 55 & 56 in Doncaster. None of the independents carried route numbers so, over time, they modified their blinds so as to display numbers. A similar situation also occurred with the former Doncaster Transport vehicles. The re-numbering scheme was phased, starting on 2nd February and 2nd March 1975.

Timetables and Maps

Historically Sheffield, Rotherham and Doncaster had produced public timetables, as had NBC subsidiaries. Some of the independents also produced timetable leaflets or sheets. Sheffield and the NBC subsidiaries produced route maps, and Doncaster Transport's Souvenir Timetable included one. The Executive decided that it would take responsibility for the future production of timetables and route maps. Sheffield had very substantial sales of its public timetable, traditionally published twice a year in the Spring and Autumn. As Operations and Marketing Manager, Philip Baggaley decided that in future public timetables should be produced in two volumes: one covering Sheffield and Rotherham, the other covering Doncaster and Barnsley. They would be issued twice yearly. Similarly the route map would be produced in two sections one for the North of the County, the other for the South.

The first SYPTE-produced timetable for Sheffield and Rotherham was published in May 1974. It included all operator's services in these two Metropolitan Districts, and had summary tables of Inter City and Local BR services – a new feature that would be a hall mark of SYPTE timetables. It is of interest to note – having regard to comments earlier in the book – that the cover was pale cream and brown (the PTE's corporate livery) but the County symbol was emblazoned on the cover, with 'South Yorkshire Passenger Transport Executive' written around it. When the Doncaster District timetable was published by the Executive in April 1975, a similar cover was adopted. It was some time later that a combined Doncaster and Barnsley timetable book was published. It was in 1976 that the first route maps were published. These were produced by Cartographic Services of Manchester and looked very smart. The routes were shown in brown on the cream background with the service numbers and names being shown in black. They had exemplary clarity. From then on the Sheffield/Rotherham timetable came out twice yearly, but the Doncaster/Barnsley volume never sold as well and subsequently came out annually. A second edition of the route maps was published in the early 1980s.

Service Reliability

As referred to previously the shortage of staff was affecting the reliability of bus services. Even with staff working as much overtime as they could be persuaded to do (within the limits of the Driver's Hours Regulations) many journeys were being missed throughout the week. On Friday evenings and on Saturday, when overtime working was least popular, there was widespread cancellation of journeys and the service that did run was irregular and haphazard, with passengers never being sure if their bus would turn up.

The Executive were starting to negotiate locally on a comprehensive package of pay and conditions, but the effects of this were unlikely to be felt on the road for some time. An interim agreement to pay higher rates for Saturday overtime was having only a minor effect. Even when the main pay settlement was agreed, recruitment and training of drivers would take some time. There was no way of overcoming the staff shortages quickly.

Application was made to the Traffic Commissioners for authority to reduce services on Friday evenings and Saturday, to a level at which they could be guaranteed with the numbers of staff available. Although there was no statutory objection, the Traffic Commissioners decided to hold an Enquiry in Sheffield and invited comments from some of those who attended. There was considerable resentment at the PTE's proposals by individual passengers and various user groups, who saw it as the start of the slippery slope. Such moves were also at odds with the 'Grand Design' and were reluctantly accepted by the County Council, being introduced in February and March 1975.

A shortage of serviceable buses had also affected operations at various times during the first year. A large increase in maintenance costs, that had been reported to the Passenger Transport Committee because of its effect on the year's budget, had been mainly caused by the failure of the manufacturer to deliver new buses. 82 Daimler Fleetline chassis had been ordered by the former Sheffield Corporation Transport in 1971, and none had been delivered in the year 1975/76. In addition to delays caused generally by the fuel crisis of 1974 manufacture of this model had been disrupted by the move of production from Coventry to Leyland. In consequence, 40 old buses, due to be withdrawn from service, had to be given costly overhauls. Spare parts also were in short supply, some being supplied up to fourteen months after being ordered and numbers of buses were frequently off the road waiting for spares. At this period a substantial number of buses were hired temporarily from other operators.

There was concern that continuing shortages of this kind would restrict opportunities for service development being planned for 1975/76. By 1976 increased numbers of platform staff had been recruited and driver training stepped-up. Service unreliability, because of staff shortages, had been largely eliminated, and confidence in the published timetables was being restored Some service improvements had been made and in total more than a million extra bus miles were run than in the previous year.

OTHER DUTIES

The PTE , of course, had a dual role under the Act, for not only had it to manage its own inherited operations, but it had also to co-ordinate the operations of the other bus companies in the County, both NBC and private. When the PTA resolved, very early on, to achieve this objective by acquisition, the scene was set for a particularly interesting few years. The story of those Independent Operators who chose to sell to the PTE is told in Chapter 9.

The PTE implemented the County Council's aggressive acquisition policy, although without much enthusiasm. Perhaps with all the other pressures it is understandable if insufficient thought was given to this first acquisition. However, it created a number of precedents. The decision to integrate Booth & Fisher staff pay and conditions was unavoidable in those days, but little benefit to the travelling public was seen until the introduction of the X29 service in 1979. Halfway Garage was neither 'fish, flesh nor good red herring' – it was, quite literally, halfway between an independent unit and a PTE District. Mervyn Pillinger, as Operations Manager, had a difficult job and, initially, little guidance as to what was expected of him. The Booth & Fisher purchase was a tale of missed opportunities until the major service developments in the early 1980s.

Planning

The Transport Development Plan[17], which the Transport Act 1968 required the PTE to publish with the approval of the County Council, had been produced during 1977 and published in 1978. It set out immediate and longer term proposals for developing local road and rail services, and for the design of future systems and vehicles. The implications of the County Council's transportation policy, and the South Yorkshire Structure Plan were examined, and an increase in the use of public transport was envisaged because of the effect of these. During the year an Integration Group had been set up to cover future bus/bus and bus/train integration. The examination of future provision of public transport in Sheffield had also required considerable analysis of passenger and operational data.

Traffic Management

The former Sheffield City Council had been in the vanguard of establishing urban clearways on most of the city's radial roads. This legislation pre-dated bus-only lanes, but had similar effects. These arrangements were extended and developed by the County Council and the North Central Area Traffic Management Scheme was introduced in August 1974. This covered the city centre from the end of The Wicker to The Moor and included bus gates and bus lanes.

The traffic management schemes designed by the County Council, as highway authority, were not always as helpful to public transport as could have been hoped for, despite the County's pro-public transport policy and the existence of the JPTU. Indeed the latter had little input to bus priorities and traffic management schemes, which was a quirk of the County's arrangements. At the time comprehensive traffic management schemes were necessary, but their implementation inevitably affected bus routing and the position of bus stops in major shopping areas. Baxtergate, Doncaster; The Moor, Sheffield; Mayday Green, Barnsley; and College Street, Rotherham were all the locations of heated debate between the PTE and the highway authority.

An exception concerned Doncaster town centre. The opening of the A1(M) in the 1960's, and the construction of the inner relief road (cutting the railway station off from the town centre) had removed through traffic from the central area. In spite of two bus stations – North and South – there were still numerous bus stands in Duke Street, St. Sepulchre Gate and at Christ Church and Cleveland Street, as well as many picking up places. There were a myriad of narrow streets and a complex one-way street lay-out The whole lot called for a comprehensive central area plan. This came – eventually and at the suggestion of the PTE – only after considerable resistance, largely from the Police, the local Divisional Superintendent having a strong car bias, which meant that even if the County Engineer could obtain the 'yellow line' orders, he could not, or would not, ensure their enforcement. The first bus lane did not occur in Doncaster until 1994! North Bridge and the approaches thereto, particularly on the A638 from Sun Lane and Sprotbrough Lane, as well as the A19 in from Bentley, were perpetual problems for bus operation. The improvements introduced on the south side of the town, Bawtry Road and Cantley Lane junction, showed just what help could be given to buses.

The Executive was also consulted by District Planning Authorities, and over the years had assisted in the preparation of plans for the centres of Barnsley, Doncaster and Sheffield. At an early stage of the planning process, where new housing or industrial areas were being developed, the Executive aimed to ensure adequate provision for efficient bus operation. Sites on which the Executive had been consulted included Gawber in Barnsley, Edenthorpe in Doncaster, Thorpe Hesley in Rotherham and sites in Mosborough, including the District Centre in Waterthorpe.

Pedestrianisation

It has been said that the Executive worked with the County Council to obtain bus priorities to facilitate operation, and a modicum of success was achieved. However, not all highway schemes were beneficial to buses, and one such exercise highlights the conflicts within the County Council, and between the County and the Districts.

Politically, South Yorkshire supported public transport. But while the Transport Committee was pushing for bus priorities, the Highways Committee was set on pedestrianisation. One of the thoroughfares along which all vehicular traffic was to be banned was The Moor in Sheffield. The Moor constituted an extension of Sheffield's town centre shops and was, in effect, a subsidiary or second shopping area with various major stores represented. The road was traversed by 23 bus routes (and by the trams before them); in fact, all of the routes which served the environs to the south-west of Sheffield passed along The Moor and with bus stops literally in front of the shops, passengers enjoyed maximum convenience. But this ideal for bus passengers was not to last. The Moor was on the City Council's list to be pedestrianised.

Alternative routes for vehicular traffic were available on either side of, and parallel to, The Moor. But the bus stops would no longer be in front of the shops, and the routing was circuitous and more tortuous. A need to negotiate several new roundabouts and corners increased the chances of passengers falling inside buses and the substantial additional miles per annum, which meant increased expenditure which could have been better spent on service development. MVA in its Sheffield and Rotherham LUTS exercise, and the PTE in its Development Plan, both recommended that the use of The Moor be retained for buses only and had also recommended the safeguarding of a tramway alignment along The Moor. It was noted at the time that the tram was an ideal vehicle to mix with pedestrianisation, as witness the numerous highly successful examples on the Continent.

The case to retain buses in The Moor was weighty. Any public transport minded authority would surely see the value of a buses-only road, and spare the passengers the need to carry heavy shopping baskets to some other place before boarding a bus. Now was the time to prove the value of the bus undertaking being under the same umbrella as the highway and planning authorities. This is what the 1972 Act was all about, to see how the principle would work in practice. Accordingly, the PTE made strong internal representations against the closure of The Moor to buses. But its protests fell on stony ground. County Council policy was to close The Moor (it was certainly the wish of the Highway Committee if not all of the Transport Committee) and the PTE was, to all intents and purposes, a part of that County Council. It had had its orders and therefore became powerless to pursue the matter. Had it been an independent undertaking it could have taken the matter beyond the County

Council. It might not have been successful but its voice would have been heard. To be in on the ground floor and all under the same umbrella was not necessarily beneficial to all parties.

The Moor was finally closed to traffic in July 1979 and the buses were diverted. More bus priorities were introduced including bus actuated traffic lights at the junction of Eyre Street, a re-alignment in South Lane and a 'bus only' slip road up to Furnival Square. Ornamental seating, a street market and even a bandstand now occupy the space where the buses used to be. The only vehicles to be seen cross at right angles half way down are private cars proceeding to a car park located inside the bus circulatory area and therefore slightly better placed for the shops than at the bus stops! To make quite certain that any future tramway would never use The Moor a mammoth office block was erected astride the thoroughfare at Moorfoot! A further irony was the construction of stylised brick-built tramcar ends on a short length of track bed.

Transport for the Disabled

On a more positive note the PTE, with the financial support of the County Council, was instrumental in meeting the needs of the disabled and all who experienced difficulty in getting around. The kneeling bus and the special split step at the entrances are matters for Chapter 7. Also mentioned in that chapter are the buses that were specially adapted to carry wheelchairs. But it was these vehicles which enabled a very special type of service to be introduced. A group of routes was inaugurated in Doncaster, which served all of the surrounding neighbourhoods, to give a return facility to the town centre shopping complex. The buses rotated day by day on to a different route thereby serving all communities once a week. With a lift to enable wheelchairs to be carried safely anchored to the floor with some normal seats retained for any necessary attendants, the service enabled disabled people to see modern shops that some had never seen for years. It was a social, if not a commercial, success.

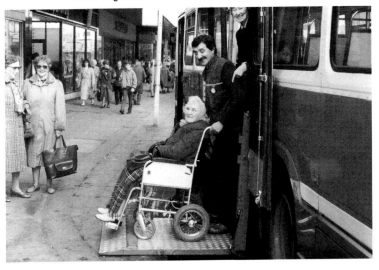

One of the Leyland National buses converted to carry wheel chairs unloading in Doncaster town centre. *(Audley Forrester)*

OPERATIONAL FEATURES

One-person operation

Reference has already been made to the high level of crew operation and to the problems of introducing one-person operation. SYPTE was unusual in keeping conductor operation working well into the 1980s and as late as 1983 there were still 500 conductors on the South Yorkshire staff. Indeed some buses, specifically designed for OPO, were withdrawn without ever having been used as such. The ticket machines used by the conductors were Ultimates – a wonderful machine for the nimble fingered – and Setrights, whilst the OPO staff were using electric TIMS in Sheffield and Almex 'A's in Rotherham and Doncaster. 'Videmat' self-service machines were also used on some of the cross-city routes in Sheffield and on a small number of routes in Doncaster.

As OPO conversion programmes gathered a-pace, the complexity of industrial relations matters once again manifested itself in industrial action. The Sheffield staff were adamantly set against the use of Almex 'A's for OPO. As a result of earlier extensive consultations the Executive had purchased a quantity of motorised Almex 'A's (unique to South Yorkshire). These were demonstrated in all the garages, and installed on a number of buses. The Sheffield staff refused to use them and a one-day strike ensued. The machines were withdrawn and negotiations begun which resulted in the fledgling Wayfarer Mk 1 being tested with remote thermal printer that was situated behind the cab in an effort to speed up passenger flow. The potential of this machine was immediately recognised and eventually the system was introduced fleet wide, although inevitably Doncaster and Rotherham were to be different and insisted on the simple integral version.

Express Operation

With the inauguration of the White Rose Group of express services, introduced in 1969, the predecessors of SYPTE had their first involvement with such activities. Although Sheffield JOC ran a number of long distance services they were stage carriage by nature and not express. The White Rose opened new horizons. South Yorkshire was well-served by motorways: the M1 running throughout its length and the M18 giving motorway access to Doncaster and the eastern part of the county. The A1 was dual-carriageway throughout with the central section – A1(M) – being motorway.

At the PTE's establishment local rail services were unfocused and services were those that BR felt were worth providing. There was an hourly service to Leeds via Barnsley and an hourly service to Hull and Cleethorpes, providing a half-hourly service to Doncaster. A key element of support for the development of local rail services was their ability to provide fast links both within the county and between the county and other neighbouring areas. These matters are dealt with more fully in Chapter 10. It was necessary to see where these express links could be provided by coach, utilising the motorway network or other 'fast' sections of road.

Links to be looked at were:

Barnsley-Doncaster
Barnsley-Huddersfield
Doncaster-Sheffield
Sheffield-Worksop-Retford

Following protracted negotiations and with a minimum revenue guaranteed, Yorkshire Traction introduced an

AEC Reliance 1016 acquired with the business of Felix in the PTE's original coaching Traveline livery. *(Mike Fowler)*

Fastline Dennis Dominator 2486 leaves Rotherham bus station en route from Doncaster to Sheffield. *(Mike Greenwood)*

express service between Barnsley and Doncaster (North Bus Station) via the A635 which was a fast and direct route. It was an immediate success – although the guaranteed payment was not discontinued! The Barnsley – Huddersfield link was provided by diverting and supporting the Sheffield–Penistone–Huddersfield railway service (See Chapter 10). Not mentioned, because it was already in existence was the 512 Sheffield – Chesterfield limited stop service – basically peak-hour duplication on the basic service 10. The Sheffield–Worksop–Retford route was covered by service 85 which provided quite fast journey times. In the event the local train service was supported.

There remained the Doncaster – Sheffield link. This was eventually provided by the X24 service with an X25 providing certain services via Bawtry. The remoteness of Rotherham Masbrough station and the tortuous nature of the former rail route meant that rail journey times were extended. Yet analysis of 277/278 route loadings showed the value of an end-to-end express service In 1982, it was decided to adopt 'Fastline' as the brand name for all express and limited stop services, which were given an 'X' prefix. In due course a network of express services was introduced to serve the Mosborough area, but these are dealt with later in the Chapter. The development of the Fastline services led to a requirement for coach-seated double-deckers with special branding livery. They became an attractive feature of SYPTE's operations, most still continuing under Mainline's banner.

Coaching

Towards the end of its separate existence, Doncaster became interested in coaching work. Although Sheffield had some coaches for JOC services, and bought others for the White Rose services, it was not involved in any coaching activity. Rotherham had no coaches. With the acquisition of independents (see Chapter 9), the PTE bought both Excursion and Tours (E & T) Licences and vehicles and, in some cases, the supporting infrastructure of booking agents.

The raison d'être of purchasing the independents was to gain control of the stage-carriage business. The Executive saw itself as a local bus operator. As described elsewhere it had problems with service reliability – principally because of staff and vehicle shortages – so that the Executive felt disinclined to become involved in such extraneous activities as coaching (This was in marked contrast to the way Tyne & Wear PTE were developing similar opportunities.)

The Author, as Controller of Operations was convinced, along with the District Manager, Doncaster, and Operations Manager, Halfway, that properly organised coaching could be a profitable and worthwhile activity. However, it proved impossible to negotiate satisfactory pay and conditions that would make such activities profitable.

The coaching market – excursions, tours, private hire – is entirely different from the local bus market. The only common feature is the use of passenger-carrying vehicles, although even here coaches are a world apart from buses. It required a different type of person both to develop and sell suitable coaching programmes, and to drive the vehicles. Only coach drivers understood this point. Bus drivers saw it as a 'soft job' or a 'perk', largely because they went to 'nice' places and did nothing while they were there. Accordingly every garage wanted a coach, which was completely the wrong way to organise the business. The Controller's ideas were to consolidate coaching activities on two garages: Halfway (as a base for its own immediate market and a springing-off point for Rotherham and Sheffield) and Doncaster, where a nucleus was being created and there were keen staff. Over time the Doncaster-based activity grew with the acquisition of independents, many of which had coaching activities.

The Trade Union never accepted this view and was not prepared to negotiate the necessary flexibility in pay and conditions to make coaching profitable. Three of the Sheffield garages and Rotherham had coach-seated single deckers – dual-purpose vehicles (DPs) for either express or the longer distance (often ex JOC) routes. They tried to set up their own competing programmes, thus diluting the effort and reducing the quality branding SYPTE was trying to adopt with Travel-line.

Vehicles were a perpetual problem and it was not until the early 1980's that new vehicles were purchased. The best of the acquired coaches were refurbished and repainted, including a large number acquired from Dearneways. Eventually the Executive gave the Trade Union an ultimatum, either agree with the Executive's proposals on pay, flexible conditions and coach allocations, or they would pull out of the business. As was so often the case, the Union refused to move and the PTE got out of the coaching business. Eventually common sense prevailed after a few years and a dedicated group of drivers were eventually chosen and trained to drive the new Dennis Dorchesters and second-hand Leylands Tigers that were acquired. Coachline activities were then based on Leadmill Garage.

Further Consolidation

The first two years of the PTE's operations had been characterised by the consolidation of the municipal inheritance into a composite, efficient and effective whole, by the need to improve service reliability with all that meant in engineering and staff recruitment and training terms, by a staged implementation of a County-wide fares policy and by improved and County-wide passenger information and publicity. None of these items was particularly eye-catching or headline grabbing but all were essential to the establishment of sound foundations upon which to build. In parallel with these were the improvements to vehicle design and maintenance, belated delivery of new buses and the development of new vehicles for the future, all described in the next Chapter. Work in this period also included the research into and drafting of the PTE's 'Transport Development Plan'[17] which would, in due course, lead to substantial infrastructure developments.

On-going issues

There were perpetual concerns about the operation of the Central Bus Station (CBS) in Sheffield, built for shorter, narrower, rear-platform buses; the continued existence of Bridge Street Bus Station, inconvenient for everywhere except, possibly, the markets; the growing congestion in High Street and timekeeping problems with the City Clipper service. Additional bus priorities were needed in Sheffield and a campaign for such measures was required in Rotherham and Doncaster, particularly the latter. Both Sheffield and Doncaster had a proliferation of terminal points, including on-street stands. Interchange arrangements between services were inadequate, yet none of the bus stations could accept more services without investment and even then all but Sheffield were confined by the existence of multi-storey car parks above them.

SERVICE DEVELOPMENT

It was apparent that from the effects of improved service reliability, the holding of the fare levels (particularly during a period of inflation) and the availability of new vehicles that passenger numbers were growing, as was to be expected from the implementation of the County Council's policies. It also became clear that such improvements could not be introduced in an ad-hoc manner if they were to achieve maximum effect with still-scarce resources. Furthermore, extensive consultations were required both internally with the staff and externally with the County and local District Councils, Area Advisory Sub-Committees, User Groups, industrialists, etc., etc. Accordingly it was decided to develop an annual Service Development Programme, and this began to take effect in 1976/77.

The phrase 'Service Development' covered a whole range of improvements:
- increased frequencies on existing services
- extended or altered routes.
- new routes
- area re-organisations, where a complete network would be re-appraised so as to provide a new pattern more in line with current needs
- introduction of special services

There was also the need to react to external developments, such as town centre traffic management schemes, pedestrianisation proposals, re-development in city centres or of derelict industrial sites.

New residential developments were springing up all over the area as the housing boom continued. Areas such as Mosborough, Chapeltown and Stannington in Sheffield were all areas beyond the traditional 'city' and therefore did not benefit from the high frequency services provided within the City. These areas were probably the most extensive in so far as population increases were concerned and traditional bus routes quickly proved to be inadequate. At the same time some of the traditional heavy industries were in decline (steel and coal eventually almost disappeared).

The 'Grand Design' (Chapter 3) had made reference to Service Development which gradually built up in its momentum over the years. The foundations for annual service development programmes had to be laid by improving the reliability of the existing operations – particularly in Sheffield – and by negotiating satisfactory arrangements with other operators. Given the commitment of the County Council towards public transport there seemed to be a wonderful opportunity to expand the system. The County Council was pouring substantial sums of public money into the system to maintain low fares and this was fuelling the demand for better services.

Re-organisation of the Sheffield – Dronfield – Chesterfield corridor in 1980 was a scheme sponsored by Derbyshire County Council (DCC) in whose area 75% of the business lay. DCC provided financial support for the services, but did not operate a low fares policy. Dronfield lay in Derbyshire but was a dormitory of Sheffield and its centre for public services was in Chesterfield. Housing had expanded rapidly to the west (Gosforth) and east (Coal Aston) but the bus route network had remained unchanged for years. The new network ensured that all areas of Dronfield had links to both Sheffield and Chesterfield and enabled DCC to reduce its financial contribution

The scheme took almost 3 years to implement, due to squabbles over which garage of the PTE did which work – the PTE's subsidiary Booth & Fisher (see below) became involved and this was resented by Sheffield. But it was a good scheme and many of the elements have survived through deregulation to be commercially viable.

Mosborough, some six miles south-east of Sheffield, where new housing was planned to accommodate some 80,000 people, was almost like a mini 'new town'. An independent operator, Booth & Fisher, had its operating base and garage at Halfway which was within the designated development area, and was an ideal centre from which to expand the necessary facilities for the new Mosborough area. In the event the PTE acquired this company (see Chapter 9) and eventually transformed the undertaking from a few single-deck buses running on semi-rural and rural routes plus some colliery and school workings, into a major operating unit to serve the new resident population. The enlarged network included an important double-deck trunk route into Sheffield.

The initial stage in the development of Mosborough was made by the introduction of Service X30 which ran between Sheffield, Woodhouse, Beighton, Westfield and Halfway. It quickly became heavily used despite its routing and on most occasions the hourly service ran full to capacity. Even so there was a reluctance by the Sheffield District to find resources to increase the frequency. Eventually Booth & Fisher were organised to operate a half hourly direct service between Sheffield and Halfway. It was an instant success although it was initially operated by elderly single deckers which had been displaced from Doncaster. The Sheffield Trade Union were furious at this action and their relationship with the Halfway staff remains unfriendly to this day.

Additional mileage was run and extra passengers were carried in 1978/79 and again in 1979/80. Service developments continued in both years. In 1979 eighteen additional peak hour vehicles were put into service and 10,000 miles per week added to services.

A major restructure of services in North Derbyshire and Mosborough took place and was another example of Derbyshire County Council seeking network changes to cater for expanded housing at Killamarsh and Eckington. East Midland Motor Services (which had an operating agreement with the PTE for its South Yorkshire operations) was also involved and this time the two operators exchanged routes so as to ensure the best networks could be achieved. Always an emotive act, the words 'transfer of mileage' were guaranteed to cause apoplexy to a trade union representative.

The PTE gradually entered into Operating Agreements with all the various bus companies in the area. Initially the PTE sought to acquire operators, and while some were willing (Booth and Fisher, Severns, Dearneways etc.) many were not. Agreements were made with companies such as Leon, East Midland and Yorkshire Traction, who still continue in business. These agreements gave the companies a financial arrangement as a basis to enable services to be changed. Examples were the increased frequency between Doncaster and Barnsley by YTC and the diversion of the Doncaster to Leeds service by South Yorkshire Road Transport to service a northern part of Doncaster which the Doncaster District was reluctant to serve with one of their own routes.

A major highlight was the introduction of articulated buses, 'Bendibuses' to use the expressive local name for articulated single-deckers on the City Clipper circulatory service in Sheffield. The Bendibus saga is dealt with more fully in Chapter 7.

As the service development programme's momentum built up, the Executive and County Council found themselves under increasing financial pressure, as has already been described. Pressure for new services and/or increased frequencies did not ease, although additional resources were limited. Thus resources for service development had to be found increasingly from savings and reductions from other parts of the network. This 'teeming and ladling' approach posed a number of problems.

Firstly, with the cheap fares and increasing number of passengers it was not easy to find spare resources at the times they were most needed. Secondly, there was increasing resistance from the Area Advisory Sub-Committee to any reductions in service, however trivial. Thirdly there was also resistance from the trade unions to change, because this often had the effect of transferring work from one District or garage to another. Furthermore, the Trade Unions were sensitive to the pressures being placed upon the County by the government and felt that the future of the policy was clouded.

A great deal was achieved by the Service Development programme from 1974 to 1985 as shown in the Appendix on pages 153-155. Over the twelve years 329 existing bus services were the subject of major change, 76 new services were introduced and 166 services were being diverted or extended. Thirty-seven services were cut back or withdrawn. Significant developments were the introduction of 'Nipper' services, the introduction of articulated buses; the development of a network of express bus services and the introduction of special services for the disabled and those living in inaccessible areas[20].

In retrospect there is an overwhelming feeling that a great challenge was unfinished, and that subsequent events have lost for ever the opportunity to complete something worthwhile. It was an exciting period in the development of South Yorkshire's transport, but it was also an endless war of attrition to achieve anything. That delayed the implementation of the County's 'Grand Design' and compounded the problems created by hostile government policies – evident even under the Labour administration up to 1975.

Under Section 59 of the 1985 Transport Act, Passenger Transport Executives were prohibited from operating buses themselves. Thus came to an end an era that had lasted from 1969 (1974 in the cases of South & West Yorkshire). More importantly, the municipal inheritance of nearly a century was broken. The PTEs (and municipalities) were required to establish their direct operations as separate limited liability companies which, in due time, were to be privatised. SYPTE established South Yorkshire Transport Ltd., now trading as the Mainline Group – but that's another story, dealt with in Chapters 12 and 13.

Angel Street Sheffield, one of the many busy loading points in the city centre. *(Mike Fowler)*

7 ENGINEERING DEVELOPMENTS

VEHICLE ENGINEERING

Inheritance

SYPTE took over the bus fleets of Doncaster, Rotherham and Sheffield – a total of 903 vehicles, 128 from Doncaster 125 from Rotherham and 650 from Sheffield. The inherited fleet was predominantly double-deck, although there was a very wide diversity of designs reflecting both the operating characteristics and engineering policies followed by the predecessor authorities. Each of the former municipalities had vehicles on order in April 1974, some of which were several years late, and thus continued to have some influence on vehicle design. There was little standardisation in this fleet and, in general, it was an 'old' fleet with a high average age. Whilst adequately maintained, this had been done on the basis of 'maintenance or failure' rather than under a system of preventative maintenance.[14]

There was a widely varying mix of front and rear-engined double-deckers with open platforms and single or double-door configurations. The single-deck fleet, albeit small, consisted of underfloor and rear-engined vehicles with one or two doors, as well as dual-purpose (DP) vehicles. There were 33 different chassis from five manufacturers – with bodywork by fourteen different bodybuilders. Thus in the fleet there were 126 different types – clearly some rationalisation was required.

The diverse nature of the fleet stemmed from the policies of the previous undertakings. Sheffield, contributing 70% of the initial SYPTE fleet, had historically favoured AEC and Leyland chassis with bodywork largely by Weymann and, in earlier times, the local firm of Cravens, primarily a railway rolling stock builder but which built bus bodywork in the periods before and after the 1939-45 war. In the 1950s, Charles H. Roe of Leeds became a regular supplier and in the 1960s more diversity of bodybuilders became evident, Park Royal, Alexander and East Lancs all delivering batches. Examples of the last-mentioned concern's design were built locally in 1964-6 by Neepsend Coachworks, a subsidiary of East Lancs.

From 1960, Sheffield began to adopt the rear-engined double-decker, at first favouring the Leyland Atlantean, AEC not offering such a model and continuing to supply front-engined Regent V models until 1963/4. From the mid-1960s the Daimler Fleetline was adopted, latterly being supplied in similar large numbers as the Atlantean, though there was also a batch of Bristol VRT in 1972. Sheffield was unusual in choosing the longer 10.6-metre option in conjunction with two-door layout for many of its

late rear-engined double-deckers instead of the more widely-favoured 9.5-metre versions. Sheffield had operated 49 single-deckers latterly, the more modern of these being AEC Swift rear-engined models with Park Royal bodywork.

The Doncaster fleet consisted of 128 vehicles: 3 coaches, 5 midibuses, 48 single-deckers and 72 double-deckers. The coaches were Fords; one with a Caetano body, the other two with Duple bodies. The midibuses were Seddons with Pennine bodywork similar to those operated by SELNEC PTE. The single-deckers were either Roe-bodied Leyland underfloor vehicles or Seddon RU's with Pennine bodies. The front-engined double-deck fleet consisted of 12 Leyland PD2 or PD3 and 29 Daimler CVG6. All had Roe bodywork, 11 of the Daimlers having former trolleybus bodies. There were also 31 Roe-bodied Daimler Fleetlines.

Rotherham had the most standardised fleet – all Daimler and most with Roe bodies. It had shown a consistent policy of vehicle and body development, was well-maintained – although the garage premises left a lot to be desired – and was always well presented. It reflected the pride and competence of the General Manager, Ken Griffiths and the Chief Engineer – Charlie Duke – a kind man of many talents and high standards.

Operating territory

Sheffield was well-known as a graveyard for buses because of its very hilly and demanding terrain. It is the hilliest city in Britain and all routes, except those going along the Don Valley, involved a climb from the City Centre, which was only about 200ft above sea level. Even the valley routes faced stiff climbs as they neared their destinations, such as Totley or Dore. One notorious Sheffield route was the 51,

A chart showing the undulating nature of service 51 in Sheffield.

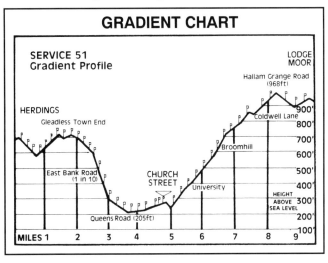

the gradient profile and operating characteristics of which are shown overleaf – it climbed 763ft in one direction and 500ft in the other. Such routes tested vehicles to the full – notably engines, gear boxes and brakes. There were over-heating problems in summer and cold or overcooling problems in winter on the long descents.

Whilst there were some hilly sections of routes in Rotherham, notably in the Greaseborough, Kimberworth and Clifton areas, the territory was much easier and very compact. Doncaster's operating area was virtually flat. However, some of the longer distance services required some relatively fast timings for stage carriage services.

Two-door buses

In April, 1974 there were still substantial numbers of front-engined double-deckers in the fleet. Sheffield purchased its first rear-engined double-deck buses in 1960. From 1966, 225 dual-door double-deckers were purchased as compared with 94 single-door buses. It was a requirement of the Bus Grant conditions introduced in 1968 that all buses had to be capable of one-man-operation (now OPO). The two door buses were designed for, but not necessarily operated by, one-person. Sheffield adopted the front-boarding, centre-exiting (two door) arrangement, with the foot of the staircase opposite the central exit. Apart from the convenience for passengers leaving the upper deck, the forward ascending configuration had the distinct advantage of throwing passengers forward to relative safety and not down stairs if the bus had to brake heavily. There was, therefore, a preponderance of two-door double-deckers in the STD fleet by 1974, compared to the front entrance/front exit arrangement adopted by Rotherham and Doncaster. There were very good reasons for Sheffield adopting the double-door policy: heavily loaded routes with simultaneous boarding and alighting with many routes being cross-city. Most of Rotherham and Doncaster routes were radial by nature, terminating in the town centre or bus station, with little simultaneous boarding and alighting. Most of Sheffield's services were at this time (1974) crew-operated for reasons discussed in Chapter 6. Sheffield's adoption of two doors was in line with other large city operators at the time such as Manchester, Newcastle, Glasgow, Edinburgh, Coventry and so on.

The polka-dot fleet inherited by SYPTE, together

One of the London Transport DM type Fleetlines, No. 1523 in the Wicker, Sheffield. *(Mike Greenwood)*

The first of the Van Hool-McArdle bodies on Volvo Ailsa chassis was fitted to No. 370. It is seen here in Dublin, as yet unregistered and fitted with CIE destination blinds for the photograph. *(SYPTE)*

The only Van Hool-McArdle body to be received not fitted to a Volvo was No. 431, a 1976 Leyland Atlantean. After withdrawal from passenger service it was converted to a mobile sales/exhibition unit. *(Mike Greenwood)*

with its age and the arduous operating terrain, led to both high bus operating costs and frequent occasions when services were missed. Whilst buses had been ordered by the previous municipalities, deliveries were taking four to five years. Furthermore, the availability of spares was also poor. The bus industry was still geared up to maintaining the inherently reliable front-engined bus and not the 'box of tricks' which typified the first generation of rear-engined buses. As increasing proportions of services were being operated by the Atlanteans and Fleetlines, so the problems mounted and became more apparent. As will be considered later in this Chapter, most of the garages were 'over-bused' and thus maintenance facilities were inadequate.

New bus orders

To overcome these problems SYPTE surprised the industry by two moves. First it ordered 29 Daimler Fleetlines with MCW bodywork to the same design as was being supplied to London Transport as the type DMS, the only differences being the front destination layout, the moquette and the external livery. Originally these had been part of an order for 60 bodies from Alexander[15]. The second, and bigger surprise was the order for 60 Ailsa double-deck buses. The Ailsa design had been developed in Scotland at Irvine, with the encouragement of the Scottish Bus Group (SBG) as an alternative to the Atlantean, Fleetline and Bristol VR designs, all built by the British Leyland group. By adopting a front-mounted engine it was hoped to overcome many of the problems experienced with the rear-engined designs. SYPTE's buses were to have a turbo-charged, 6.7 litre Volvo TD 70E engine capable of developing 201 bhp, but initially governed down to 185bhp. Although these figures were above those of contemporary Gardner or Leyland engines in the 10-11 litre class, they depended on using the much smaller engine's fast-revving characteristics. This engine was coupled to an automatically-controlled electro-pneumatic gearbox (GB 350) made by Self-Changing Gears Ltd.

Originally it had been hoped to have these buses bodied by Alexander of Falkirk, but they could not achieve the required delivery dates.[16] No other British bodybuilder could meet the PTE's delivery requirements. However, in October 1975 an order for 60 bodies was placed with Van Hool McArdle of Dublin for a two-door design, suitable for OPO, and with 75 seats. The design was based upon an all-welded steel box section frame – a first in Britain at the time. The PTE had come across the Van Hool McArdle design earlier in 1975, when it had hosted a CIE Atlantean with their bodywork. The first bus – No. 369 – was bodied in Belgium, but all the remaining buses were bodied at the Spa Road Works in Dublin[17]. Originally, this works had been owned by Dublin United Tramways, a predecessor of CIE, who had, in turn sold the works to Van Hool McArdle. A unique Atlantean, No. 431 was also bodied with a Van Hool McArdle body, and was exhibited at the 1976 Commercial Motor Show at Earls Court, London[15].

The Ailsas gave stalwart service in Sheffield and Doncaster, but due to the lack of torque at the bottom end of the scale they suffered from poor acceleration in the lower speeds and were not a reliable vehicle in the long run. SYPTE phased them out well ahead of their sell-by-date. They were more at home on the flat routes in the Doncaster area. Although designed for OPO, Sheffield staff would never accept them as being suitable – because they could not go from the driver's seat into the saloon direct. Doncaster staff had no such inhibitions. They were striking looking buses – unique in their design – and were sorely needed.

Gradually orders placed by the previous undertakings began to come through in the form of Atlanteans, bodied by East Lancashire Coachbuilders for Doncaster and by Alexanders for Sheffield. Some Roe-bodied Fleetlines also came for Rotherham. In those days new buses had to be shared between garages so that they all had 'some new toys', such was the influence of the T & GWU.

Against this background it is not suprising that SYPTE decided to develop a standard double-deck bus although the operating regime in Doncaster and Rotherham was much less demanding than in Sheffield. Within Sheffield there were the cross-city routes and the terminal routes, the former requiring two-door buses, the latter only one door. Of course a standard bus offered greater flexibility than the 'horses-for-courses' approach which was to be adopted later. The 'standard' bus was very much in-line with the thinking of the time and was developed particularly in London, SELNEC, West Midlands and Greater Glasgow. SYPTE engineering was following the main-stream of current thought. However, prior to developing its own standard it undertook extensive analysis and development work, both internally and with the manufacturing industry.

BUS DEVELOPMENT

In the period 1976 – 1980, it was considered that the double-deck bus would continue to be the backbone of the SYPTE fleet. Operationally the area was predominantly urban and the County policies were going to lead to increased passenger usage. The industry was moving towards a vehicle 9.5m. long, 2.5m. wide and 4.4m. high although, as previously indicated, Sheffield had preferred the 10.6m length. This pointed to the need to determine the 'door question' once-and-for-all.

There was also the need for an underfloor or rear-engined single-deck bus with the ability to accept one or two-door design of bodywork. There were already in existence the City Clipper and Early Bird services in Sheffield, and this type of service was likely to develop under the County's policies. Also required were DP coaches for the White Rose Express services and the longer stage carriage routes, such as Sheffield – Gainsborough. An 11 m. long underfloor engined design would suit here, although 12m. long coaches (the maximum permitted) were not ruled out.

Doncaster had been an early operator of midibuses in the form of the 6.3m-long Seddon Pennine IV 236 chassis. These had been used to initiate a town centre service, as well as a number of other services penetrating housing estates. This chassis had been developed, initially, to meet SELNEC's requirements for its Centreline service. It was considered that the demanding work, both in terms of passenger loadings and traffic, required a 'big bus cut down' rather than a 'minibus built up'. The Seddon design had shown itself very effective in traffic. Readers will appreciate that this was well before the minibus revolution which was to take place ten years later, in the mid-1980s. Articulated buses had been under investigation and trial since late 1977, and the subject will be dealt with later. However, they were at this time illegal in Britain and a number of other fundamental issues had to be resolved. Accordingly priority was given to the development of reliable components to be incorporated into future bus orders.

Componentry

For the first four years of the Executive's life engineering developments had concentrated upon overcoming the severe mechanical problems besetting the bus fleet, in an attempt to improve vehicle availability and thus improve service reliability. South Yorkshire was not, of course,

alone in the problems it faced with buses, particularly the rear-engined designs. However, the problems were exacerbated by Sheffield's hilly terrain and the 'polka-dot' fleet with such a profusion of designs. In particular, braking systems required almost constant attention to maintain acceptable levels of efficiency. When dealing with this subject in the PTE's *Transport Development Plan*[17], it was said: 'The Executive accepts that there is a need for vehicles of a higher engineering quality and reliability than those currently in service'. At the time the PTE's fleet was totally inadequate to meet the demands being placed upon it – certain groups of vehicles tended to be unreliable and costly to run. To overcome these problems it was essential to react to the operating needs by improving the vehicle specification and reduce the many different types within the fleet. With hindsight it is difficult not to overstress two points: firstly, the truly awful reliability problems and the consequential effects to service on the road, even with 25% spare vehicles: secondly, the importance of service in those regulated days.

Development of bus specification

Chapter 8 of the PTE's *Transport Development Plan* set the objectives of present and short term developments, which sought to achieve '... a marked improvement in urban transit standards and an emphasis on fuel economy, transmission reliability, lower engine emission, lower noise emissions, improved passenger comfort and safety through improved transmission systems, and a high degree of vehicle quality and reliability'. Written in the Spring of 1977, and published in 1978, this statement sought to put South Yorkshire in the vanguard of bus development. Particular note should be made of the concerns for noise and fume emissions, and the concept of 'urban transit', rather than just bus transport. This was also the thinking behind investigatory and trial work with articulated buses, trolleybuses, battery powered vehicles and light rapid transit. All this was a far cry from the 'cheap fares policy' which became the public persona to many outside South Yorkshire. All these developments were supported by the County Council

The South Yorkshire developed Standard split step entrance is seen here on No. 1764, which in addition operated from November 1979 until March 1982 with a Rolls Royce LPG engine. *(SYPTE)*

who provided or authorised the budgets for them.

A high degree of standardisation was seen as being essential to reducing costs. 'The Executive is actively pursuing a policy which will ensure that all bus systems are designed to allow for the reasonable needs of elderly, infirm and disabled people experiencing difficulty in movement or impairment of vision'.[17] Again South Yorkshire was leading the field, well before the disabled requirements of the 1985 Transport Act. Considerable attention was given to reducing floor heights, entrance design and step heights. The 'Kneeling National' and split-step entrance were examples of these. Throughout this vehicle development programme the policy was one of 'active engagement with manufacturers in producing future bus designs...'.[17]

A large part of the Engineering Department's development work concentrated on resolving the transmission, gearbox and braking issues which, of course, were fundamental to passenger comfort and safety, and giving a good in-traffic performance. The rear-engined buses of the day had semi-automatic (clutchless) gearboxes manufactured by Self-Changing Gears or Leylands's own Pneumocyclic gearbox, usually with CAV electrically-operated control. These required relines of the internal brake bands and overhauls after as little as 10 weeks in service. A recently delivered batch of Atlanteans had the then new G2 automatic gearbox which gave a variable performance and could be lethal in icy conditions, when some vehicles had to be taken off the road! The Executive's engineers knew of the reputation for reliability enjoyed by the Voith D851 gearbox used extensively abroad, and this also had a built-in retarder which was reputed to reduce brake liner wear by 50%. Later in-service experience proved this to be very much on the low side in many areas of the PTE's operation. In fact, liner wear was so low that there were more problems with brake glazing than with wear, and linings were lasting up to two years. These gearboxes would not fit in the double-deck chassis produced in Britain without alteration, and none of the Executive's suppliers was prepared to modify a chassis to fit one. SYPTE took an ordinary Leyland AN68 Atlantean and re-engineered it to its own standards, including the fitting of a Voith D851 automatic transmission, incorporating a hydraulic torque converter and integral hydraulic retarder system. Improvements were also made to the cooling system, revised engine power outputs and general detailed improvements. The fitting of the Voith showed a 10-fold improvement in brake and brake drum life with the consequent cost savings and improvements in reliability. Add to that increase in gearbox life of around 400%, and the reduction in operating costs and improvement in lost mileage comes into clearer focus.

When a trial of the modified gearbox had demonstrated its success, the chassis manufacturers agreed to fit them in future vehicles. By 1984 these gearboxes had been fitted to over 50% of the Executive's fleet and they were being used in four different types of chassis. Subsequently all the manufacturers of double-deck buses offered this gearbox as an alternative, and many hundreds are in use elsewhere in the country.

In spite of the Executive's policy of working with the manufacturers, Leyland not only refused to help in the work with the Voith gearbox, but actually withdrew its warranties on the vehicle concerned! In today's climate it is hard to realise that such action would be possible, particularly having regard to the fact that the majority of the SYPTE fleet consisted of Leyland group products, hundreds more were on order (and late) and the PTE was laying out the specification of its future requirements. Of course, the long-term effect of that attitude contributed to the total demise of Leyland as it then was. A year later Leyland offered the Voith gearbox as an option on its AN68, although it never acknowledged SYPTE's work!

Whilst the Voith gearbox was seen to be the solution to many of the problems, it could not be retro-fitted. There was, therefore, a need to do development work on new braking materials and braking system design. The PTE policy was also to do away with asbestos-based materials – another first in the field. Additionally the objectives were to achieve longer brake lives and reduced costs, as well as achieving an improved braking performance. These developments were pursued in association with Mintex, Duron and Don International. The PTE also had a joint venture into the latest technology braking system with GKN Ltd., relating to the development of disc brakes on heavy vehicles. (These had been pioneered many years earlier by Guy Motors Ltd on their revolutionary Wulfrunian double-decker design, where lack of development work revealed many problems.)

The Executive made a big contribution to the design and specification of buses, and had a record of successful innovation. It is doubtful whether Dennis would have been able to make a success of re-entering the bus manufacturing market without the support of SYPTE. Many items of the Executive's specification were adopted as standard by Dennis in the 'Dominator' chassis, more than a thousand of which were produced for use in this country, and an even higher number abroad.

Comparative Trials

Also during this period the Executive decided to carry out comparative trials with a number of existing double-deck bus designs, to determine either the most suitable design for future SYPTE bus orders or those features that were best suited to South Yorkshire's operating conditions. The notorious route 51 in Sheffield (mentioned earlier) was selected for the trials and five different types of vehicle were tested:

> Leyland Titan, developed from the B15 for
>   London Transport
> MCW Metrobus, recently launched into production
> Foden-Northern Counties prototype
> Hestair-Dennis Dominator
> Ailsa Mk II, a development of the 61 in service

The Leyland had a Pneumocyclic automatic gearbox

The Dennis Dominator built as a demonstrator for Dennis with East Lancs body, and pictured when new in Downing Street in connection with the receipt of an export award to the company, became No. 521 with the PTE. It continued to carry its blue and cream livery for some time after entering service. (Martin Llewellyn)

The small batch of Metro-Scanias did not last very long with the PTE (London Transport experienced similar problems) – No. 503 is seen here (Geoff Atkins)

Before the Dennis Dominator with Alexander R-type body was finally chosen as the standard vehicle, a number of experimental types were tested. Here, posed outside Halfway garage in the centre of the line up is the only Foden purchased (only seven of the type were ever built) No. 511, with East Lancs body. The four Dennis Dominators pictured also have East Lancs bodies; to the left are 523 and 524 which were originally ordered by Morgan and Store (see chapter nine), whilst to the right are 521 and 522. The history of the latter vehicle has been touched upon on the previous page, whilst 521 was the vehicle retro fitted with a Rolls Royce Eagle engine and used on the service 51 trial. (Gary Nolan)

and a Leyland TL 11 engine. The Metrobus had a Voith gearbox and a Gardner engine. Both these vehicles were integrally constructed; the Leyland from the Leyland National plant at Workington and the Metrobus from MCW's works at Washwood Heath. The Foden was also powered by a Gardner engine driving through an Allison gearbox. This was a semi-integral vehicle, the Foden underframe being designed to derive rigidity from the body. The Dennis Dominator was a latter-day Fleetline and was supplied with a Gardner engine driving through a SCG unit with auto-control gearbox when delivered in March 1978. Subsequently it was fitted with a Rolls Royce Eagle 220 engine and re-entered service on 24th July 1978. It had a body built by East Lancashire Coachbuilders of Blackburn. (Both Foden and Dennis were encouraged in their efforts by engineers in the operating section of the bus industry concerned with Leyland's cavalier attitude and also with the ever-increasing complexity – and cost – of its new generation double-deckers.) The Mark II Ailsa incorporated operating experience with the 61 already delivered to SYPTE. It incorporated the Turbo-charged Volvo TD 70E and a Self-Changing Gears automatic gearbox. The body was by Van Hool McArdle. The vehicles, therefore, incorporated 'something old, something new, something borrowed and something blue'.

The tests on the 51 route in Sheffield were spread over the first part of 1978 and included an operating assessment as well as detailed engineering information. Passenger and crew reactions were also studied. The vehicle that came out best overall was the Dennis Dominator, with the MCW Metrobus coming second. Since the PTE had a dual-sourcing policy the Dennis and the Metrobus were selected for the double-deck fleet. Up to this point the Dennis had not sold in large numbers and there had been no export orders. Whilst the Dominator had come out best in the tests SYPTE engineers considered that it still required some further development to bring it into line with the PTE's specification.

Standard buses

The key components were seen as: Dennis chassis, incorporating air suspension; Rolls Royce engine; Voith gearbox and Alexander body. A loose consortium was put together by the PTE, involving Dennis, Rolls Royce and Alexander, and thus all the PTE's design and development expertise accumulated over the previous four years could be brought to bear. Surprisingly it was not traditional in the British bus industry for chassis and bodybuilders to work closely together: it was very much a case of 'there's my chassis – you body it!' By working together, a much stronger and more effective design was produced.

With regard to the choice of engine SYPTE had considerable experience with Leyland and Gardner engines, the designs of which were old. Current designs had been 'stretched' to power the bigger rear-engined buses and/or to provide an improved performance. What had once been reliable designs were showing poorer reliability in contemporary service. Conceptually what was required

As well as the large fleet of standard Alexander bodied Dennis Dominators that entered service between 1981 and 1986, two small batches were ordered from Northern Counties and East Lancs. Seen here under construction at Wigan in 1983 are some of the Northern Counties batch. *(Mike Greenwood)*

was a big engine, probably down-rated, and working well within its limits. Detailed technical studies had been carried out prior to the comparative tests of route 51, and these had identified the Rolls Royce Eagle engine as one that would fit the bill. Since Rolls Royce were seeking to enter the PSV market, mutual benefits could be seen from developing the 'Eagle' to become the power unit for the Dennis Dominator Mark II. The engine was capable of developing 230 bhp, but in the SYPTE's application it was governed to180 bhp.

SYPTE had experience of most British bodybuilders, particularly Charles Roe, East Lancashire, Park Royal and Alexander. Those people who had come from SELNEC also had wide experience with Northern Counties' bodies. A large batch of Roe-bodied Atlanteans had required extensive structural work within quite a short time. East

Lancashire bodies were built in two sections – top and bottom – and then married together which gave long-term concerns about their integrity. The new vehicles were expected to have a twelve/thirteen-years life. Alexander produced aluminium framed and clad bodies in a production line process. Jointly SYPTE and Alexander developed a body, including an anti-corrosion specification, which enabled the bodybuilders to give a fifteen-year body warranty. Thus developed the Alexander 'R' type body – one of the most handsome double-deck bus bodies ever built – and certainly the most handsome on a rear-engined chassis.

The first of the SYPTE Standard buses – 2101 – entered service at Doncaster garage on 1st June 1981. Subsequently 293 were produced. Ten, numbered 2311 – 2320 were built by Northern Counties and 15, numbered 2351–2365 were bodied by East Lancashire Coachbuilders, but to the SYPTE spec/Alexander 'R' type design. This was done because Alexander's prices became uncompetitive. Subsequently similar bodies were built by East Lancs for Hull and Leicester Corporations. Thus SYPTE's influence spread to new places. As part of the dual-sourcing policy 170 Metrobuses were bought over a period of five years in five batches (15). Leadmill garage became an all-Metrobus garage with an allocation of 75 vehicles. It consistently achieved 100% turnout and minimum lost-mileage with less than 10% spares – an achievement not seen since the heyday of the PD2s and Regent IIIs! Later, express, coach-seated versions were delivered to the Fastline specification in twenty Dennis/ Alexanders and ten Metrobuses. In the former case a 10.5m vehicle, incorporating an additional centre section, was built.

Prior to developing the SYPTE standard bus, Sheffield had specified two-door vehicles for reasons outlined previously. Early PTE deliveries – to previous municipal orders – also incorporated the two-door layout. There were also a few two-door double-deckers in Rotherham and Doncaster. When OMO (as it then was) operation was first developed for double-deckers, two doors, ie separate entrance and exit, had been considered obligatory if boarding times – and hence journey times – were not to become greatly extended. Manchester and Coventry had done much pioneering work in double-deck OMO operation and London Transport had done some work using Operational Research Techniques. Conceptually it seemed to be right to have two doors, provided there was simultaneous boarding and alighting, and subject to careful design of the lower deck, to ensure adequate circulation. It was also essential to have an appropriate ticketing system. In turn this led to putting the second door midway in the wheelbase or towards the rear axle. This made it more remote from the driver and there were concerns about passenger accidents. In SYPTE's case there were two or three centre-door accidents in close succession, although fortunately in none of the cases was the PTE found to be at fault. PTE deliveries of two door buses had the centre door immediately behind the front axle – as opposed to the Sheffield arrangement of amidships. This, of course, reduced the circulation area within the vehicle.

The argument raged both within the industry and SYPTE as to the pros and cons of one-door v. two-door buses. As Controller of Operations and Planning, the Author was

Pictured here with the Chairman of the PTA, Councillor Alec Waugh and Eric Kay (front), inspecting a new vehicle are Councillor G Bennett a Rotherham member of the PTA and Bill Bland, the PTE's Development Engineer. *(SYPTE)*

concerned to resolve the issue on a factual, scientific basis – since little such information was found to exist – although there were plenty of 'opinions' around. Both London Transport and SELNEC had undertaken studies into one-door v. two-door operation, but the Sheffield union were reluctant to accept these results. Accordingly, a detailed method study was commissioned followed by a series of time studies on one-and two-door double-deckers, including those two door buses fitted with Videmat self-service ticket machines, thus permitting two-stream loading. To the very considerable surprise of many – and to the relief of others – the studies showed that in Sheffield two door operation had no benefits over one door operation, in fact one-door operation was shown to be marginally quicker! There was the usual tussle with the Trade Union, but from thence forward SYPTE came into line with the other PTEs (and much of the industry) by adopting a one-door layout. By that time very few UK operators were continuing to buy two-door double-deck vehicles. The reason why two-door operation was found to be slower was because the Sheffield drivers were letting passengers off at the centre door *before* opening the front door – thus negating the whole concept. They did this for several reasons: to be able to carefully observe the centre door and ensure nobody was trapped or nobody boarded by it, and to ensure that the bus was not overloaded. Interestingly enough these issues barely figured where articulated bus operation was being considered! However, the door gear on them was more reliable and there were interlocks on the remote doors.

Throughout the whole of the period during which these developments were taking place, the Engineering Department was under the Direction of Eric Kay. Early appointments had been Bill Bland as Development Engineer, and Dr. John Jordan as Research Assistant. Bill had come from BR where he had been Depot Manager at BR's Heaton DMU Depot in Newcastle – before it became the Metro Maintenance Depot. Bill brought a refreshing and hands-on approach to bus engineering and development. These three laid the foundations for the Standard SYPTE bus which was progressed following the arrival of Bill Kirkland as Controller of Engineering and Property Services. Bill came to the PTE from Greater Glasgow PTE, where he had been Chief Engineer. He had been apprenticed to Manchester Corporation before going into private industry, where he gained experience of manufacturing industry and production engineering. Bill often commented about the 'agricultural' nature of bus engineering. He re-joined the bus industry at SELNEC PTE where he was the Chief Engineer of the then Central Division (ex-Manchester part) based at Hyde Road.

ARTICULATED BUSES

In 1977 the Director of Engineering reported that there seemed to be scope for running articulated single-deck buses in South Yorkshire and he had been looking at the technical aspects of this.

Left: The visit of the Leyland-DAB demonstrator to Sheffield in July 1977 has been well documented. *(E Kay collection)*

Below left: The chassis of one of first batch of Leyland articulated buses before bodying. *(E Kay collection)*

Increasing numbers of them were being used abroad, whereas in this country we had continued with the traditional use of double-decked road passenger vehicles, that went back beyond the days of the horse tram to the stage-coach era. Even though articulated single-deck buses had obvious advantages in some situations, the Ministry of Transport's Vehicle Regulations did not, at that time, permit their use in this country. The Director of Engineering had discussed this with the Ministry of Transport officers, and with the bus manufacturers, and he was convinced that it should be possible to change some of the Regulations, and to modify the vehicles to comply with the rest.

At the UITP Conference and Exhibition in Montreal in 1977 there had been displayed a Leyland-DAB-Saurer articulated bus designed for the Swiss market. It was 17.3 m. long and had a capacity of about 175, of which around 50 were seated. Following Swiss practice it had four doors, one being at the very rear. Arrangements were made by Eric Kay for this bus to visit South Yorkshire on its way back to Switzerland. Alec Lee, SYPTE's Chief Driving Inspector, went to Harwich where he received tuition from the Leyland people before driving it to Queens Road, a dispensation from the DTp having been obtained for it to be driven in Britain – since they were illegal at the time.

The dispensation also permitted passengers to be carried free for trial purposes.

Initially it was tried all over Sheffield, including a trial with the full PTA and PTE on board around the City Centre, before visiting Rotherham and Doncaster for trials on their routes. It even ventured into Barnsley – the fiefdom of Yorkshire Traction – much to the consternation of some of their crews! Everybody was most impressed by its manoeuvrability and performance – except Sheffield taxi drivers who saw it (rightly?) as a threat! With its steering rear axle, the articulated bus was *more* manoeuvrable than a 9.5-m. rigid double decker, let alone a 11-m. or 12-m. single-decker. It had ample power from the Saurer engine and stormed up hills. After extensive trials in South Yorkshire, it toured other parts of the UK, including London where there was a memorable photo of it negotiating Parliament Square. However, most busmen's minds were already made up: "It's too big, it won't do here", etc., etc.

There were four main characteristics that appealed to SYPTE at the time, where an articulated bus scored over a conventional double-deck bus. These were:-

1. The ability to provide additional doors with reliable safety features which, given suitable fares and ticketing systems, enables additional passengers to board and alight without excessive stop times.
2. They can carry up to 150 passengers in a variety of seating/standing combinations, eg 40 seated, 110 standing, 50:90, 75:30 etc. Thus they have higher productivity than a double-deck bus.
3. The ability to offer at least double-deck capacity on routes where low bridges preclude the use of a double-decker. (It was noted that low bridges in the Dearne Valley were a major hindrance to the reshaping of bus services there.)
4. More than half the double-decker's seats were upstairs. It was noted that whilst many passengers appreciated

the view, they found the stairs difficult to negotiate particularly with shopping and young children. With the increased consideration being given to the elderly and less active passengers, it gave added importance to having only one deck. It was also becoming apparent that for short journeys there was increasing passenger resistance to using the upper deck, even if all the seats were taken downstairs.

Whilst the Executive realised that some important and fundamental problems would have to be resolved, and the law would have to be amended, it felt it was worthwhile to pursue articulated bus operation on certain specialised or problematic services. The particular service it had in mind was the City Clipper service in Central Sheffield, where adding additional rigid buses was not a solution. The problems to be resolved related to the fares and ticketing system, the rates-of-pay and scheduling arrangements for wholesale introduction. It was also essential to get first hand operating experience and to see what traffic management measures would be required.

With the original articulated bus there had been a passenger participation exercise involving over 2000 people, who answered a detailed questionnaire about the vehicle and their own travelling habits. Clearly the vehicle was very favourably received. It was also interesting to note that most passengers were quite prepared to stand for at least ten minutes (and some for up to fifteen minutes) on a bus that was designed for the purpose and was given priority in traffic. The artic was seen as much more than 'just another trial'. When dealing with operational issues reference was made to bus priorities. There had to be another major leap. Passenger shelters, information, bus-location systems, etc, all needed to be combined. There were a number of examples from the continent and Scandinavia. West Midlands PTE produced its 'Trackline' package in due course. The concept in South Yorkshire was that, subject to satisfactory financial, economic, technical and operational performance, artics were envisaged as taking over from double-deckers on all the major cross city routes.

Following the initial success with the Leyland-DAB-Saurer nothing more was heard from Leyland! However, a salesman from MAN – Peter Crewe – called to say that "he had a left-hand drive 16.3 m. artic demonstrator available and would we like to try it?" SYPTE jumped at the chance. When the bus came Peter also asked for SYPTE's articulated bus specification, since they were about to build a right-hand drive demonstrator. "We couldn't believe our luck" recalls Bills Bland. The midnight oil was burnt, whilst operations and engineering staff produced a spec. Similar trials were carried out with the MAN as had been done with Leyland – from whom still no word had yet been forthcoming.

South Yorkshire was now well on the 'artic map'. Volvo beat a path to Exchange Street with an 18m-long coach-seated version that SL were then using for airport services. Even this added length posed no insuperable problems – at least under the expert eye of Alec Lee. The final artic to be tried was a 17.5m. pusher artic from Mercedes Benz. All the other artics had had an underfloor engine, whereas the later Mercedes design had its engine in the rear section. This permitted a lower floor height for most of the vehicle. However, it was interesting to note that experiments and trials involving the elderly showed that floor height was less important than well designed step arrangements. These included wide steps with adequate grab-handle arrangements as well as 8in or 10in risers. Note all these considerations were being undertaken in 1978/80 – well before the advent of low floor trams, let alone low floor buses – yet another 'first' for South Yorkshire.

Whilst these trials were taking place there were a number of management visits abroad to look at articulated bus operation. These included visits to Cologne, Bochum (Sheffield's twin city), Bremen, Copenhagen and to Silkeborg to visit the DAB factory. These culminated in a joint management/union visit to Bochum.

Had the officers had their way ten MAN 16.3 m. artics would have been ordered as that company had been very helpful and positive from the start, and had produced the RHD demonstrator. At the eleventh hour Leyland announced their Leyland-National artic – in reality a Leyland-DAB chassis with a body structure made up from Leyland National components – and it came in due course. SYPTE had never been consulted by Leyland about its development and their requirements. The PTE had hoped originally to purchase ten Leyland-DAB-Saurers – one complete vehicle from Silkeborg – and nine mechanically complete vehicles to be fitted out by a UK coach-builder – Plaxtons or Duple were in mind. (The reason for this arrangement was the high cost (and quality) of the complete vehicle from Denmark.) These ideas had been discussed and 'agreed' informally with DAB, but either Leyland did not know or did not want to know of them. Notwithstanding this the first Leyland-National artic was a disaster – far too heavy and cumbersome which caused the articulation to 'sag' and catch the ground. The Executive and DTp were concerned that British manufacturers should be in on this development with its future potential. Since there was now a Leyland option available, the Executive insisted on splitting the order between Leyland and MAN.

The articulated buses were leased from the manufacturers with a two year cut-off clause. The Unions were told of this, but did not believe the Executive would let them go. They were allocated to Greenland Road to provide service on the Sheffield City Clipper services, for which special dispensation had been given, albeit at free fares – which suited the County Councillors! The artics entered service in 1979 and by March 1980 had carried over 400,000 passengers safely and uneventfully.

Before the vehicles were delivered careful consideration had been given as to how the artics were to be marketed. Eventually it was decided that they would be painted white with a green and orange stripe and they would be called 'City-Liners' continuing the 'Line' theme: 'Link Line' (local rail services) and 'Travel-line' (coaching and private hire activities). However, as soon as the artics went on the

Left: MAN No. 2004 is seen here at the terminus of the City Clipper service on Pond Hill, Sheffield. *(Mike Fowler)*

Below: The same fleet numbers were used for the second batch of articulated buses, and the second 2002 is seen turning out of Castle Street on the City Clipper. *(Mike Greenwood)*

Sheffield streets 'The Star' called them the 'bendibuses' – it was such an appropriate name it caught on immediately, including within the PTE! From thence forward Sheffield became synonymous with bendibuses.

The MANs performed consistently well, requiring little maintenance. The Leylands were a different story: the first one was dreadful. Prior to delivery Bill Kirkland had inspected it and told Leyland to make various modifications. These were not carried out and this was only found out on delivery. It was returned to the manufacturer immediately. The second was not much better, the last three were better and eventually settled down to be reasonable performers. They were popular with passengers and drivers alike, they posed no problems to motorists or the Police. The free fares on the City Clipper yet further increased their usage and consistently high loads were carried in one pre-Christmas period, which would have been impossible with double-deckers, let alone

Before the initial two year trial terminated it was determined that as fare collection was not felt desirable on the City Clipper, a brief experiment would take place to establish the facets associated with such a feature on multi-stream boarding vehicles. Number 2001 is seen here operating on service 56 to Wybourne during these experiments in July 1981.

(Martin Llewellyn)

works in Leeds for the installation of the sophisticated and quite complex equipment required for ticket-issuing and cancelling on a three-door vehicle. A figure of around £10,000 per vehicle was mentioned for this work. Unfortunately, right at the last minute when all other hurdles had been surmounted, agreement on pay rates could not be reached and in 1981 the buses were returned to the respective manufacturers from whom they had been leased. This was a sad end to a very brave experiment which had resulted in the articulated single-deck bus being accepted for use in Great Britain. The MANs eventually found their way to Australia; some of the Leylands went to McGills, whilst the others saw very little service other than as specialised vehicles for exhibitions etc.

However, the artics had shown their worth and the Executive was not for being beaten. Renewed negotiations took place on a pay and productivity package, acceptable to the government of the day, which included driving artic buses as a normal part of the fleet. It took a couple of years, however, before the deadlock was broken and an agreement for artics was concluded and one of the requirements was to train all Sheffield staff, although the initial batch of any further artics were only to be allocated to Greenland Road garage. Only after the conclusion of this Agreement was the order placed for further articulated vehicles.

By this time MAN had gone out of the frame – disillusioned by only having five artics when they had expected 10, having been so helpful at the early stages of the project and by the IR problems in South Yorkshire. (MAN had also hoped to sell some DP buses to SYPTE who were then in the market for 10 for the White Rose Services, and/or the longer distance stage carriagework. The Engineering and Operations Departments recommended their purchase, but the Executive refused, on the basis that there were suitable British alternatives.

The subsequent purchase of ten Leyland Leopards – with Duple bodies – went some way to calming Leyland after their being cut out of the SYPTE double-deck market. Leyland was now – at long last – in 'listening mode' – so when the Executive had resolved the IR problems and felt confident to go forward with a second batch of artics, it suggested Leyland-DABs. When quotations were called for, Leyland tendered a price without a specification. It seemed they were going back to their bad old habits of telling customers what they could have and ignoring the customer's stated specifications. At the Board Meeting to discuss the tenders, Bill Kirkland advised that Leyland-DAB artics were as good as, if not better than most and the Executive should enter into discussions with them to see what specification they would or could offer. The upshot

additional single-deckers. The artics were operated under a temporary scheduling agreement, it having been impossible to negotiate an economically satisfactory agreement. (The Executive thought, wrongly as it turned out, that since the artics were so popular and the drivers were receiving such prestige, that the rank and file would persuade their negotiators to accept the deal, which is why the two-year clause was inserted in the lease agreement.)

Perhaps the most controversial of the industrial relations issues which were tackled within the PTE, understandably, was that surrounding the use of articulated buses (the Bendis). The Ministry dispensation which had allowed the vehicles to operate in passenger service, though without charging any fares for passengers, had been replaced by normal licence and certificate of fitness proceedures following the satisfactory trial period and the way was clear to proceed with carrying fare-paying passengers. Whilst negotiations were conducted with the Union and platform staff the vehicles began to go to Charles Roe's

The name plate "Cutty Sark" is clearly seen over the entrance to No. 2001 of the second batch. *(Mike Greenwood)*

was that Chris Dyal, the Engineering Contracts Manager, accompanied Bill Kirkland to the DAB plant in Denmark to negotiate both a specification and price. They were able to confirm the quality of the manufacture of the product at a very competitive price. The PTE decided to place all its eggs in one excellent basket and ordered thirteen 17.3-m DAB artics.

Thirteen Leyland DAB Bendis were ordered, ten for the Clipper in Sheffield and three, of a coach-seated two-door variety, for Rotherham on the long Thurnscoe route.

After some market research it was decided to relaunch the City Clipper with its own unique image and livery – to be carried through in the publicity – and to name each of the ten artics destined for the City Clipper service, after a famour tea clipper. A schools competition was organised by Traffic manager Bob Rowe and the ten 'best' chosen. Each bus contained a plaque giving the name of the school that had chosen the name of the particular bus. The numbers and names allocated are set out below:-

2001	Cutty Sark	2006	Flying Cloud
2002	Samuel Plimsol	2007	Pegasus
2003	Storm King	2008	Queen of Clippers
2004	Fiery Cross	2009	Challenger
2005	Sir Lancelot	2010	The Great Republic

A photocall on the delivery of 2001, 'Cutty Sark', was made at the Greenwich location of this famous tea clipper. One of the artics was exhibited at the 1985 UITP Congress and Exhibition in Bruxelles – a nice return compliment to the initiation eight years previously. Unfortunately the artics did not have long on the City Clipper route before deregulation. Throughout the vicissitudes of SYPTE, SYT, Mainline, etc., and the abandonment of the route itself, the artics are still going strong and now offering good competition to the Supertram. Three artics were delivered with 63 seats to a Coachline specification and allocated to Rotherham. These were for the X91 Sheffield-Thurnscoe service formerly run by Dearneways. Technically they

As indicated on this page, the last three of the 1985 deliveries werecoach seated for use on service X91. 2011 is seen here at Rotherham bus station. *(Mike Greenwood)*

were an operational success, but the revamped service failed to retain the market, which itself was changing, as described in Chapter 9.

MISCELLANEOUS DEVELOPMENTS

Small buses

Being good bus territory the municipal predecessors of SYPTE had seen no need for small buses – in common with most other urban operators. Doncaster was an exception, acquiring five Seddon Pennine IV 236, similar to SELNEC Centreline buses, for its own town centre service. When the need came for small buses to serve remote parts of the housing estates, examples of the short versions of the Bristol LH were purchased second-hand, since the Seddon was now out of production. However, in

Duple bodied Leyland Leopard No. 15, seen here returning from Manchester on service X48 was on of the batch of vehicles purchased from Leyland as mentioned at the top of this page. *(Mike Greenwood)*

anticipation of such a need, and in the knowledge that SELNEC (now Greater Manchester) required to replace its first generation fleet of Centreline buses, discussions were held between SYPTE and GMPTE to see if a common specification could be developed. Dennis of Guildford – builders of SYPTE's Standard bus – indicated that they would be prepared to design and build a purpose-designed midibus provided there was an order for 50 vehicles to the same spec. This gave added incentive to SYPTE and GMPTE.

In the event a common chassis specification, covering engine, transmission and other mechanical parts was achieved, but the conflicting nature of the proposed services for which the vehicles were destined, prevented a common body specification being agreed. The power unit was to be a Perkins diesel engine driving through a Maxwell automatic gearbox. This gearbox included a retarder, but was entirely mechanical and it proved the weak spot of the design. GMPTE required a lower seating to standing ratio than did SYPTE, and this led to the two different body designs built onto the Dennis Domino chassis. GMPTE went, as usual, to Northern Counties, who designed a body remarkably similar to one seen on a Bedford JJL rear-engined midibus some years earlier. After inviting tenders from a number of body builders, SYPTE chose Optare to build their bodies. Optare was a management-led worker buyout of the former Charles Roe works, at Leeds. In the event SYPTE's first Domino midibus turned out to be the first bus built by Optare. Number 41 entered service on 8th August 1985 at Herries Road garage. The total fleet eventually consisted of fourteen vehicles allocated to Herries, Greenland, Rotherham and Doncaster. The design and spec were formulated in the pre-deregulated world when service and reliability were paramount, but with hindsight these vehicles were over-engineered and too expensive, even though regard needed to be given to the poor reliability and comfort features of the lightweight mini/midibuses at the time.

the work was to bid for it, using minibuses. Three Ford Transits with the 'bread van' body shell were acquired. One had coach-type seats. The NCB contracts were won and the vehicles fulfilled their objective.

SYPTE watched the 'Blundred experiments' in Exeter with minibuses, and kept itself abreast of minibus developments generally. It was also clear that things were going to change in a big way, as happened – see Chapters 11 & 12. An Optare demonstrator, based upon a Volkswagen LT chassis and the prototype MCW Metrorider were tested, partly relating to the Service Development

A popular place for posing new vehicles was Park Grange Road, with the City skyline as background. The first of the Dennis Dominoes to be delivered, No.45, was the subject of this particular study. Today Supertrams can be seen at this point. *(Mike Greenwood)*

Sometime before the fashion for minibuses took off in South Yorkshire, three Ford Transits were delivered. Number 62 was based at Halfway. *(Mike Greenwood)*

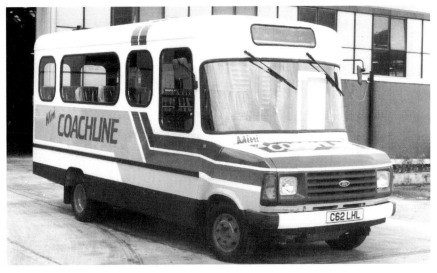

Minibuses

SYPTE's first purchase of minibuses was in July 1986 when three were acquired for National Coal Board contracts at Halfway Garage. This garage was dependent upon NCB work which was reducing in quantity and becoming more price-sensitive. It was felt that the only way of retaining

programme, as discussed in the previous chapter. Having regard to the operating area and the needs of the elderly passenger or typical shopper, it was felt that a vehicle with 25 seats was the minimum requirement. Such a design would permit a wide and reasonably designed entrance, a luggage stowage pen, reasonable aisle width and adequate seat spacing.

Midibuses

Eventually an order for 25 Reeve-Burgess bodied Dodge S50s was placed. A marketing campaign was developed, and the title 'Little Nipper' was chosen, together with a bright and cheerful livery of red, white and yellow. Before placing the order there was considerable discussion as to whether manual or automatic transmission should be adopted, and whether or not a retarder should be fitted. In the event an automatic gearbox was specified, but no retarder, so SYT's midis suffered from severe brake wear problems. Other operators who had plumped for a manual gearbox suffered clutch problems! The problem was overcome by beefing-up the brakes, but repeat orders specified a retarder in addition to the automatic gearbox. In 1989 some midibuses were marketed as 'Eager Beavers' and had a red, yellow and blue livery for use on service 52 initially. Other bodies were supped by Northern Counties as well as Reeve Burgess, who had how become part of Plaxton. Mercedes & Iveco midibuses were also purchased, usually with Reeve Burgess bodies.

Buses for the Disabled

South Yorkshire PTE was a pioneer in making adaptations to ordinary service buses to make them more accessible for elderly, infirm or otherwise handicapped people. In the late '70s work was done on bus entrances, steps, handrails, stanchions, seats, and the fitting of tactile information plates for blind persons. This was done in conjunction with organisations representing those for whom using buses presented difficulties. The Cranfield Institute of Technology was closely involved and several of the innovations were incorporated in the Department of Transport's code of practice – the DipTAC specification.

The realisation that so many bus passengers had difficulty boarding buses, and in using the stairs on double-deck vehicles, coupled with the fact that an increasing proportion of riders were either elderly persons or children had prompted the Executive to conduct trials with articulated buses, to which reference has already been made.

Later developments, in 1983, included modifying second-hand Leyland Nationals, by removing the centre door and replacing it with a wheelchair lift. The front section of the bus was modified by removing the seats and replacing them with wheelchair clamping arrangements and horizontal rails. The bench seats over the wheel arches were retained. The seats in the rear section were also retained for the ambulant disabled or those who could get out of their wheelchairs, which were then folded and put in a special pen built for the purpose. The fixed seats were also for 'accompanying persons'.

A network of services was introduced in Doncaster and Barnsley – the latter being operated by Yorkshire Traction. Lynda Chalker MP (now Baroness Chalker) who was the Minister of State for Transport, took a keen interest in the service. She visited the Doncaster operation and shared a Radio interview with Bill Kirkland on the topic. Those were the days when at least some government ministers were interested in investment in Public Transport, to meet purely social and not only financial needs!

Battery Buses

A theme pursued throughout SYPTE's life related to traction options and concern for the environment and noxious emissions. Under G.G. (Geoff) Harding's direction, SELNEC PTE had advanced battery bus technology, but on his departure this momentum flagged. Geoff himself became Managing Director of Lucas Battery Vehicles and continued the work, albeit applied to small delivery vans.

Once again South Yorkshire tended to lead the way. Leyland National 22, in this view by now painted in the new SYT livery, was modified to carry wheelchairs.
(Mike Greenwood)

On its establishment SYPTE took over from where SELNEC had left off. SYPTE acquired the two battery buses from the Department of Trade & Industry, re-engineered them and numbered them 1000 & 1001. It also acquired the Lucas-powered Seddon Midibus (of SELNEC's Centreline design) and the Chloride Silentrider I (a battery version of the Seddon/Pennine RU). Comparative trials and evaluation enabled the specification for Silentrider II to be prepared. This was to have incorporated sodium-sulphur batteries.

Whilst progress was made, there was no breakthrough – the perfect traction battery has lain round the corner for a long time. Whenever the question of 'How near are we to the ideal traction battery?' was asked, the manufacturers would reply with one voice 'ten years'. What they could not answer was 'when will the clock start running?'

Trolleybuses

Both Doncaster and Rotherham had operated trolleybus systems, as had Mexborough and Swinton Traction (later a subsidiary of YTC). A watching brief was held on trolleybus developments, with particular regard to developments in France, Belgium and Germany.

The way ahead was seen in the Transport Development Plan[17] as follows: continuing programme of bus priorities with increasing use of articulated buses on the busiest routes. Then, for Sheffield, either busways with artic trolleybuses or light rapid transit. For Doncaster, Barnsley & Rotherham: trolleybuses for the main routes and motor buses for the secondary routes. Accordingly the PTE deposited a Bill in November 1984 to seek trolleybus operating powers for specific routes in Doncaster and Rotherham and general Powers for the whole of South Yorkshire – to the surprise of YTC! The SY Bill[18] was modelled on the West Yorkshre Bill of the previous year, since by this time WYPTE were actively interested in re-introducing trolleybuses in the south-west sector of Bradford. Also in 1984 SYPTE acted as the catalyst for a consortium to come together to design and build Britain's first trolleybus for 30 years.

GEC Traction were under pressure, from their main board, to enter the lighter electric vehicle market. Towards that end they approached the Department of Transport concerning grants and were told that if they 'got into bed' with a reputable operator the development would receive government financial support. When the project landed on the engineer's desk, their first task was to select their bed mate.

Before re-joining the public transport business, Bill Kirkland had worked for GEC and was the only senior manager in the public transport industry known to the light electric vehicle design team. So, he was invited to Manchester to draft an outline agreement for a trolleybus development programme. The PTE Management board supported the proposals which required SYPTE to supply a Dennis Dominator/Alexander without its engine and

The Lucas battery bus. *(SYPTE)*

81

The trolleybus based on the Dennis Dominator motor bus was delivered unpainted (above). The livery can be seen below when it was operated in connection with an open day at Doncaster's Leicester Avenue garage in October 1985. *(Mike Greenwood)*

Part of the auxiliary air cooled diesel engine seen with the rear 'engine' compartment open *(Mike Greenwood)*

gearbox. GEC Transportation Projects would supply the electric traction package including a small diesel engine for off-line capability. GEC TP were also to provide the power supply , with Balfour Beatty supplying the overhead and Insul-8 the overhead collection gear.

The use of the Dennis Dominator has an interesting history behind it. The chassis was conceived in three parts:

A – the front axle and forwards thereof was to be common to all vehicles, double- or single-deck or articulated

B – the middle section was to be able to accommodate battery packs for a battery bus or battery/trolleybus or an underfloor motor for a trolleybus

C – the rear axle and rearwards thereof was to be able to accommodate either a horizontal traction package or a turntable (for an articulated vehicle) and in fact had to be modified for the normal diesel-engined version.

In the event, of course, only one trolleybus was built – 2450 – and 328 diesel double-deckers. No articulated versions were ever built – but the foresight was there – it would have been assembled as A + B + C + B + C.

When the proposal was put to the government they advised GEC that government funding was no longer available – how different a response would have been forthcoming in France or Germany! The PTE team decided to argue the case for going it alone and got full agreement. A few discussions with the Doncaster Council led to the private road alongside the racecourse being allocated to the scheme as the test track. The consortium was a major example of the Executive's efforts to stimulate private sector industries, with developing new and improved products that could be of value to the public transport industry. The trolleybus arrived at Doncaster on 8th September 1985, in unrelieved cream. The choice of name and livery was to turn out more difficult than anything else. The name 'Electroline' had been suggested, but fearing another 'bendibus' naming fiasco, the Author suggested it be called a 'trackless' – which everybody jumped at until the parentage of that name was pointed out!

A striking hybrid livery was designed: front half – standard SYPTE livery – rear half bright red with thin horizontal stripes in cream. The name 'Electroline' was written on the sides and back, as were the names of the consortium that had built it. The test track was set on the land owned by Doncaster Council adjacent to the Race Course. A single track with turning loops at either end was installed, and different types of catenary tried. Using the SY Act powers[18] the track crossed Leger Way to reach Leicester Road depot whence the power was supplied. Unfortunately the experiment came too late: nobody could see how to run trolleybuses in the future deregulated world, and the efforts of all in SYPTE were needed to concentrate in turning SYPTE into SYT. The experiment was a success as far as it went; however the trolleybus 2450 has been given on loan to the National Trolleybus Museum at Sandtoft, near Doncaster. The overhead was removed from Sandall Beat Road in 1994 and placed in storage.

INFRASTRUCTURE

PASSENGER FACILITIES

Barnsley

The original bus station had been opened in 1938 to provide mainly for Yorkshire Traction services and was described in contemporary reports as 'one of the best in Yorkshire'.[19] The site was bounded on the west by the railway viaduct leading to the former Court House Station, and on the south by the boundary wall of Exchange Station (the present station). The arches of the viaduct were used to house YTC's booking and enquiry office, various ancillary facilities and shops. A staff canteen was housed in a separate building next to Exchange Station. The bus station was laid out for through running with two side platforms and a large central island platform, which included passenger waiting rooms. All the platforms were covered.

Following the closure of Court House Station in 1960,

the approach viaduct was demolished, except for that part housing YTC's offices. The site was re-developed with two-storey commercial units facing onto Midland Street and a 22-stand bus station designed for end-on loading. This was a more suitable layout for front entrance buses, although it required buses to reverse off. Vehicle parking was provided on the other side of the bus station backing onto the rear wall of the railway. There were also stands in Midland Street. Passenger facilities were poor, waiting facilities meagre. Whilst there was a cafe, a newsagent and some shops, the whole feeling of the area was one of decrepitude. There were staff messing and booking on/off facilities, but these looked none too wholesome.

At one time YTC, then a member of the BET Group, owned land on the east side of the railway station. Unfortunately in the late 1960s this was sold to another BET Group Company who built a Bingo Hall and thus frustrated for ever the development of a decent bus station, let alone a proper bus/train interchange.

When it became clear that the Sheffield-Barnsley-Wakefield-Leeds rail service was to be supported by SYPTE, the idea of developing the interchange began. Added emphasis was given to the idea when the effect of

the County's policies started to generate more passengers. Further impetus was created when the idea of pedestrianising May Day Green was promulgated – although both SYPTE and YTC were unhappy with this proposal. (See remarks about pedestrianisation in Chapter 6). Meetings were held to consider alternative schemes, from 1978 to 1988, to no avail. YTC proved to be intractable negotiators under a succession of General Managers. The County even threatened to acquire the land compulsorily.

Progress was only made after the demise of the operating PTE, when the railway station was rebuilt, and the land between there and the Bingo Hall was laid out as an interchange. However, to date, the existing bus station remains an eyesore as it has done for the whole period of this story. Being right at the heart of the old County and quite literally under the nose of County Council members and Officers, this was particularly galling. Perhaps the Councillors were right in wanting NBC subsidiaries to be transferred to the PTE's ownership. Certainly a golden opportunity to create a beneficial facility to the passengers, the town and the operators – YTC and BR – was missed.

Doncaster

Doncaster County Borough, as it was before 1974 and the establishment of SYCC, had prepared an overall plan for the development of the Town Centre. The opening of the A1(M) in 1960 had reduced through traffic volumes greatly. The construction of an inner ring road, Trafford Way, from the south end of North Bridge to Balby Road, reduced traffic further on High Street and Hall Gate. As part of this plan two bus stations were built: the North Bus Station had eighteen stands and was adjacent to the Railway Station. The South Bus Station had sixteen stands and was by College Road. Apparently consideration had been given to having only one bus station, but either a sufficiently large site could not be found or the traffic volumes generated were unlikely to be acceptable. Doncaster really did not have the size to justify two bus stations in addition to having four major bus loading points at Christ Church, St. Sepulchre Gate, Duke Street and Cleveland Street.

Realistically, there was little that could be done, other than to refurbish the two bus stations which were both under multi-storey car parks. This has been done at least twice in the period under review. Doncaster town centre is very compact, but a maze of narrow streets. The PTE's efforts were, therefore, concentrated on persuading the County Engineer to produce a comprehensive Bus Priority/ Traffic Management scheme for the town centre. This was eventually done and implemented in the 1980s.

Rotherham

Rotherham Bus Station had 32 stands and was located in the ground floor of a multi-storey car park, backing onto the river and fronting onto Frederick Street adjacent to the town centre. However, many of the bus services still used Effingham Street, until it was pedestrianised in the 1980s. Bus routings had to be rather tortuous to get into and out of the bus station. The station itself was exceedingly busy both with passengers and vehicles. As the result of an initiative by the then District Manager, A. J. (Tony) Dobson, and the Area Advisory Sub-Committee, a cost-effective refurbishment programme was implemented about 1984.

Sheffield

Sheffield Central Bus Station (CBS) had been built as a temporary facility in 1956 and was inherited, largely unchanged, by SYPTE in 1974. The site had been laid out for 7ft 6in by 26ft rear platform buses and was now being used by 8ft 2½in by 30ft or 36 ft long buses and coaches. Scrapes, grazings and broken mirrors were legion. The bus station had 44 stands. Passenger facilities were poor, although not quite as bad as at Barnsley! There were passenger enquiry and staff facilities, the former being quite good. There was also a cafe and some small shop units.

During its operating years numerous ideas were developed by the PTE for the re-development of CBS which handled all terminating services in the city. (The numerous cross-city services used on-street stands.) The Bus Station lay between the (Midland) Railway Station and the town centre, being separated from the former by Sheaf Street and the latter by Flat Street. It was adjacent to the Polytechnic – now Hallamshire University – and the GPO's Main Sorting Office. The bus station was not ideally sited, being 5/7 minutes from the main shopping areas and about 100ft lower than them, but there were no obvious alternative sites. Better bus/train interchange could have been developed – at a price – by building over part of the railway station, but that would have added three to five minutes onto the journey to the shops. In any case the costs of such an arrangement were unrealistic to contemplate – at least in Britain!

The redeveloped Transport Interchange in Sheffield incorporated a small shopping arcade marketed as the Archway Centre. In the background, below the Hyde Park flats, runs the Supertarm route to Halfway. *(SYPTE)*

It is also kept scrupulously clean either by the public or by PTE staff – one suspects the latter!

Meadowhall

When SYPTE was established Meadowhall was the site of Hadfield's Steelworks employing 9000 people. It generated a considerable amount of bus traffic. The low bridge under the former Midland main line made the area difficult to serve, except for single deckers, or artics. Following the steel strike in 1980, Hadfields closed and the shock reverberated around the 'East End' and Sheffield generally. The site lay as waste land until 1988 when it was bought for what was to become Meadowhall Shopping Centre.

As part of railway developments, initial thoughts had been given to either re-instating the north-to-west side of the triangle, thus permitting trains to run direct from Barnsley to Rotherham/ Doncaster or to building a station at the junction with the Barnsley line. Alternative station layouts offered cross platform

The opening of the new Transport Interchange at Meadowhall (above) coincided with the opening of Europe's premier shopping development in September 1990. A more modest bus station (below) had previously been built at the Crystal Peaks shopping development. Both are served by Sheffield Supertram. *(SYPTE)*

interchange in one direction, but there would be the need to close the (little used) Brightside station. The remoteness of the location led to nothing being done until the coming of the Meadowhall development, which led to a four-platform station on the junction being built.

The size of the proposed development, and its location midway between Sheffield and Rotherham, and near to major housing areas such as Shiregreen, Thorpe Hesley, Blackburn, Kimberworth and Brinsworth, meant that a major bus station would be required. A site between Meadowhall Road (adjacent to the River Don) and the railway line was chosen for the interchange, which offered connectional facilities between local and express buses, local trains and Supertram. There is a direct, covered footbridge link to the Meadowhall Shopping Centre itself. There is also a car park for park-and-ride passengers. The architectural integrity of the whole interchange is first class, as is the signing and passenger information.

A re-signing and re-painting was achieved by the 'old' SYPTE, but the real and dramatic changes were brought to fruition by the 'new' PTE. A completely new layout on the site of the old, but also incorporating land previously occupied by the Sheaf Baths and a bus parking areas, were incorporated. The new bus station is basically 'L' shaped with a shopping mall and passenger facilities at the join of the 'L'. It incorporates shallow saw-tooth design stands. There is an architectural symmetry about the place, signing and lighting are excellent, and there is real-time passenger information. Links to the railway and Supertram are not improved, but otherwise the new bus station is exemplary.

Minor developments

Minor bus station schemes were at Mexborough and Crystal Peaks, Mosborough. Mexborough was the largest of the five towns – Wath, Wombwell, Kilnhurst, Swinton & Mexborough – in the Dearne Valley and served by Yorkshire Traction. The main street was narrow and a by-pass had been built in West Riding County Council days, as a precursor to both pedestrianisation and town centre redevelopment. Unfortunately the by-pass had cut off the railway station from the town, otherwise quite an effective interchange could have been built, since many YTC services terminated in Mexborough. Eventually a small bus station was built convenient to the town centre, and on the other side of the road to the railway station which was reached by a subway.

transferred to the other garages. Leadmill was an awkward triangular site, formed from the conversion and amalgamation of the former Shoreham Street tram depot and Leadmill garage. This fusion and reconstruction was undertaken in 1959/63. Leadmill garage was the closest remaining garage to the City Centre and to CBS. It was also the smallest of the Sheffield garages, with a capacity of about 90 vehicles. The other three garages were relatively new, Herries having been opened in 1952, Greenland Road 1958 and East Bank in 1961. They were built to a standard design by the City Architect, modified to suit the individual sites. East Bank was the biggest, but on a difficult site with a large retaining wall behind it which, during SYPTE days, was to be a major source of concern and cost.

Had the passenger decline experienced by STD continued there would have been adequate capacity in the

An aerial view of what was opened by Sheffield Transport as East Bank Road garage. When subsequently re-occupied by Mainline it was termed Olive Grove. To the right of the picture is Charlotte Road garage, originally the home of Sheffield United Tours. Subsequently it was used by National Travel (East), Sheffield & District and finally Sheafline/SUT. *(SYPTA Ltd)*

Crystal Peaks is the shopping centre for Mosborough. It was developed jointly by a property developer and Sheffield City Council – the first out-of-town development permitted by the City. The development of Mosborough had led to a progressive revision of bus services to cater for the ever-expanding population. After much negotiation a four-stand bus station was built at Crystal Peaks.

GARAGES

Sheffield

In the latter days of STD there had been six garages: Bramall Lane, Townhead Street, Leadmill, Greenland Road, Herries Road and East Bank. The first two had been closed in 1963 and 1968, respectively, with vehicles being

four remaining garages. However, with the gradual increase in passengers, and the increase of fleet size because of additional spare vehicles, all garages were over-bussed, i.e. there were more buses than capacity. The addition of spare vehicles was brought about by the increasing percentage of rear engined vehicles entering the fleet. The earlier ones were much less reliable than their predecessors. This meant that a lot of time was wasted shunting vehicles around to get at those needing attention overnight. It also meant that a proportion of vehicles at each garage had to overnight in the open, with the attendant problems for the run-out on winter mornings.

The maintenance capacity of a garage is largely determined by the number of pits and a programme of both increasing the number of pits, and to provide additional covered parking, was put in hand at Greenland, Herries and East Bank. There was also a general enhancement of engineering facilities. At Leadmill additional and secure parking facilities were provided.

Rotherham

Rotherham garage was situated between the River Don and the canal (the South Yorkshire Navigation) off Rawmarsh Road. It was a constricted site and the garage was a steel-framed building, covered by asbestos sheeting. The whole area was decrepit and showed signs of scrimping – in contrast to the vehicles which were well-maintained. When the river was in flood the pits in the garage filled with water. Investigation showed that the land was unstable. There is little doubt that of all the inherited garages, Rotherham was the worst.

In 1976 it was decided to look for another site. The option of closing the garage and transferring the vehicles did not exist, because all the other garages were overbussed and only Greenland would have offered a practical alternative in terms of dead mileage. Internally the PTE gave brief consideration to expanding YTC's Rawmarsh garage if YTC were to be acquired in the near future (as was the County's policy). Another alternative considered was to reach an agreement with YTC whereby they and SYPTE would share an expanded garage. However, this was thought, quite rightly, to be impractical; furthermore the Rawmarsh site was not very big.

Some 30 or 40 potential sites or buildings were looked at in the Rotherham area, before the Midland Road site

was selected. Not only had a large flat area to be found, but also the effect it would have on crew changeovers and positioning mileage needed careful consideration. To save design costs and to reduce time it was decided to use the design Fairhurst's had produced for GMPTE for their new Tameside garage. Plans produced in 1978 for a new garage to house 200 buses in Rotherham were considered over-ambitious and it was decided that fresh plans should be produced for a 160 bus garage, with a smaller workshop area. This could accommodate 160 vehicles in herring-bone parking, together with the supporting engineering facilities, offices, cleaning and fuelling areas, etc. There was considerable discussion and modelling as to the required capacity at Rotherham, and a view had to be taken on the future fleet size.

A very fine garage was constructed but the standard of finish and amount of office provision required by the agreements and operating standards of the day produced a facility that today's more commercial need could not support. In the 1970s and 80s both Revenue and Capital budgets were developed to meet the PTA's policy of raising service efficiency, and enhancing the 'standards of life of the citizens of the SYCC'. The consequences in today's less caring world is that the overhead costs involved adversely affect the financial performance of Rotherham's operation.

Doncaster

The PTE's garage at Doncaster was situated about 1½ miles from the town centre at Leicester Avenue and adjacent to Leger Way. It was a well-built, well-maintained structure with 'Trolleybus' proudly proclaimed above one entrance and 'Motor Bus' above the other. The offices were integral with the garage. There was a large yard out at the back. The workshops, pits, tyre and paint booths were along three sides of the building, with the parking area in the centre. These were built for shorter and narrower front-engined buses, not for the current bigger underfloor and rear-engined designs. After a lot of deliberation it was decided to build a new workshop unit in the yard at the rear, and to make the original garage a running depot only. The new workshop unit was a massive space-age construction, providing excellent engineering facilities as demanded by the policy of the day, but at a price burdensome to today's purely commercial operation.

Other garages

The garage at Halfway came with the acquisition of Booth & Fisher, discussed in Chapter 9. The garage was square in plan, brick built and located in the middle of quite a large site. Although the door entrances and roof beams permitted full-height double-deckers (B & F had a single-deck only fleet), double-deckers could not exit through the

The PTE offices in Doncaster were situated in Leicester Avenue and were built for the Corporation Transport Department, whose name appeared over the entrance. *(Bob Rowe)*

main way out, because of the steep rise onto the road. The offices were an integral part of the garage. There was a filling station and car showroom facing on to Station Road. With the planned expansion of the fleet and the introduction of double-deckers, the J & C Ash building, also owned by Booth & Fisher, was refurbished and extended to provide a four-pit workshop.

Severn's garage at Dunscroft was opened in 1951 and was in the best condition of the acquired Doncaster independents. More importantly it was the best located of the garages, being in the middle of this diffuse territory. Some minor improvement works were undertaken. The main work was to tarmac the hard-standing surrounding the garage and to plant trees and landscape the periphery of the site to reduce objections from the neighbouring properties.

Queens Road Works

Queens Road opened as a tram depot in 1900, but the new car building shop was not opened until 1911.[1] Following the cessation of tram operation in 1960, it became the Central Works for the six Sheffield garages. The role of Central Works was continued through the life of the 'operating' PTE. It was managed by the Works Superintendent, firstly one Jim Gregory, who had previously been in Manchester, and subsequently by Brian Keith. Whilst the majority of its workload related to the Sheffield fleet, it also provided services to the PTE's other garages. Regrettably it became a casualty of the changes effected in 1985 (See Chapter 12) when it closed. The building lay unused until 1993 when it was finally demolished.

8 NATIONAL BUS COMPANY

To appreciate the part played by the National Bus Company subsidiary companies in South Yorkshire, it is necessary to chronicle first their immediate background history.

The National Bus Company (NBC) subsidiaries providing public transport facilities in the area at the time were:-

- East Midland Motor Services Limited, Chesterfield.
- Lincolnshire Road Car Company Limited, Lincoln.
- Ribble Motor Service Limited, Preston.
- Trent Motor Traction Company Limited, Derby.
- West Riding Automobile Company Limited, Wakefield.
- Yorkshire Traction Company Limited, Barnsley.

Typifying the NBC presence in South Yorkshire, No. 650 of subsidiary Yorkshire Traction operates into Sheffield on service 265, provided jointly with the PTE as successors to SJOC *(Mike Greenwood)*

Additionally, coaching facilities were provided by the NBC subsidiaries, National Travel, National Holidays and National Express.

All of the companies had a long and proud history of bus and coach operations, dating back in some cases for over 80 years. Except for Lincolnshire and West Riding, they had been in the British Electric Traction (BET) group prior to agreeing to sell its bus-operating interests in Britain to the State-owned Transport Holding Company (THC) in 1967. Lincolnshire, once also under BET control had been in the Tilling group when that organisation sold its bus activities to the State in 1948. West Riding had been an unusual case of a one-time tramway company which had remained independent until it was sold to THC in 1968. Each company employed skilled staff (many with very long continuous service records), modern vehicles,

adequate training and engineering facilities and not least managements which were commercially oriented with wide experience of both a competitive and co-operative approach in the market place.

The 1968 Transport Act proposed the acquisition of the BET interests which should be wholly absorbed into the THC and the two should then be thoroughly integrated. These would then become vested in a newly-established National Bus Company (NBC). It was envisaged that it would be run on a commercial basis, as one in which the Company would pay its way, having made appropriate provision for asset renewal and for servicing out-of-revenue the interest on what was called its commencing capital debt to be funded by the Exchequer.

Contiguously, the principle of fuel tax rebates was to be extended, and capital grants towards the purchase of new buses designed for OPO use were to be introduced for all operators – important principles at a time of declining user demand and escalating oil prices.

Powers to make agreements

Where Passenger Transport Executives were to be established, the NBC subsidiaries would be required to co-operate as a special duty and were empowered to make agreements with the relevant PTEs to ensure that the Executive's responsibilities for planning public transport services, through integrated patterns, would be achieved within, and near, their areas of influence. Service 'swaps' between the parties were envisaged, always conditional that any such arrangements should not destroy the profitable basis of NBC subsidiary companies' activities.

On 28th November 1968 the National Bus Company was formed as laid down in the Transport Act, 1968. The creation of the South and West Yorkshire PTEs had to wait until 1974.

From 1974 the companies maintained their operations consistent with the statutory duties of the NBC. However, following creation of the SYPTE, the subsidiary companies had to have regard to SYCC's policies. The companies' policies for service re-organisations, to equate supply with demand, and fare scales and conditions approved to achieve their financial duties, commensurate not only with the

1968 Transport Act, but also with all other relevant legislation, were maintained.

All of the companies operated commercially providing a mix of stage carriage, limited stop, express and contract services within South Yorkshire and across its boundaries into neighbouring counties. Leisure-oriented services were also provided extensively by the coaching companies, and Yorkshire Traction in particular. These services encompassed long distance express services, excursion and tours, holiday tours and private charter.

Yorkshire Traction

Of the subsidiary companies only the Yorkshire Traction Company provided stage carriage services wholly within the South Yorkshire Metropolitan County. The remaining stage carriage companies, and Yorkshire Traction, provided cross-boundary stage carriage services into adjacent counties. All the town services in Barnsley, and virtually all other bus services in that Metropolitan District and in the Dearne Valley towns, were provided by YTC. Yorkshire Traction was represented at the meetings of the Barnsley Area Advisory Sub-Committee.

Yorkshire Traction's main sphere of influence was around its depots at Barnsley, Doncaster, Rawmarsh, Shafton and Wombwell. The majority of the internal services were provided by YTC on an exclusive basis, but there were wholly internal and cross-boundary services operated jointly with the PTE's predecessor municipal operators.

Both the internal and cross-boundary services operated under the cross-subsidisation principle, with some unremunerative services and sections of routes cross-subsidised out of profits on the remainder, within an overall umbrella of profitability. Contract services provided mainly for education authorities, local works and the National Coal Board, were all 'tailor-made', some being provided on a fares revenue guarantee basis.

By their very nature, the provision of such services necessarily involved a high degree of co-ordination and co-operation between the provider and user, and it was not therefore surprising that a high degree of liaison existed between the operator and such bodies as Local Education Authorities, Chambers of Trade and Commerce, employer organisations, industrialists and all relevant Local Authorities. Liaison was also long established between the NBC subsidiary companies and other road passenger transport providers.

Important relationships existed also between the NBC subsidiary companies and the relevant Area Traffic Commissioners, Police, Highway Authorities and Government Departments (including local Members of Parliament).

Each of the NBC subsidiary companies was responsible, through its General Manager, to a Board of Directors and to the National Bus Company. The latter's hierarchical structure encapsulated a central Board to which the Companies had responsibility through a Divisional and Regional Structure.

NBC structure

All of the companies were subject to policies determined by NBC, which in turn was required to meet the financial targets determined by the Transport Minister. It follows, therefore, that each company was required to prepare capital, revenue and expenditure budgets for its Board's approval, and was subject to regular report and monitoring of performance against those budgets, and for any remedial action which might become necessary in the year of account. The subsidiary companies' budgets were required to be consistent with those of NBC as a whole, having regard to the latter's External Financing limits determined by Government, and with the Statutory financial framework within which NBC operated.

Given the structure of NBC, the subsidiary companies were able to take advantage of the

One of the other NBC subsidiaries to be found in South Yorkshire was East Midland Motor Services. Here Olympian 328, in non-standard NBC livery, awaits departure from Rotherham bus station on jointly operated service 19.

(Mike Greenwood

facilities provided on a divisional and regional basis and most importantly of those which derived from the central organisation. In this context, centralised vehicle purchase policies, central negotiation of fuel discounts, large scale tyre purchase facilities and centralised banking facilities, gave benefits of scale.

Similarly, systems development in operational, financial and engineering fields were of immense value to the companies which both prior to 1974, and subsequently, enabled them to modernise their procedure through centralised research and planning, again on a 'benefits of scale' basis. In 1974, for example, the adoption of a common costing system within the NBC subsidiaries meant that all activities in South Yorkshire, no matter which of the Companies was concerned, could be viewed by the PTE in the knowledge that like systems of accounting techniques and principles were common in all the subsidiaries.

Although each company, for example, had individual responsibility for staff training, it could, too, call on Regional and Centralised facilities – important not least in the field of management development. Such developments as the CIPFA operational route costing system and MAP (Market Analysis Project) were other relevant features of commonality.

The National Council for the Omnibus Industry, formed pursuant to the Transport Act 1968 (Section 137), and the National Joint Council for Non-Manual Staff, established in 1969, were the Councils through which the wages and conditions of employment of the subsidiary companies' platform, engineering and non-manual staffs were determined with their demise under changing circumstances, respectively in 1985 and 1986. Middle and Higher Management Staff, likewise, had appropriate centralised negotiating arrangements in the pay and conditions fields. Generally speaking, the pay and salaries of the subsidiary companies' staffs was below that of their counterparts in the SYPTE and this gave rise, subsequently, to 'parity pay' claims within the companies.

Co-ordination

Directors of SYPTE had already met NBC subsidiary company officers on several occasions before the PTE commenced operations on 1st April 1974. The companies were acutely aware that they would be considerably affected by any co-ordination activities of the Executive, and by the policies of the County council. They already had agreements with the original PTEs and wrote to the Executive in March 1974 suggesting Heads of Agreement for similar mutual arrangements in South Yorkshire. The Executive examined the proposals and advised that they found them unacceptable. They also told the companies that the County Council had not considered necessary an agreement between the PTE and NBC subsidiary companies, because in April 1974 the council's Passenger Transport Committee had passed a minute that expressed the wish that Yorkshire Traction and the other operators' relevant operations in South Yorkshire should be acquired. The Council's view was that this was the only way they could ensure their

passenger transport policies were carried out on these operations.

Under section 24(2) of the Transport Act 1968 the PTE and NBC had a duty to co-operate with one another in the re-organisation of bus services within, to and from the area, and to enter into agreements as to the services to be provided, and the terms on which those services were to be provided.

Fares rationalisation

The Council had general ideas for rationalisation of fares and concessionary travel and for support for, and development of, service. They had a duty, along with the PTE, to co-ordinate and integrate services in the County, but at that time they had not been in office long enough to assess what was needed, what it would cost, and whether they could finance it.

The costs of operating services were rising rapidly because of inflation, which averaged 19% year-on-year in the four years 1974-77. The NBC subsidiary companies, having already increased fares in South Yorkshire in April 1974, applied to the Traffic Commissioners in August for another increase. In accordance with former practice they asked the PTE to submit 'in line' proposals for increases on its services running on routes where the subsidiary companies were the main operator. The Council's approval was needed for the PTE to do this, but the Budget Sub-Committee members, unfamiliar with the practice, were reluctant to agree because the general policy for fares in the County was still being considered.

The subsidiary companies asked the Traffic Commissioners to direct the PTE to 'come into line' when they applied the new fares in September. The PTE told the Commissioner they were hoping to get early approval from the Council but this was not received until November. The companies made an adjustment to the revenue paid into the joint operator's pool to compensate for the period when the PTE had charged lower fares.

A pattern for agreement

In November 1974 the Council approved the proposals for fares and concessions set out in Councillor Thwaites' report *Tomorrow's Transport for South Yorks*. (See Chapter 3.) The PTE's Director of Finance & Administration (DFA) and the Director of Operations & Planning (DOP) had been meeting the NBC subsidiary companies and other operators to try to reach an agreement on the method of calculating payments for standard schemes of elderly persons' concessions and reduced fares for children, which the Council wished to make available on all bus services in the County, notwithstanding the difficulties inherent in the wider principle.

The County Chief Officer's management team, including the Director General, discussed in December the Agreement which West Yorkshire PTE and the NBC subsidiary companies were actively considering. (In due course this was to become The Metro-National Agreement.) It included proposals for a joint company to control certain aspects of operation, and had been hailed by West Yorkshire as a model way of achieving the co-ordination required by the Transport Act 1968. Some senior Council Officers in South Yorkshire were in favour of SYPTE making a similar agreement. The Executive had already obtained copies of the proposals and had met WYPTE and NBC subsidiary company representatives separately to discuss them.

Although WYPTE were satisfied with the terms of the Agreement in their operating circumstances SYPTE could not see that it would give adequate control to the PTE in South Yorkshire conditions. The Executive met the Council leader and some of his senior colleagues to discuss arrangements with the NBC subsidiary companies. The Executive advised that NBC had not changed its decision not to sell their operations in South Yorkshire, and with the forthcoming need for county-wide changes in fares and conditions, an agreement was needed urgently, but the terms of the proposed West Yorkshire Agreement would not meet SYPTE's needs. Sir Ron Ironmonger agreed that the Executive should discuss an agreement with the NBC subsidiary companies and should aim at one that would give the fullest control to the Executive, short of acquisition.

Rural service subsidy

East Midland Motor Services applied for financial assistance, under Section 34 of the 1968 Act, for rural bus services. This went to the County Council Joint Planning and Transportation Sub-Committee, along with similar claims from the other NBC subsidiaries. A special meeting was held to discuss Section 34 payments and ways of comparing social factors relating to unremunerative services in the County, regardless of the operator, and of the possibilities open to the County Council for holding down fares. If a decision was made to hold down such fares then the fares increase recently proposed would be modified. The Executive had been advised of proposals by NBC subsidiary companies for increased fares to be charged from March 1975. This could be an opportunity to make a significant move towards a countywide scale of fares for all operators.

Rationalised fares

A rationalised scheme of increased fares had been introduced in all three SYPTE Operating Districts on 19th January, 1975 and this had brought many SYPTE fares, particularly those for the shorter journeys, closely into line with those already charged by the NBC subsidiary companies. If only those NBC fares still below the PTE level were permitted to increase to that level, and the remainder were stabilised also at that level, this would produce a countywide standard scheme. Most of the fares charged by the independent operators would be brought automatically 'into line' by established custom and practice. However, this required a major decision to be made by the Council and the cost would be high, making it a severe test of their commitment.

The Director General discussed this with the Chairman, who said the Labour Group at their next meeting, were being recommended to propose a standard scheme for all operators, based on the Executive scales. The Chairman would submit to the Group a modified proposal to the effect that the County should compensate other operators for not increasing fares to a level above the Executive standard scale for Sheffield District. Because the Council could not ratify this decision before the Traffic Commissioner's hearing on 12th February, it would not be possible to give the companies any firm undertaking before then. In fact, the Council decided not to make a decision on compensation until after the Traffic Commissioner had approved the increase and the NBC subsidiary companies were advised that no decision had been made so far.

Meanwhile the subsidiary companies had been producing and printing two sets of fares tables and the Director of Operations & Planning had reported on practical details that had been agreed, such as cross-boundary fares where each individual fare had to be agreed separately to ensure anomalies were not created. The NBC subsidiary companies were anxious to get a decision as quickly as possible, but they did not get it until about a week before the increase was due to be applied early in March, and they had then to get a dispensation from the Traffic Commissioners to substitute a modified scale. The cost to the County Council was estimated at £853,000 in 1975/6 and £70,000 in the remainder of the current year.

Meetings had also taken place with the NBC subsidiary companies about compensating them for the loss of revenue involved in them granting the County Council standard concessions to elderly persons. The DFA and DOP had reached agreement for the estimated loss to be paid in four-weekly instalments with relevant adjustment at the end of the year after a financial review. The NBC subsidiaries had submitted a revised costing for the children's fares of an extra £150,000 which had not been provided for in the budget. Discussions on concessionary fares had also been taking place with the private operators and in February there was a meeting with twelve of them in Doncaster where they were asked for an early reply. When the Countywide concessionary schemes started in April 1975, they were applied on 99% of the services in the County. Against the nationwide generality of passenger user decline, the Yorkshire Traction Company, for example, experienced an increase of around one million passenger journeys in 1974 by comparison with 1973 (some 1.5%).

The February 1975 Fares Application was commercially based, whilst that of September 1975 was the first made on a 'rolling year' basis. Whilst this, too, was commercially based credit was given for assumed revenue generation due to adoption of the County's fares policy for the year to 31st March 1976. The applications of February 1976 and September 1976 followed the pattern of that for September 1975.

More passenger journeys

The increased trip generation factor of 1974 was maintained in early 1975 before adoption of the County's fares policy. Up to August 1975 the Fares Policy appeared to have no immediate effect on the passenger user upturn which was maintained at pre-existing levels, and from September to year end there was actually a decline, albeit that the number of OAP journeys increased, but was counter-balanced by a fall in the numbers of fare paying passengers.

From 1976 and thereafter, passenger trip utilisation increased consistently by comparison with 1975 and 1974. Thus, the conclusion was drawn that as the fares charged in real terms diminished, a marginal ongoing increase in the user factor became evident.

It would not be wholly correct, however, to attribute the whole of the passenger increase to the adoption of the Fares Policy, since other factors were at play simultaneously. Most notable of these were the following:-

1. Improvements in maintenance standards and manning levels were achieved especially by YTC which had input considerable resources into the maintenance of improved service reliability.
2. The introduction of various bus priority measures, not least in Barnsley, were of benefit.
3. With the ongoing passenger journey increases, some service duplication became necessary to go along with the improved maintenance of service reliability. The provision of additional duplication was achieved partially from the significant economies deriving from YTC's policy to force a degree of staggering of school hours from the Autumn 1975. This policy had the effects, inter alia, of a major saving in vehicles and staff (19 vehicles) whilst still maintaining passenger demand levels. The staff savings in particular, at a time of staff shortages, obviously had beneficial effects on service reliability.
4. In due time NBC subsidiaries – particularly YTC & EMMS – introduced increased frequencies and revised routes as their part of the PTE's Service Development Plan (see Chapter 6). YTC also introduced services for the disabled, using modified Leyland Nationals.

Fares from 1975

Reverting to the Fares Applications of 1975 onwards, these were made on a commercial basis having regard to relevant legislation (including necessarily at the relevant dates, the Government's Prices and Incomes Policies), but the proper intervention of the PTE led to the fares licensed being subvented in order that the County's fares policy could be adopted, but ensuring that the Subsidiaries could revert to commercial fares policies in accordance with their stage carriage licences, should this become necessary.

At their previous Traffic Commissioner's hearing for the fares increase, the NBC subsidiary companies had also been given approval for further increases to be 'triggered' on the next occasion their costs rose by £200,000. Yorkshire Traction and West Riding operated these triggers in August, 1975 and were compensated for not increasing the fares. The process established, when the companies applied for further substantive increases in August 1975 and February 1976, was for the NBC subsidiary companies to apply to the Traffic Commissioners and send copies of the evidence to the PTE. When the Traffic Commissioner

approved the application, and if the PTE were satisfied, the Council would approve a payment to the companies for obtaining a dispensation to apply the new fares approved. This was a roundabout process but at the time the only check on the amount paid to the companies was through examination of the financial evidence presented to the Traffic Commissioner. The Executive had not been able, at this juncture, to get agreement for them to carry out any audit of NBC subsidiary company records. Primarily this was because the PTE appeared to the subsidiary companies to require audit of NBC centrally – an anathema to the companies.

In November 1975 the Director of Finance and Accountancy (DFA) produced a summary of the existing financial arrangements with the NBC subsidiary companies for the different concessions and general fares subvention. The Director of Operations and Planning (DOP) said there was a need for the NBC subsidiary companies to provide further uneconomic services and new arrangements would be needed for the payments required for this. A copy of the DFA's report was sent to the Council Chief Executive with a letter saying the Executive were pressing NBC to enter into an overall financial agreement to give control over the subsidiaries as an immediate step, and in the longer term an overall operating agreement would be desirable.

The view of the County Chief Officers at that time (the Treasurer in particular) was that it was better to make separate arrangements each time there was a need for further payment to the NBC subsidiary companies. They had heard that their counterparts in West Yorkshire were by then disenchanted about the Metro-National Agreement, and the Treasurer was concerned about Government pressures on the Council because of their public transport policies. His view was that an overall agreement would given an automatic commitment which could upset budgets. But this line of argument could only be followed if one accepted the idea that NBC subsidiary companies and PTE fares levels could be treated differently, which would have negated the whole idea of a County Standard Fares Policy. If the budget could not stand subsidy to hold fares, the whole of the Council's fares policy had to be questioned, not just the fare increases of the NBC subsidiary companies.

There was also a discussion with the County Chief Executive and the Treasurer about new services that the Executive wanted the NBC subsidiary companies to run, and how these were to be financed. There was concern that the Council were reluctant to treat the NBC subsidiary companies and other operators as they would the PTE, and sometimes wanted the PTE to run new services even when it was more economical, and more likely to get the Traffic Commissioner's approval, if other operators ran them.

A financial agreement that gave the PTE powers to check and audit NBC subsidiary companies' accounts to verify amounts claimed would give greater, not less, control over budgets. PTE budgets were agreed at cost levels on a particular date. The inflation provision which was meant to cover all likely cost increases and contingent liabilities in the budget year, included provision for the NBC subsidiary companies and other operators also. The more the Executive knew about NBC finance the better the

The Doncaster-Barnsley service introduced by Yorkshire Traction (see page 61) utilised vehicles painted in their version of "Fastline" livery. It will thus be seen that whilst the operational span of SYPTE virtually parallelled the lifetime of the NBC, with all its dictates concerning livery, exceptions as shown in the illustrations for this chapter were made!

(Mike Greenwood)

inflation estimate was likely to be. The DFA was attempting to get a four-weekly financial return from NBC companies.

In January 1976 the DOP reported to the Executive that Yorkshire Traction were only prepared to put on extra journeys if the operation was fully subsidised. So as not to prejudice discussions on overall financial arrangements, he had agreed for the PTE to make payments that would be treated as traffic revenue by the Company.

A request was made for a subsidy by Leon Motors for the part of a route run in South Yorkshire, the other part being supported by Nottinghamshire County Council. At the fares hearing an objection was made by SYCC but the application was approved and some fares were then higher than the Council standard.

A check on NBC subsidiary company claims for subvention for elderly persons concessions in the year ended 31st March 1976 had revealed an overpayment, the amount of which was disputed: the NBC companies estimate being much less than that of the PTE. This difference had arisen, at least in part, because the estimates for County-wide concessionary travel had been based on figures derived from passenger use in Sheffield. A suggestion had been made that a compromise payment of £94,000 should be made by the Companies on the grounds that any higher payment would only bring an earlier requirement for a fares subvention payment. The Executive said they could not accept any arrangement that appeared to transfer part of the true cost of fares subvention to the elderly persons travel scheme, and asked that the DFA pursue the issue further with NBC.

On examination of a YTC fares application in September 1976 the DFA considered it would produce an excessive surplus, even though it conformed to the Government's price code. YT were not prepared to modify their claim and the Executive made representations at the Traffic Commissioner's hearing. The Traffic Commissioners granted the application and accepted the NBC company's assertion that they had to obtain sufficient revenue to cover, inter alia, the cost of replacing assets in accordance with their perceived statutory duty. Similar applications by the other NBC subsidiaries were also granted. The Executive considered that experiences like this confirmed the need for a financial agreement that would give an opportunity to obtain more information from the companies. The DG agreed to take up this matter with the County Officers and ask them to support a proposal to the Passenger Transport Committee that they should agree to the PTE pressing NBC for a comprehensive agreement in place of the separate ad hoc agreements that the Council had hitherto favoured.

Service reduction option

When the 1977/78 budget was being drawn up the NBC Regional Director was asked to identify possible service reductions in case these were requested by the Council, to keep the total cost within an amount they might specify. The NBC company's opinion was the same as that of the PTE – that cutting necessary services just to avoid increasing fares was a negation of Council policy. The Executive was aware that senior Councillors had the same opinion, and that one reason for the exercise was to demonstrate how impractical the idea was.

It was not only the National Bus Company that was affected by proposals for fare increases. In December 1976 the Council were asked if they would subsidise Rossie Motors if the fares application was approved by The Traffic Commissioners. The Council's decision was deferred. In January 1977 a similar request was made by Morgan and Store, and again a decision by the Council was deferred. In May the Council leader agreed to subvention, pending the purchase of the two undertakings.

Leon Motors had a fares application approved by the Traffic Commissioners in June 1977, in spite of an objection by the PTE. This is likely to have been the origin of the higher than standard scale fares which were the subject of continuing discussion between the PTE and Leon for several years.

An operating agreement was entered into with South Yorkshire Road Transport Ltd. in October 1978, the first of its kind, and also one with A & C Wigmore Ltd., and in 1980 a similar agreement was reached with Dearneways, but one for Leon was deferred. In the following year agreement was reached with H. Wilson. Further details of these developments are given in the next chapter.

Hesitant progress towards agreement

In 1977 and 1978 reports were still being made to the Executive about the inadequacy of financial information from the NBC subsidiary companies. A Working Party had been set up by the PTE/NBC Bus Working Group to formulate terms for an overall agreement, and it was asked to concentrate on the financial aspects first. A summary of proposed financial arrangements was put to the Passenger Transport Panel and the Passenger Transport Committee in December 1978, and finally in February 1979 the Council approved the financial arrangements with the NBC subsidiary companies and noted that an overall agreement was still under discussion.

The PTE's Chief Finance Officer (CFO) reported in October and December 1979 on current problems with the NBC subsidiary companies, insufficient financial information being given and difficulties put in the way of PTE staff commencing the 1979 audit. This was taken up with Joint Committee and with NBC Company Management. The latter maintained that differences between the parties as to the audit procedures were as to matters of interpretation of the precise audit entitlement which had been agreed.

Talks continued about an overall operating agreement and a draft sent by the Executive in October 1981 had still not been accepted as a basis for progress fourteen months later. The NBC subsidiary companies were asked to state the principal points of disagreement by the end of January 1983. Serious disagreements had also arisen on several financial matters, principally on contingency payments, interest on balances, and on the interpretation of the principles laid down for calculation of peak hour bus and provision for depreciation. On the latter a case was to be prepared to go to CIPFA for their interpretation.

The Director General reported that the response of the NBC companies to queries on the validity of contingency payments had been unco-operative. They had been told no more payment would be made after April 1983 unless it could be shown to be justified. The NBC subsidiary companies had threatened legal action.

A special meeting between the Executive and the NBC subsidiary companies had been held in Harrogate, resulting in a decision to send to arbitration the following two items:–

– withholding contingency provision
– interest on balances

The Executive had obtained Counsel's opinion, but further information was needed. The NBC subsidiary companies had presented a schedule to the Executive at Harrogate but CFO said the figures in it were difficult to reconcile.

The business dragged on, with the Companies issuing a High Court Writ because contingency payments had been withheld, and refusing to go to arbitration on this issue. The Executive sent the Counsel's opinion to NBC Solicitors to try to persuade them they could not win the High Court Action. The Chief Executive of NBC was informed of Executive's displeasure and the Council Chief Executive advised of the situation.

In November the CFO summarised problems in relation to operation and interpretation of the Memo of Financial Arrangements. He prefaced his notes with a comment that if these arrangements had not been entered into, the matter under contention would probably not have come to light. The points at issue were:-

– Peak vehicle requirement (which determined vehicle depreciation charges) for EMMS. NBC to be asked again to go to arbitration failing which legal action to be considered.
– Treatment by EMMS of interests on balances to be raised at next meeting of Joint Committee.
– CFO to ask YTC for sight of appraisal of relative effects of six year or twelve year life for vehicles which had recently been carried out for them.

The PTE Secretary reported NBC refused to accept some of the proposals in the draft overall operating agreement. The Director General had met the Regional Director who suggested that if the PTE would agree to 'withholding payments of contingency' being described as 'pending the outcome of arbitration', NBC would consider referring matters to arbitration. However, the Regional Director later refused to implement the arrangements.

In January 1984 the Director General referred to press reports about the various disputes with NBC and said the matter should now be reported fully to the County Council. There had been two meetings of Executive Board Members with the Chief Executive of NBC during this period of dispute, and some of the matters had been cleared up, but on others they had continued to be less than helpful. On the 5th March 1984 it was reported to the Executive Board that many of the minor issues had been resolved and that further discussions would take place on the rest. On 3rd May 1984 it was recommended to the Board that the Memorandum of Agreement on Financial Arrangements between the PTE and the NBC subsidiary companies, dated 7th May, 1979 to be terminated having regard to current parliamentary proposals.

However, at an Executive Board meeting on 14th June 1984, it was decided that notice of termination should not be sent yet and that an attempt should be made to conclude a full operating agreement. Leading members of the County Council were to be advised of the implications of this decision. In overall terms the difficulties for the PTE and NBC subsidiary Companies principal officers in devising a full operating agreement rested on the differing standpoints of the parties. In essence the PTE looked to outright ownership of all the Company's interests in the Metropolitan County, whilst the subsidiary companies, for their part, were equally convinced that they had the right and duty to meet the statutory requirements of both the PTE and PTA (as evidenced by their transport policies) without ceding sovereignty or ownership of their assets. This could be achieved provided that they were not inhibited by any arrangements which they might enter into from meeting in full their statutory duties of whatever nature.

The NBC subsidiary companies pointed to the fact that in other Metropolitan Counties – West Yorkshire, Tyne & Wear and Merseyside being examples – comprehensive agreements between the respective PTEs and the local NBC subsidiaries, had been freely negotiated and adopted. (They did not, of course, draw attention to the solutions adopted in SELNEC or West Midlands, where each of those PTE's had acquired a substantial part of the local NBC subsidiary!) None of the agreements in these three instances was identical as they were designed to ensure that the parties concerned were able to meet their respective duties. One of the principal themes of commonality in each of the three examples mentioned, was that none of the NBC subsidiary companies had ceded either sovereignty or ownership.

With the continuing pattern of passenger user generation the subsidiary companies, as in earlier years, continued to modify service levels and to meet changing demand. Cross-town services in the Barnsley area were developed, for example, as patterns changed and there was a marked effect on increased 'off-peak' usage during the day. In many instances, re-deployment of resources was the main means of meeting demand changes i.e. the use where possible of larger capacity vehicles.

This need was evidenced too in the companies' capital programmes which reflected increased intake of large-capacity OMO buses (eg the Leyland National) and of double-deck vehicles, against replacement by smaller capacity single-deck vehicles. Improved platform staff productivity was therefore achieved, albeit subject to increasing demands by the relevant Trades Unions for pay parity with their SYPTE counterparts.

Within the National Bus Company YTC was one of two companies with the highest ratio of miles per vehicles operated. From 1974 this position was maintained – indeed the ratio itself showed consistent betterment as passenger generation was reflected in improved vehicle utilisation.

As a corollary to this of course, engineering unit costs tended to be at the higher end of the NBC scale as a whole, and the factor itself tended towards a higher plane, as the utilisation factor moved almost imperceptibly upwards. Whilst more and more of the County's road maintenance deteriorated there was consequential impact on the bus maintenance cost elements.

The presence of low bridges on numerous important urban bus routes also became an inhibiting factor for the subsidiaries, as they sought to divert from smaller capacity to larger capacity vehicles, but some road re-alignments and traffic management measures by the County authority were, in some instances, feasible and were implemented.

To adequately maintain the bus fleet with their high work rate, capital expenditure programmes of the companies were kept under constant review, within their individual company procedures, constrained as expenditure was, within financing limits and the Corporate Planning procedures of the NBC Group.

A new Barnsley maintenance depot, new bus wash facilities at Shafton, Wombwell and Doncaster, and new pits at several depots, are but examples of the sustained efforts of the subsidiary companies, on Capital Account, to retain a commercial approach to their businesses, consistent with all other relevant factors.

As mentioned earlier, fares subvention policy was adopted initially, and continuingly, as the vehicle for financial arrangements between the PTE and the NBC subsidiary companies. However, an overall financial framework to better reflect the actual relationship between them and the Executive, and to ensure adoption of County Policies as to fares and service levels, was clearly desirable, and this was achieved when the parties concerned entered into a binding financial arrangement.

The development of services into inaccessible areas (see Chapter 6) was not confined to the PTE's own operating area; here a sister vehicle to that shown on page 55 is in Yorkshire Traction's version of "Nipper" livery. *(Mike Greenwood)*

9 INDEPENDENT OPERATORS

As will be apparent from previous chapters, the formal establishment of both South Yorkshire County Council and South Yorkshire Passenger Transport Executive on 1st April, 1974 did not actually represent the start of work for both organisations, as their existence had long been planned, and a considerable amount of preparatory work had been carried out beforehand. Thus the Passenger Transport Authority was able to resolve on 9th April, 1974 that ' ... it is desirable for the PTE to seek to carry out the duty laid upon them under the Transport Act 1968 to achieve the integration of public passenger transport services in the County, by acquiring those operations of the NBC and private operators which are relevant to the achievement of that end'. It will be noted that this resolution specified acquisition. No consideration was given by the County Council to negotiating Operating Agreements. Matters relating to the NBC have been dealt with in the previous Chapter.

In April, 1974 there was a total of 16 private (or independent) operators and the list is shown on page 105. Most of them were originally family firms dating back to the 1920s. There were exceptions – Dearneways was a post-war operation which had initially been founded in 1949, and whose principal stage operation only pre-dated the PTE by ten years. Many had joint operating agreements with their fellow private companies; agreements also existed with NBC subsidiaries and also with the PTE itself (as successor to the local authority operator), although these tended to be confined to the Doncaster area. Over the years, most turned themselves into Limited companies, but the family influence was still strong. In some cases, however, the absence of a subsequent generation to continue the business assisted in the owners' decision to sell. Whilst coach operations formed a varying part of their operations some concentrated on stage carriage almost exclusively.

The fact that the County Council wished the PTE to acquire the businesses of the NBC subsidiaries and of the privately owned operators had been well publicised. This had not helped when the Executive started arranging meetings with representatives of NBC subsidiaries and the private operators, to explain the PTE's role as planner and co-ordinator of public transport services in the county, to discuss the development of a Countywide fare scale and providing concessionary travel. They were reluctant to supply financial information and passenger statistics.

The private operators were particularly suspicious. With two exceptions, they asked the Executive to meet them as a group, accompanied by their advisers. As all were well established operators who had run successfully for years, and although inflation and other problems were causing them the same kind of difficulties other bus operators were experiencing, most of them did not seem to doubt their ability to survive, if left alone. They were worried about what they had read about takeovers and free travel, and had doubts about what the people in an office in Sheffield knew about operating buses in the rural parts of the county.

Several further meetings were needed with each of them before they had enough confidence to talk about proposals for standard fares and conditions, and how payments would be calculated. Eventually good relationships were established with them, and when a scheme of free off-peak travel for all elderly persons commenced on 1st April 1975, the passes were accepted by all operators in the County. At first the passes were only available in the Metropolitan District of residence, but from 1st September 1975 they permitted travel anywhere in the County. Also from 1st April 1975 standard concessionary fares for children were available on 99% of bus services in the County.

At the first meetings the PTE representatives had said they had not gone to talk to them about acquiring their businesses, but that they would be prepared to do so separately if desired. Two of the companies said they were interested in the prospect and one of them, Booth & Fisher, was the first to be acquired. The other one still operates independently.

When the local press commented on the Council's wish for the PTE to take over the services of the small operators, they usually assumed this was just a politically motivated commitment and, to be fair to the press, some of the councillors referred to it as if this was the case. But there were quite valid planning and operational reasons as set out in an internal PTE memo of the time:

'It is already apparent that it will be difficult, if not impossible, for the Executive to implement fully the Authority's county-wide policies unless ownership of the stage carriage services of the sixteen private operators can be acquired.

The approval of the individual independent operators will be required before the level or quality of their services, or their fares policies, can be influenced, and generally compensation payments will need to be agreed. But in addition to this, they will in many cases have the right, as operators, to object to changes which the Executive wish to make in their own services or fares. The recent Traffic Commissioner's hearing on the elderly persons' and children's concessions was an example of this.

Now that we are involved in the details for

compensation payments for concessionary fares, and in the collection of statistical information needed for TPPs, there are growing administrative problems in dealing with so many operators.

As wider transportation policies are developed, possibly requiring changes to be made in other operators' services and affecting their profitability, the problems will increase. When consideration is being given to new route patterns and to new forms of service such as dial-a-ride, rail feeders, rapid transit, etc, a great deal of consultation and agreement will be required.

It will also be difficult to deal with so many operators on marketing issues such as the quality and consistency of service, interavailability of tickets, through booking, travelcards and the standardisation of operating practices, etc. Many of these issues will involve payments to the operators.

The type of agreements we are likely to require for these matters may need to go beyond what would be needed merely to compensate the operators for running specific uneconomic services, or for accepting OAP concessionary passes, or for holding fares down. The agreements might need to be on a virtual 'cost plus' basis and will be difficult and costly to control from an accountancy and audit point of view. There is less incentive for the operator to hold down costs if subsidies are being paid by the County'.

All parties were conscious of the need to discuss with the Unions arrangements for bringing in the concessions, but this would also have to be co-ordinated so that NBC could raise the matter with their staff first, because of the greater effect of the changes on their operations.

Independent operators with which the PTE and Felix Motors ran jointly in the north-east of the county had put in fares increase applications, but the new fares were not higher than the County scale. The Council agreed to the PTE and Felix putting in 'in-line' applications which would yield £33,000 pa. These operators, who had not hitherto applied the standard children's fare, then agreed to do so.

Some independents had long tradition of always buying new vehicles, whilst others had tended to purchase second-hand ones. The advent of bus grants from 1968, however, tended to result in even these operators buying new – sometimes for the first time. The vehicles acquired with the businesses subsequently bought, therefore, tended to be a 'mixed bag', but for a PTE that was having to come to terms with a rationalisation of the three municipal fleets it had inherited, it was generally in no position to pick or choose the vehicles it acquired, with the exception of some of the older stock which never saw service with the PTE.

Within a month of the PTA's decision, the PTE's Director of Operations and Planning was able to report that interviews had already taken place with the Directors of three companies, namely Booth & Fisher, Rossie Motors and Leon Motors. From this a pattern began to emerge, which set the standard for subsequent acquisitions. In each

of these cases it became clear that the owners were prepared to sell at the 'right' price, and also that they wished to include all the activities associated with their stage carriage interests in a 'package' deal. In one case this meant buying a cycle shop and repair business and some very dilapidated properties. In other cases it meant buying a petrol station and car showrooms. There was a considerable amount of work in valuing the businesses to arrive at price, consideration also had to be given to the integration of the management and control arrangement, and also arrange for operation of the extensive excursion and private hire activities, in which many of the private operators were involved. These latter features tended to be-devil the PTE for as long as it remained a bus operator. It is interesting to note Philip Baggaley's thoughts in August, 1975 with regard to the acquisition of Booth & Fisher.

'Recent statements in the Press since Monday give the impression that there is unlikely to be any change, even in timetables, let alone in anything more radical, for a period of 12 months. Surely this cannot be intended to be the case. In view of the adverse publicity given to the sum of money involved in the transaction, the public will at the very least expect some declaration of intent, if not actual visible progress, toward some measure of integration.

Whilst the Executive have expressed the intention of retaining the Company as a separate legal entity for at least that period, every endeavour must be made to facilitate the proper integration of services into the Executive's Undertaking as a whole, and to work towards that end. In particular, the corporate image of the Executive must be projected. When Tyne and Wear PTE acquired a similar, albeit somewhat smaller independent operator, they converted the outward signs to their own image whilst still preserving the legal identity of the absorbed company.

In order the avoid the problems which still exist in the former municipal undertakings absorbed into the PTE, whereby certain reluctances to conform to standard procedures and to be properly integrated have been observed, it will be necessary to lay down clearly defined channels of communication and limits of responsibility if any progress is to be made in this respect.

The main difficulty is likely to be if there is a prolonged period of time during which basic wage rates etc., are different from those in the rest of the PTE. It will readily be appreciated that there may be problems if we desire to operate buses on a Booth & Fisher route, alongside those from another garage where higher rates apply and it may be that there will be resistance to any form of service re-organisation, additional duplication or even assistance in case of emergency until some harmonisation has taken place. It would, therefore, seem to be desirable that whilst we have asked for a 12 month breathing space, the matter should be dealt with more urgently and certainly by 1st April, 1976 when the next year's budget will be in force'.

The memo continued at some length identifying the practical issues that had to be dealt with if the benefits of acquisition were to be reaped. These included:-

– pay and condition issues
– provision of service numbers and new destination blinds
– acquisition of vehicles and their repainting
– assessment of the prices of the Schools and Coal Board Contracts
– analysis of private hire business
– ability to render assistance to other PTE buses in the area.

In pursuance of the County Council's policy of control by acquisition, whilst the PTE recognised that it could not allow any opportunities to pass by, it was desirable to consider an order of priority which would greatly assist in achieving the objective. It was determined that the priorities would be to:-

1. strengthen the PTE's proportion on routes where it only had a small influence
2. to acquire services which (at that time) had an inhibiting effect on the development of neighbouring PTE services
3. to move into new areas where the PTE had no influence

It was further recognised that since co-ordination with, or acquisition of, Yorkshire Traction was also part of the policy there was little benefit in acquiring the one or two operators which existed in Yorkshire Traction's area. Furthermore, the acquisition of these operators by the PTE would not strengthen their influence materially, although elsewhere it was felt essential to avoid independents falling to other hands. The most useful acquisitions were identified as some of the services centred on Sheffield and Doncaster, and an assessment of these, together with a review of all the other operators follows.

SHEFFIELD

Serving Sheffield there were three independent operators, Booth & Fisher, A & C Wigmore and Dearneways.

Booth & Fisher Motor Services, Halfway

This was the largest operator with over 40 vehicles and relatively modern premises (including non-bus activities) within the expanding area of Mosborough. In 1973 approximately 42% of the Company's revenue came from Stage Carriage service, 44% from Contract Carriage (mostly NCB), 12% from Private Hire and Excursions, and 2% from other sources. At that time some of the Company's services were in direct competition with the Executive's

services. Removal of this competing element would give greater flexibility. There were two main stage carriage services which both ran out of South Yorkshire into Derbyshire and Nottinghamshire, and which both ran parallel or crossed routes of the East Midland Company. Booth & Fisher's main services ran through areas which were being extensively developed. These include Mosborough, which was the main residential development area in the County, and in which it was vital for extensive and completely adequate public transport services to be provided.

For the Executive to be able to develop the facilities required, it was essential that they should not be inhibited by having to obtain the agreement of the Company to necessary service changes. There were also numerous contract colliery and school buses, as well as excursions and private hire. The established private hire business could be extended, and the Excursions licences would be valuable because they covered picking up points in this developing area. The depot at Halfway was ideally placed to serve this and there would be economies if the Executive could operate some of their own services from the Booth & Fisher site. The main garage, which contained a workshop, was then of recent construction with scope for expansion both on the main site and across the road. A well-laid out petrol station and garage forecourt faced onto Station Road which offered considerable potential with the expansion of Mosborough. Other activities of the Company, including vehicle repairs, filling station and driving school, were all considered capable of development and would give the Executive an opportunity of extending into these fields. Booth & Fisher was the largest of the independent operators in the area and had recently acquired the private hire and excursion business of Sharp Bros. (Beighton).

There would be advantages, from the recruitment point of view, in the Executive having a garage in the area. There was less competition for staff from other industries than in Sheffield, and increased operation from Booth & Fisher's garage would also create more local job opportunities. There could be considerable economic advantage in the Executive's use of the Company's garage, without the necessity to provide expensive new buildings in this area.

The optional development of the PTE's routes were being inhibited and whilst some of these were just in Derbyshire, they were well within the PTE's traditional operating area, and there was an indivisible community of interest with the city of Sheffield. Housing development was taking place in three distinct areas along the routes, i.e. Mosborough, Dronfield and Kiveton. The existence of different operators had for a long time prevented route and timetable alterations being carried out, which would probably have occurred if there had been a sole operator. It was important that the PTE should be able to fulfil its functions in these expanding areas.

A & C Wigmore, Dinnington.

This firm provided, primarily, a stage carriage business of an hourly service between Sheffield and what was becoming the expanding area of Dinnington. It was competitive with several of the PTE's services and was also partly covered at the Dinnington end with East Midland routes. It was interesting that some years previously, before the advent of the PTE, negotiations had commenced jointly by Rotherham and Sheffield Corporations to acquire the business, but they fell through. In the event it was not until 1987, and after the advent of deregulation, that the Company was sold, not to any existing operators, but to persons new to the business, who have subsequently developed the Company as Northern Bus. These developments must wait until Chapters 12 and 13.

Phillipson (Dearneways), Goldthorpe

Dearneways provided an hourly limited stop service with high minimum fares between the Dearne Valley and Rotherham/Sheffield. Considerable battles took place in the traffic courts prior to the commencement of the Dearneways service on October 5th 1964 (the service ran right through both Yorkshire Traction and Mexborough & Swinton's territories, besides running through both Rotherham and Sheffield). It also operated through well populated areas. In view of the foregoing it is perhaps surprising to learn that it was not regarded by the PTE as 'an immediate embarrassment' and of less priority than the other two operators . Furthermore, the Company was lead by the charismatic Maurice Phillipson, who had pioneered the route. He was strongly independent. It was only ill-health that persuaded him to sell. The Company also operated a number of services to army camps at Catterick, in the South West and in Scotland.

DONCASTER

Serving Doncaster, it was felt particularly important that some (although not necessarily all) of the Independents running into Doncaster should be purchased. The former municipality had kept its operation very much within the former County Borough boundaries and had, in any case, poor representation in the north-east quadrant of Doncaster. Furthermore, Doncaster was expanding rapidly both industrially and residentially. In particular, expansion was taking place in Cantley, Bessacar, Armthorpe, Finningley and the villages north-east of the town. The main areas or operators identified for acquisition are set out in the next paragraphs.

Rossington Route

It was noted that the PTE only had a quarter share of this important route and that the NBC (in the shape of East Midland) also had a quarter share. This itself had been acquired from Don Motors of Bessacarr in 1962, it being rumoured that right up the point of sale Don Motors were about to sell to another Doncaster independent. The other operators were Blue Ensign (based in Doncaster – in fact, of all the independents, the only one so situated) and Rossie Motors (based in Rossington). Neither had extensive non-stage carriage operations.

Rossie Motors received approximately 80% of its revenue from stage carriage services; the remainder being from private hire. They had recently disposed of their excursion licences (which were little used) to Harts of Adwick-le-Street. Because the PTE already ran on the route the service could be easily absorbed into the PTE and run from Doncaster garage. The existing premises could be sold. Large areas adjacent to the route were scheduled for future housing development.

Leon Motors (Finningley)

This Company was regarded as the only 'sole operator' independent having a free-standing route which ran through a developing residential area, where it was felt Cantley might present integration possibilities. Stage carriage operations accounted for only approximately 50% of the revenue, the remainder coming from school contracts 25%, excursion and express work 10% and Private hire 15%.

The Company's stage activity was based on the Doncaster – Finningley route with some buses extended or superimposed through to Misson and Wroot. The route was run independently and competed with PTE services between Doncaster and Cantley, with no restrictive conditions. There was considerable housing development along the line of route and the services had potential for development. The stage activities could be integrated conveniently with, and run from, Doncaster District of the PTE, but consideration could also be given to using the existing garage as a dormy shed. Leon also had a medium sized excursion, coastal and Private Hire business, which it was felt could be integrated with the PTE's Doncaster district operations. Stage carriage activity could be conveniently split from the others, and consideration could be given to using the latter as a nucleus of excursion and private hire operation in the Eastern part of the County. The excursion licences were for a large number of destinations from Doncaster Bus Station with authority to run seven vehicles (increased on Sundays and Bank Holidays). The trips were extensively advertised and were among the biggest excursion operations in the County by a non-NBC Company. In retrospect it is interesting to note that of the sixteen operators identified in 1974, only Leon Motors remains with its original owners, albeit almost twice the size following deregulation.

Thorne Corridor

The Thorne corridor lies either side of the A18 trunk road, as an ever-widening wedge. It runs past the Doncaster Royal Infirmary and through the Wheatley suburb of Doncaster (served originally by a trolleybus route). Villages served off this spine road include Armthorpe, Edenthorpe, Kirk Sandall, Dunscroft, Stainforth and Hatfield. Many of these were colliery villages. Whilst Thorne provided the outer terminus, with some services extended to Goole, the 'scatter' of the villages and limitations of the highways network made it difficult to serve the area effectively. With a multiplicity of independents the problems were compounded.

Operating along Thorne Road were services from Doncaster to Armthorpe (on which the PTE already had a

¹/₃ share); to Thorne and Moorends; and to Stainforth and Dunscroft (on which the PTE again had a ¹/₃ share); and beyond the County boundary to Goole in Humberside. Four operators were involved, none of which operated on all of the services, namely Felix Motors Ltd. of Hatfield, T. Severn & Sons, based at Dunscroft, Harold Wilson Ltd., Stainforth (trading as 'Premier'), Samuel Morgan Ltd (trading as 'Blue Line')/R. Store Ltd (trading as 'Reliance'), the latter being regarded as one firm. Wilson had many coaches in the fleet and was not considered a first priority. (It is interesting to note here that it was not until 1988 and post-deregulation that this Company sold out to South Yorkshire Transport Ltd, as successors to the PTE).

Morgan and Store's operation included the Goole route and had some fairly old rolling stock when compared to some of the others. So the priority was given to Felix and Severn, both of whom it was felt ran good vehicles, but more importantly, by virtue of the combination of services run, would give the PTE the majority interest in three services (excluding the Goole route) viz Armthorpe (66.6%), Thorne/Moorends (75%), and Dunscroft (66.6%). Severns had a comparatively modern, purpose-built garage at Dunscroft. It was a flat site capable of expansion. It was also well-located to serve the whole corridor. Since none of the other properties were suitable, they would have to be disposed of. The Severn's site provided the best location on which to concentrate future bus operations consolidated from the previous independent operation. Additionally, Severn's bought new vehicles – usually Leyland Atlantean with Roe body to the 'Leeds/WYPTE standard'.

OTHER SERVICES

The other services which operated into Doncaster, and which were identified by the PTE, were those of two firms whose premises were situated in West Yorkshire. United Services (W. R. & P. Bingley and Cooper Bros.) of Kinsley and South Kirby, respectively, who ran an hourly service between Wakefield and Doncaster. This was exactly duplicated (and provided a half-hourly frequency) along a Yorkshire Traction route within the County of South Yorkshire. The other operator was South Yorkshire Road Transport of Pontefract. They ran hourly between Leeds and Doncaster and also Pontefract and Doncaster, duplicating to an extent the routes of West Riding, another NBC subsidiary. It was felt that both these operators could well best be dealt with by a purchase by West Yorkshire PTE who had no representation in the South part of their County and were thus anxious to purchase United Services operations. This they achieved in 1977. They left the operation as a free-standing unit, but rapidly repainted all the vehicles into WYPTE livery so as to make their presence known in Wakefield and Doncaster.

South Yorkshire Transport had been established by the McCloy family earlier in the century and was part of much wider bus machinations in the Wakefield/Castleford/ Pontefract area. Although based in Pontefract they were well-known as South Yorkshire Transport with a traditional dark blue/light blue and cream livery. With the advent of South Yorkshire PTE, they sought the assistance of a local designer to come up with a distinct livery, not so much in the colours (dark blue and light blue were retained and white added) but in their application which achieved the objective of providing a strident looking vehicle. SYPTE negotiated one of the first, if not the first, Operating Agreement with South Yorkshire Road Transport. The question of buying them outright was often discussed with them, but never achieved. The Company finally sold out in 1994 to the West Riding Group of Wakefield.

BARNSLEY

There were two operators serving the Barnsley area, neither of which was regarded as being of particular importance to the PTE.

Larratt Pepper, Thurnscoe.

A two-hourly service between Barnsley and Thurnscoe was operated in the heart of, and co-ordinated with, Yorkshire Traction services. The PTE did not feel that the service could be run satisfactorily by them in isolation. Although consideration was given to this acquisition which, together with Dearneways, could have provided a point of leverage on YTC, in the all-important Doncaster-Barnsley corridor, which the PTE was keen to up-grade and where YTC were well-entrenched and conservative.

One of the few South Yorkshire independent operators not to sell to the PTE was the long established firm of A C Wigmore. In typical Wigmore operating area scenery a typically well presented Duple bodied Bedford RWX 178M is heading for Sheffield on what became service 209 under the PTE's comprehensive county route numbering scheme. (Gary Nolan)

A large proportion of the Booth & Fisher operation, which was the first business to be acquired by the PTE in February 1976, was linked to the then numerous collieries in the area, although in this photograph 332 NKT, which was new to Maidstone and District, was operating a stage carriage service. *(Mike Fowler)*

The first of the Doncaster area independents to be purchased was that of Felix, in April 1976. The Felix fleet consisted of AECs whilst Guys predominated with Blue Line/ Reliance, Leylands with Severns and Daimlers with Rossie Motors. That such a variety of manufacturers could be available to bus operators today! *(Mike Fowler)*

The PTE was not the only South Yorkshire operator to use the Volvo Ailsa Alexander combination (see chapter 7), although only one unit was supplied to H. Wilson Ltd (Premier). It is seen here in its original version of Premier's livery. Bob Wilson (the proprietor) eventually sold out to South Yorkshire Transport Ltd (as successors to the PTE) as described in chapter 13. *(Mike Fowler)*

Baddeley Brothers, Holmfirth.

At the other side of the County services were operated in what was very sparse rural territory on the fringe of the Yorkshire Traction and West Riding areas, south of Huddersfield, between Penistone and Holmfirth. This area was in West Yorkshire. It was considered that even if Yorkshire Traction was acquired, the operation would be more suited to West Yorkshire PTE, who acquired it in due course, integrating the operation into their Huddersfield District.

SUBSEQUENT DEVELOPMENTS

The scene was set for the next step in the South Yorkshire story to unfold. Whilst negotiations had commenced concurrently with the formation of the PTE, it was not until February 1976 that an announcement of the first acquisition was made, that of Booth & Fisher. The arrangements for day-to-day management were not, however, to be repeated. The premises at Halfway were retained and remain today as one of the six depots retained by the current successor, Mainline. Control was not, however, placed under one of the PTE's three District Managers, as with subsequent purchases, but placed with Mr M. Pillinger, a former Booth & Fisher Director, who became Operating Manager, Halfway, reporting direct to the PTE Board. This arrangement in fact continued until the PTE ceased to be bus operator.

Booth & Fisher had gained a certain interest with enthusiasts as a last refuge of the Bedford OB. By the time of acquisition these had been replaced, largely by a collection of assorted 'Albion Nimbuses, (Nimbii ?). There was also a large collection of AEC Reliances and also a very rare AEC Monocoach. The retention of a homegrown manager was probably wise, in view of the amount of contract work operated; there were a great many colliery contracts together with an intensive service between Sheffield Midland Station and the motive power depot at Tinsley, run and paid for by British Rail, for its Staff. For many years Halfway continued to operate its own excursion and tours, as it had done in Booth & Fisher days. For a period also the petrol station, car maintenance and MoT Testing facilities were continued. Perhaps the most significant change that subsequently occurred was the commencement of service X29 and the introduction of double-deck buses to the garage in 1979. This led to a gradual replacement of the acquired stock by new standard PTE Leyland AN68s, although the final Booth & Fisher vehicles were to last until 1986.

The second anniversary of the formation of the PTE saw Felix Motors of Hatfield acquired (1st April 1976) but on this occasion the whole of the operation was transferred to the PTE's Doncaster Garage at Leicester Avenue, and the Garage at Dunsville was sold. This acquisition made the PTE the majority operator on the Armthorpe service, beside introducing PTE vehicles onto the A18 (the 'top road' in Independent parlance) for the first time. On order at the time of purchase were two Daimler Fleetlines which materialised into the bus fleet in due course. The Executive

also brought their useful Excursions and Tours Road Service Licence, although when attempting to expand this facility, they gave rise to conflict with those independent operators who also held E & T licences, and who still remained outside the PTE's control.

The next acquisition by the PTE did not take place until two years later, but in the meantime West Yorkshire PTE had purchased both Baddeley Brothers and Cooper Bros. in March, 1976 and April 1977, respectively. In April 1978, Blue Ensign's operation came under the control of the PTE. Although the garage was situated in Union Street, only a stone's throw away from Doncaster South bus station, the premises were not retained and the operation was quickly assimilated into the Leicester Avenue operation. This time the acquisition gave the PTE an uplift to a half share of the Rossington route, and a trio of coaches which were added to the rapidly growing coach fleet at Leicester Avenue. Alone of the three municipal operators, Doncaster Corporation had, prior to 1974, attempted to build up an expanding Private Hire business, together with a limited Excursions facility.

As already indicated, expansion in the Excursions and Tours business was achieved quite often only after long and protracted battles in the Traffic Court, and it was not until 1980 that licensing for this type of operation was abolished. The initial acquisitions had brought useful facilities, based on Dronfield/Mosborough, Killamarsh and Doncaster, and it made sense to attempt to capitalise on these by virtue of the linking of some longer distance destinations. This work was also a useful complement for the Private Hire drivers. However, the difficulties in undertaking this work were not confined to external sources. The difficulties of convincing the Trade Unions of the need for flexibility, already referred to in Chapter 5, led in 1979 to a complete abandonment of this work almost overnight.

For the record it should be noted that the following month, in May 1978, Yorkshire Traction acquired the stage service of Larratt Pepper, although no vehicles or premises were taken over, and Larratt Pepper Coaches still exists today. The end of this financial year brought a flurry of activity which resulted in Morgan and Store being acquired towards the end of March 1979, followed a day later by Severns. These two events were not entirely unconnected, in so far as it was felt by the PTE that finance for purchasing other operators could well be more difficult to obtain in the financial year 1979/80. Also there was a need to consolidate operation at Dunscroft as referred to previously.

The PTE was now in a position to be able to make some sense of the various takeovers. Only H. Wilson was now left on the Thorne Road corridor, and he was confined to the A18 road on services to Thorne and Moorends. Elsewhere, the PTE now operated 100% of the Armthorpe service, as well as all of the service to Dunscroft, and also over the County Boundary into Humberside. Meaningful service development could now take place, for example, the tantalising gap on Broadway, Dunscroft which the previous operators had jealously guarded, could be served.

The Independent Operators
Annual Stage mileage figures – year ending 31 March 1976

	Total mileage	Mileage in S. Yorks	% in S. Yorks	approx. vehicles owned
Baddeley Bros.	214,180	101,762	47	27
Blue Ensign	104,985	104,985	100	6
Booth & Fisher	423,000	260,311	61	42
Felix	334,911	334,911	100	15
Larratt Pepper	75,234	75,234	100	10
Leon	256,033	248,839	97	17
Rossie	100,391	100,391	100	6
S Morgan	348,891	269,980	77	16
R. Store	274,382	195,671	71	11
Severn	399,172	399,172	100	15
S Yorks Road Trans	941,972	251,036	27	17
W R & P Bingley	241,655	80,696	33	27
Cooper Bros	97,971	28,112	31	3
Wigmore	248,242	248,242	100	7
Dearneways	207,803	207,803	100	15
Wilson	155,086	155,806	100	22
TOTALS	**4,417,908**	**3,062,230**	**69**	

Total mileage in South Yorkshire was 6.6% of total stage
mileage in County

Initially this was achieved by diverting the Goole service this way from March 1980, as part of a comprehensive review of the acquired services.

In the meantime, only the Severns premises at Dunscroft were retained, remaining even today with Mainline, whilst properties at Armthorpe and Stainforth were eventually sold. Two Dennis Dominators with East Lancashire bodywork, ordered by Morgan and Store, eventually entered the PTE fleet. Obviously in all these acquisitions large numbers of platform and engineering staff joined the PTE as employees, more often than not at improved rates of pay. But it also brought one or two well known managers into the organisation, such as Cliff Theaker and Colin Fowlston. The latter became Operations Manager at Dunscroft, reporting to the District Manager, Doncaster. Cliff Theaker had acted as Secretary to the 'Thorne Road group of independents' and was a mine of information.

The re-organisation of services referred to above went a long way to simplifying the rather complicated working arrangements enjoyed by the independents, whereby individual vehicle workings were allotted after agreement with each operator, with some workings nevertheless rotating between them. Perhaps the most complicated was found on the Thorne Road services through Dunsville to Hatfield, Thorne and Moorends and initially shared by Felix, Severns and H. Wilson, which became service numbers 186 – 188 under the PTE. In particular a 'floating'

vehicle working, known locally as 'J' week, still caused the PTE some difficulties, as it was rostered to be worked after the acquisition of the first two named operators six weeks out of every eight. For an independent operator who made use of part time staff the problem was not so great, but rostering such arrangements was not so simple for the PTE! The eventual acquisition of H. Wilson by South Yorkshire Transport Ltd. in 1988, finally resolved all these intricacies.

The final acquisition by the PTE in the Doncaster area was completed in December 1980, when Rossie Motors was purchased. Again the premises, this time in Rossington. were not retained, although a number of buses entered the fleet. The actual Company itself was also used beneficially by the PTE in due course, although that is not a topic for this narrative. As a result, the Rossington service was now only shared with East Midland, who had a quarter entitlement, and as part of a package of exchanges a few years later this was surrendered by them, in return for additional mileage on the Sheffield-Gainsborough service – so at last Rossington became the exclusive preserve of one operator. This situation subsequently enabled the PTE to link the service, with that to Edlington, as a cross town route.

A year later, agreement with Maurice Phillipson was reached for the acquisition of the Dearneway operation, numbered X91. This was transferred to the Midland Road garage of the PTE in Rotherham in December 1981. This trunk route continued unchanged under the PTE, but was always confined to single-deck operation due to low bridges. Its popularity was such, however, that considerable duplication had been, and was required, so that the PTE in an attempt to reduce costs but maintain capacity, ordered three articulated vehicles for this service. They entered service in November 1985, but unlike their counterparts used in Sheffield, had only two doors and were fitted with 75 coach-type seats. Although the introduction of the artics was a cost-saving measure, and the vehicles were liked by the passengers, passenger levels declined. Whilst there were economic reasons for this in the Dearne Valley towns, and the introduction of an express service between Doncaster & Barnsley, there were also operational reasons. With duplication, Dearneway effectively ran two services. The route, as licensed via Rotherham Bus Station, and a duplicate service by-passing Rotherham, and thus much quicker. In effect, therefore, journey times increased with the removal of duplication, on the introduction of the artics. Service X91 was discontinued in 1989, its role

having been taken over, to a large extent, by the PTE-sponsored Sheffield-Swinton-Thurnscoe-Wakefield-Leeds hourly train service. (See Chapter 10).

Spasmodic discussions continued between the PTE and the remaining Independent operators, up to 1986, but no further acquisitions were made. Only Leon Motor Services of Finningley remains recognisable from the original list of sixteen operators. The advent of deregulation in October 1986, led eventually to the sale of both the National Bus Company subsidiaries and the former PTE (local authority) operations, which from 1986 to 1993 traded as South Yorkshire Transport Ltd., so that arguably all the bus operations in the County should now be classed as 'independent'. At the last count it was asserted that there were now approximately 35 operators providing local bus services (ie at least six days per week, 52 weeks per year) in South Yorkshire, plus almost as many again providing services that require registration under the current regulations. However, that is another story dealt with in Chapter 13.

Typifying the Guy fleet of Blue Line/Reliance is Arab V KYG 299D seen approaching Christchurch terminus where stands for all of the North East Doncaster Independents were to be found.
(Mike Fowler)

The final Roe bodied Fleetline delivered to Rossie Motors was actually a Leyland Fleetline, MHE 50P, which subsequently became No 1157 in the PTE fleet. Later it was sold to Leon Motor Services with whom it still operates. Over the years sales of buses between the various Doncaster operators has been by no means unusual. *(Mike Fowler)*

10 TRAIN SERVICES

There was no history of rail commuting in South Yorkshire, partly because of the nature of the conurbation and partly because of the comprehensiveness of the Sheffield transport system. Initially this was the tramways, but subsequently (from 1928) with buses in some of which the railways held an interest. (See Chapter 1.) Passenger usage of the local railway services in South Yorkshire was the lowest of any of the PTEs. This may have been one of the reasons why South Yorkshire was not included in the first tranche of PTEs. The role of the railway in South Yorkshire was, above all, that of moving freight. Their secondary role was to connect the South Yorkshire towns to other places in adjacent parts of the country.

The South Yorkshire rail network was developed by five pre-grouping railway companies. At nationalisation in 1948 there were duplicate facilities provided by both the LMS and LNER in and between Sheffield, Rotherham, Barnsley and Chesterfield. The 1955 Modernisation Plan led to a substantial rationalisation of facilities and investment in new ones, for example the Tinsley Marshalling Yard. Not surprisingly, therefore, the Beeching cuts fell heavily on the area removing, at a stroke, the duplication. One of the results of this was that there was no Diesel Multiple Unit (DMU) depot in South Yorkshire. DMUs for the local services were mainly provided from Neville Hill (Leeds) and Botanic Gardens (Hull).

Section 18 of the 1968 Act[5] required the Executive first to prepare a statement setting out, in general terms, the policies which it wished to follow, and after that was to come the much more detailed Development Plan[17]. At the outset, therefore, the PTE had to decide, inter alia, whether it was prepared even to consider accepting financial and planning responsibility for any local railway services within its area and up to 25 miles beyond. A map of the railway lines as at April 1974 showing the grant-aid services, the inter-city services and lines which at one time had a passenger service, is shown on page 117.

The position that the South Yorkshire PTE was in at the time of its inception in 1974 with regards to its railway considerations, may be summarised as follows:-

(a) The local railway services operating in South Yorkshire were not very well used.

(b) Looking at South Yorkshire in isolation, in traffic terms, they were even less attractive as most of even the local services were cross-boundary.

(c) As a legacy from the Beeching era there were lines that might have potential for revival.

(d) The costs involved in supporting any railway services were high.

(e) The PTA, as well as the PTE, was required to be a party to the decisions. Although any line closures would invoke the TUCC procedure, public reaction might be ameliorated by the fact that the PTA members were elected representatives of the local communities.

(f) If the PTE and the PTA both decided that there was no case to justify expenditure on any line, the Minister would have little compunction in authorising closure.

Looking at the diagram on page 117, the local services open for consideration were:-

Terminal Points	via	Last intermediate station in S. Yorks
Sheffield-Leeds	Barnsley	Darton
Sheffield-Hull]	Rotherham and	[Thorne North
Sheffield-Scunthorpe]	Doncaster	[Thorne South
Sheffield-Huddersfield	Penistone	Penistone
Sheffield-Gainsborough	Worksop	Kiveton Park
Sheffield-Manchester	Hope Valley	Dore
Sheffield-York	Pontefract	Bolton-on-Dearne
Doncaster-Leeds	Wakefield	None

There were trains between Sheffield and Chesterfield as part of the inter-city network but there was no local service.

In 1974 the Executive and British Rail had set up a Joint Committee and a Rail Services Sub-Committee. Discussions had taken place on the relationship between local road and rail services, and the review of local rail passenger services had begun. Geoffrey Myers, then Divisional Manager, had shown his usual enthusiasm, and wasted no time in arranging for the newly-appointed Directors to receive, at their first meeting, a presentation on 'The potential for railway development in the area'.

BR's proposals were contained in *Rail Passenger Concepts for South Yorkshire*[21]. The preface to the publication said: 'This document sets out to indicate the part rail transport could play in the future. It is not intended to be a definitive plan, but more an expression of the concepts of rail travel as they could be applied to South Yorkshire'. To describe the proposals as 'visionary' would be an understatement. The concepts were presented to S/R LUTS[7] and evaluated as part of that Study.

BR's concepts, to be achieved in two stages, categorised services as being:

CITY – a Sheffield radial network of seven routes
DISTRICT – a radial network serving principal towns in the area, eg Chesterfield, Worksop, Doncaster etc.

EXPRESS – a network of through services linking the four main towns of South Yorkshire and Chesterfield.

Interesting ideas included:

– serving Stocksbridge off the Penistone line
– a branch to Rawmarsh
– a branch to the former Chesterfield Market Place station
– a branch to serve Mosborough and Eckington going off the Worksop line at Woodhouse

Later stages showed the Rawmarsh branch extended through Wath to Thurnscoe and a branch to Lodge Moor! The City Centre loop would have featured in many services. There was also an idea to re-route the Barnsley line between Ecclesfield and the City Centre via Shiregreen and Firth Park. Quite some detail was gone into on the new alignments and service levels to be operated. The cost (at 1973 prices) of Stage I was put at £46m. The cost of Stage II was put at £59m.

So far as local railways were concerned SRLUTS[7] recommended:

– a half-hourly all-day service from Chesterfield to Barnsley via Sheffield together with a new station at Dronfield. The service to be augmented in peak periods.
– a half-hourly service from Sheffield to Doncaster via a re-opened Rotherham Central Station
– a half-hourly service from Sheffield to Retford via Kiveton Park.

Bus/train interchanges and re-orientated bus services were recommended for Swinton, Elsecar, Dronfield, Dore and Rotherham[22].

In spite of BR's very positive vision, the immediate reaction was that the future of the railways in South Yorkshire was not very bright. To support all the eight services mentioned above involved (at 1974 prices) a total of £1,911,000 annually, being the declared deficit. This was an intolerable burden, particularly as only 2% of the total passenger journeys within South Yorkshire were made by train. The Director General of the PTE at the time said that he saw no future for the railways in South Yorkshire and that it was all bus territory. In preparing the Policy Statement it was thought prudent to at least keep the door open and it said that an assessment would be made of the railways' potential. The Director General later opined that this only got through because he was on holiday. He would have preferred to close the matter there and then! It was calculated at the time that an addition of only 18 buses would cater for all the local traffic within South Yorkshire that was carried by train. That, of course, excluded the cross-boundary traffic but there was nothing to say that had to be taken into account. Whilst the PTE might have liked to consider the traffic between Sheffield and Leeds or Sheffield and Huddersfield, for example, the PTA could not afford to be strategically minded! There was also the

knock-on effect. Taking the Leeds service again as an example, if South Yorkshire PTE set itself against its support and the part within South Yorkshire was closed, then the top end in isolation would be useless for West Yorkshire PTE and vice versa, and neither side would likely take advantage of their 25 miles beyond the boundary powers. The national railway system was being split into small parcels which individually were not attractive. Its future was bleak.

British Rail had already sensed which way the wind would likely be blowing and began their salesmanship with their input to the Sheffield and Rotherham LUTS[7] described previously. Their proposals involved a short circular single line tunnel, one-way clockwise, under the centre of Sheffield from the main line station, with a new station near the centre in the vicinity of Castle Square. It would constitute a circular terminal working for the Leeds/Barnsley service. The proposal was ingenious and the topography of the land was suitable for such an alignment. The plan was given serious consideration by the consultants, in parallel with the alternative tramway proposals. The PTE supported the tramway but BR remained optimistic and were disappointed when it was the tramway that appeared in the final recommendation.

With the events which followed, and which have just been described, BR quickly summed up the situation. They saw a pincer movement designed, in their view, to eliminate their local services. Only the local PTEs and PTAs could save them and SYPTE did not appear enthusiastic. It was no longer railway stations – it was panic stations! There followed a period of hard-sell. To encourage a favourable reaction to the local railways, BR explained, implored, demonstrated, cajoled, entreated, and at times, almost bullied the PTE into what they saw as positive action.

When the Author arrived as the new Controller of Operations and Planning in September 1976, not only had the Executive not made any decision with regard to supporting the local railway services, it was not even in a position to do so. It was clearly urgent for a factual assessment to be made, and an analysis was put in hand, much of the work being done by the Author and with Bernard Pratt, the PTE's Rail Planner.

The annual cost of supporting local rail services in South Yorkshire is shown below[22]:-

	£
Sheffield-Barnsley-Wakefield (K)-Leeds	423,000
Sheffield-Rotherham-Doncaster	428,000
Sheffield-Worksop-Retford-Cleethorpes/Lincoln	246,000
Sheffield-New Mills-Manchester	60,000
Sheffield-Penistone-Huddersfield	610,000
Sheffield-York	90,000
Doncaster-Wakefield (W)-Leeds	54,000
	£1,911,00

The ensuing report, entitled *The Future of Railways in South Yorkshire*[22] published in January, 1977, recommended a range of options, including declining to sign a Section 20 agreement, through to the signing of a letter of intent. In the event the Executive agreed to support three services for a period of two years – at least a positive decision had been made and time had been bought at an annual cost of £1.1m. It was to take just over another two years before the Executive had enough confidence to take a longer term view. The results of this were published in April 1979 in a report *The long-term future of local rail services in South Yorkshire*[23]. As a result the Executive entered into a long-term agreement and gradually started to apply to the railways the policies it had been applying to the buses.

Integration between the modes was a requirement of the 1968 Act and a major duty of a PTE. The PTE had to be encouraged (or so BR thought) to think in terms of the systems concept. Throughout those years the PTE remained unimpressed with this desperate enthusiasm but had always recognised that the railway had some potential; that was why it had agreed to consider them in the first place. It was this recognition of their latent value that had caused the PTE to recommend, and the PTA finally to accept, that the railways had a part to play in the future transport needs of South Yorkshire and in the end a Section 20 agreement was signed in 1979. Following its assumption of planning and financial responsibilities the PTE considered each line in depth in conjunction with BR and substantial improvements were made subsequently.

As is so often the case with railway stations, some of those in South Yorkshire were not ideally situated. As far as the major centres are concerned, at one time Sheffield had two main line stations, Sheffield Midland and Sheffield Victoria, neither of which were perfectly situated for the commercial centre. Sheffield Victoria has long since disappeared having been closed along with the old Great Central line, although Sheffield – Penistone-Huddersfield trains continued to pass through it until re-routed. The Midland station lies on the south-east perimeter of Sheffield and although only about half a mile from the centre involves an uphill walk (which is why BR proposed their underground circular line). The Transport Interchange was eventually planned to embrace the station area (see Chapter 7) but that, of course, does nothing to shorten the distance. Barnsley station was quite well placed, Doncaster was reasonably close to the centre but Rotherham Masborough was remote, some 1¼ miles away from the town and virtually useless.

Three groups of inter-city services served South Yorkshire:

1. London (St. Pancras)-Sheffield, certain trains being extended to Leeds, but via a different route to the local services.
2. East Coast Main Line services from London (Kings Cross) to Leeds, Newcastle and Edinburgh. These called at Doncaster.
3. North-East/South-West services which called at Sheffield and, occasionally, Rotherham.

It follows that Inter City traffic locally, within South Yorkshire, was virtually nil which meant a minor simplification in what was a highly complex costing system, though not a circumstance that necessarily meant a cheaper price to the PTE. When the four original PTEs were formed a costing formula was devised known as the 'Cooper Brothers' formula (after the firm of accountants), the principle of which was to allocate costs (and receipts) 'where they lie'. In other words, where BR and the PTE supported trains, shared the same track, stations, staff, maintenance facilities, management and administration, etc., costs were allocated strictly according to the extent of use by each category of train. Like any system of financial apportionment it was felt, by some, to be inequitable. In line with European legislation and the Public Service Obligation (PSO) concept, the 'New Approach' had the blessing of both BR and the Minister.

Under the 'New Approach' trains were categorised into three groups being inter city, freight and local passenger. On lines where inter-city trains ran (or any other BR non-supported passenger train), then those trains would bear all the costs with the marginal costs being borne by the PTE trains and freight. In other words, the costs to the PTE was reduced to the amount that would actually be saved if the PTE services were withdrawn and the remainder continued to run. It was only if a line was used solely by PTE trains that the PTE had to bear the entire costs including the overheads. Clearly it was beneficial to the PTE to share the track with other BR services (even though it did occasionally prejudice timetable flexibility), but BR was always co-operative in this respect, so far as South Yorkshire were concerned. Unfortunately, some of the local passenger lines in South Yorkshire were not shared by other BR trains, but as far as possible ways and means were found as, for example, the special summer weekend excursion train to Blackpool which used the Barnsley line!

From 1977 the following rail services were supported by the PTE under a Section 20 Agreement:-

(a) Sheffield-Barnsley-Wakefield-Leeds (as far as Darton)
(b) Sheffield-Rotherham-Doncaster-Hull/Cleethorpes (as far as Thorne North/South)
(c) Sheffield-Worksop-Retford (as far as Kiveton Park)

Service levels were increased on all three of these lines and fares stabilised at the level reached in 1977. Although the fares were slightly higher than the bus fare level, season tickets and day return tickets enabled many passengers to have fare levels similar to those for buses. Elderly passengers were able to use their concessionary passes at off-peak periods as on bus services. Even though only minor improvements had been made to services and waiting facilities, ridership increased from 26m passenger miles in 1977 to over 38m in 1982. Although there were only 22 railway stations on the supported services, a detailed review of these, the facilities provided and the bus interchange and car parking arrangements, was undertaken and published in November 1981[24].

The interim agreement to support the local railway

The Sheffield - Barnsley line crossed the A6135 by girder bridge. The opportunity was taken to promote the PTE supported services. The new Chapeltown Station described on this page was immediately on the Barnsley side of the bridge *(Author)*

major improvements to be made in the infrastructure on this line, to commence in 1984/85, and subsequently a new station was constructed at Rotherham Central together with a short length of new connecting railway – the Holmes Chord.

The responsibility of the PTE was to examine both the traffic and potential traffic to see whether beneficial changes could be made, and to investigate costs and ways of reducing those costs. A resumé of what was accomplished, line by line, now follows.

Sheffield-Barnsley-Leeds Line

This line carried reasonable traffic, much of which was end to end within the northern half in West Yorkshire. It was no use, therefore, without West Yorkshire support, but in the end they also accepted. Nevertheless, Barnsley in South Yorkshire was an important intermediate point to and from both Sheffield and Leeds. Chapeltown, a dormitory area north of Sheffield, had a strong affinity with Sheffield but Chapeltown station was not well placed, lying inconveniently some distance north of the main catchment area, and with poor accessibility.

Sheffield-Rotherham-Doncaster Hull/Scunthorpe Line

This line linked the two main centres of South Yorkshire, being Sheffield and Doncaster, and connections with inter-city trains were available at both places. There was a traffic affinity between the two towns and Rotherham, Mexborough and Conisbrough were the main intermediate stops. Some trains proceeded across Doncaster to Goole/Hull or Scunthorpe/Cleethorpes; the last stations in South

services had been made permanent from 1st April 1979. Development work had started on up-grading the Rotherham – Doncaster rail corridor. Powers were being sought from Parliament, through a British Railways Bill, for the construction of the Holmes Chord, to link the former Midland and Great Central lines in Rotherham and to permit the re-opening of Rotherham Central Station. During 1982 extra trains were put on to make a regular half-hourly service for an experimental period between Sheffield and Doncaster, the intention being to improve the track and station facilities on this line if successful.

In August 1982 a new railway station was opened at Chapeltown, closer to the town centre than the old one had been. In May 1983 the Executive began to support an additional line, the Sheffield – Barnsley-Penistone-Huddersfield line (as far as Penistone) following its diversion via Barnsley. A new station was provided at Silkstone Common. The experimental increase in train services on the Don Valley line, which produced an overall increase of 45% in passengers between Sheffield and Doncaster, was made permanent. Approval was given for

A view of Barnsley Station after PTE funded refurbishment. *(SYPTE)*

Yorkshire being Thorne North and Thorne South respectively. By their own volition, but with the agreement of the PTE, BR later converted the service from DMU operation to locomotive haulage because of reliability problems with Trans-Pennine and Inter-City DMUs and linked it with the Sheffield to Manchester service via the Hope Valley.

The drawbacks to this service were the location of Rotherham station and the non-existence of a station at Swinton. Rotherham (Masbrough) station was located about 1¼ miles west of the town centre and could not be serviced conveniently by buses. Rotherham (Central) station, along with Swinton (Central), had been closed when the former GC Sheffield (Victoria)-Doncaster service was withdrawn as part of the Beeching cuts. Accordingly, the PTE proposed and master-minded the implementation of an ambitious scheme to divert trains away from the old Midland line between Swinton and Mexborough, and on to the parallel Great Central line from which passenger services had been withdrawn. The track was still used for freight. The prize was that it passed through the centre of Rotherham, and the platforms of the disused station were still in situ. Trains were diverted and for the first time in many years Rotherham became properly accessible by rail.

The re-routing of the Doncaster services started at Holmes Junction, south of Masbrough station, where a single line chord was built to connect the ex-Midland line with the ex-GC line, a short distance south of the site of Rotherham Central. Parliamentary Powers were obtained

under a private British Railways Bill which was financed by SYPTE. The works involved moving a substantial amount of steel slag, demolishing and re-building a lock-keeper's house and constructing a level crossing. It was this latter feature that gave rise to quite a lot of Parliamentary opposition since it was held that the frequent closure of the level crossing would impede the dumper trucks shuttling between the various scrap yards and slag tips. As anticipated by the promoters, no such problems occurred in practice.

At one time Rotherham had three stations: Masbrough, Central and Westgate. Although the station buildings at Central had been demolished the platforms remained. However, it was a cramped site, close to the canal and hemmed in by road overbridges. It was close to the site of the new Police Station and Law Courts and to a large new supermarket. It was also within easy walking distance of the town centre and bus station. A number of bus services passed the station and stops were conveniently located. Car parking provision was not as generous as had been hoped originally. The requirements for disabled access posed a challenge because of the differences in levels and cramped site adjacent to the road. A solution was found for the Down platforms by adopting a circular ramp.

Prior to the decision to promote the Rotherham Central idea there had been considerable opposition from certain County Council members because they felt that it would lead to the closure of Masbrough and the loss of Inter-City Services. It was only logical that this should be the case and it could be shown that there would be net benefits to Rotherham if Central replaced Masbrough, even though it would not be served by Inter-City trains. Eventually Central was built and opened and, some time later, Masbrough closed.

The Doncaster trains then used the ex-GC line as far as Aldwarke Junction where they crossed over to the Midland line to gain access to the new station built at Swinton. (Previously Doncaster trains had crossed at Aldwarke from the Midland to the GC so as to gain access to Mexborough and Doncaster.) Aldwarke was a major double 'X' junction between the ex-Midland and ex-GC lines introduced at the time of the construction of the Parkgate Steelworks. Today it is much simplified and the signal box has been closed.

When Swinton station was conceived and in the early days of planning the ex- Midland main line was still in existence carrying NE-SW services that had come either via Burton Salmon and Altofts Junction or via the Swinton & Knottingley (S & K) line. There were also certain expresses that had come from Leeds via Wakefield Westgate and the Moorthorpe curve. There was also quite a lot of freight traffic. The four-track main line passed through the site in a fast, sweeping curve from which it was not possible to build a double junction onto the double track spur leading to Mexborough station. Consequently a long 'ladder' of single leads had to be built. In turn this lead to the construction of a three-platform station.

There was controversy as to the number of tracks there should be on the spur and to the gradient. Inter-City were toying with the idea of diverting some NE-SW trains to serve Doncaster and since the singling of the St. Philips Curve on the south approach to Doncaster a single line spur would have introduced further operating constraints. So far as local services were concerned there was also the constriction of the single line Holmes Chord to which reference has already been made. Accordingly a double track spur was re-instated between Swinton and Mexborough. The freight issue concerned some of the limestone, aggregate and oil trains and the routing thereof. For a time Up (westbound) freights continued to be routed via the ex-GC route from Mexborough to Aldwarke Junction because of the easier gradient.

It had been hoped to built a small bus/train interchange at Swinton but the road layout was not conducive to such. Mexborough was also a traffic objective of the buses although no suitable interchange could be built there because of the location of the ring road. Park-and-ride facilities were provided at Swinton and are quite well used. Swinton station is served by locally supported services to Leeds via Wakefield Westgate and to York via the S & K as well as the Doncaster line services

The re-routed Doncaster trains then continued to Mexborough and Conisborough en route to Doncaster. Initially no improvements were made to these two stations, except for improved shelters for rail and bus passengers and improved passenger information and signing. Subsequently – and with European funding assistance – Mexborough station was given a major re-vamping.

A former BR Divisional Manager commented that it was a tribute to all those involved in the early planning stages of these schemes that the original objectives of policy had been substantially achieved, notably the maximum exploitation of the existing rail network. It was also a tribute to the PTE who were successful in promoting a positive rail strategy in a difficult climate.

Sheffield-Penistone-Huddersfield Line

The line from Sheffield to Penistone was a part of the old Great Central main line to Manchester via Woodhead. Originally it had run from Sheffield Victoria and was electrified in 1951. When this route was closed everything was concentrated on Sheffield Midland, which meant that Penistone-Huddersfield trains had to reverse at Nunnery Sidings. This was a cumbersome and time-consuming process. All intermediate stations between Sheffield and Penistone had been closed, except that Wadsley Bridge was specially opened on the occasions of football matches at the Sheffield Wednesday ground. The main traffic affinity on this service was between Sheffield and Huddersfield in West Yorkshire and, like the Leeds service, would have been useless without the parallel support of West Yorkshire PTE.

The BR view at this time was that they had been seeking to persuade both West and South Yorkshire PTAs that the Huddersfield-Penistone-Sheffield service was grossly uneconomic, was incapable of value for money development and should be put up for closure. The West Yorkshire PTA supported the line on their side of the county boundary north of Penistone, but were doing so as a temporary expedient only on the basis that South Yorkshire would support their section under the Section 20 Grant arrangements. (This in itself was politically symbolic since West Yorkshire was at that time a Conservative controlled Authority. Embarrassment of their local Socialist rivals in South Yorkshire was not an unhelpful side effect.)

However, South Yorkshire PTA were at this stage not convinced that the proposal offered good value for money. There was a strong impression amongst BR managers at the time that they had other priorities for scarce financial resources, and that these did not include Railways. Bus developments to a population which had a low car ownership, and where the vast majority of journeys were made in local communities, was more important. Furthermore the financial pressures on the County Council, discussed earlier in the book, led to the PTE's caution.

BR and PTE officers had discussed a proposal to divert the Huddersfield-Sheffield service away from the direct route south of Penistone, to a more populous, if longer, route via Barnsley, which was then the County Town, with the further potential for developing new stations at intermediate points. BR had every reason to believe that the PTE officials agreed with this strategy, which would have had an additional benefit of helping to provide a more frequent half-hourly service between Barnsley and Sheffield, which was known to be a politically popular objective. Political support could not initially be mustered for this proposal, which effectively meant the withdrawal of service on the direct route between Penistone and Sheffield which was contentious for another reason. This particular section of the line was part of a Trans-Pennine

The new Rotherham Central Station was sited on the old Great Central line close to the Town Centre. Whist access to the site was somewhat cramped, requirements for access for the disabled were met by the provision of a circular ramp. *(Author)*

freight route between Sheffield and Greater Manchester, known as the MSW – the Manchester, Sheffield and Wath Railway. It was a heavily used freight railway linking the Yorkshire coalfields with power stations to the west of the Pennines which the BRB was proposing to close.

The closure case for the MSW was a freight one (through passenger services having been withdrawn previously) on the basis that there were adequate alternative routes across the Pennines, to the south between Sheffield and Manchester via the Hope Valley, and to the north between Leeds, Huddersfield and Manchester. Freight traffic was, in any event, falling off. Nonetheless this was a highly charged and very sensitive issue throughout South Yorkshire, particularly amongst the politicians who were, of course, anxious to fight for what they saw as a strategic link between South Yorkshire and Manchester. SYCC's view was also significantly influenced by the large mining and railway worker's community which existed, and which dominated South Yorkshire politics at that time. So the proposed closure of the Penistone route had to be seen in this context and when the closure hearing took place in Huddersfield Town Hall and in the Royal Victoria Hotel, Sheffield, they were attended by the largest number of individual objectors in the history of Railway closure cases up to that time.

The public hearings ran over several days and part of the BR defence of the case was to point towards the more attractive proposition of diverting the passenger services via Barnsley. The TUCC opposed the closure, but commended the alternative route via Barnsley to the Secretary of State for Transport, if he felt minded to agree the closure of the direct service between Penistone and Sheffield.

In its heyday Penistone was a two-way junction. To the west to Manchester and Huddersfield; to the south was the junction of the Sheffield and Barnsley lines. The Barnsley passenger service had been withdrawn a long time ago. Here then, was the making of another ambitious scheme proposed by BR and developed by the PTE. The line between Penistone and Barnsley was re-opened to passenger trains together with intermediate stations at Silkstone Common and Dodworth, where a new housing development had materialised. The service was provided by diverting the Huddersfield service to run via Barnsley at the expense of some twelve additional minutes running time. The advantages were considerable, being:-

(a)   New links were provided to Barnsley
(b)   Silkstone Common and Dodworth were given a
       train service

The opening of the new Silkstone Common Station occurred on 28th November 1984. The opportunity was taken to utilise the only DMU which had been painted in BR's version of SYPTE bus livery to celebrate ten years of the PTE, and seen here in company with the Author. *(Author)*

(c) It gave an increased and hence more attractive service between Barnsley and Sheffield

(d) A new station at Chapeltown

(e) The cumbersome reversing movement outside Sheffield was eliminated.

(f) No existing facilities were lost as there were no stops on the section from which the service was withdrawn.

Apart from timetable improvements, and the more recent development at Mea dowhall, two important projects were introduced by the PTE on the Barnsley line. The first was an increase in service over the Sheffield to Barnsley section, achieved by the diversion of the Penistone service described above. The other was the opening of a new station at Chapeltown with free park-and-ride facilities. The new station was south of the old one which was closed, and was situated right in the centre of the town and was conveniently accessible. Some wag wrote in the local press 'the station now approaching the Barnsley train is Chapeltown'. But never mind the jokes, it was a positive step, a convenient station with a good catchment area,

which included new housing development at Burn Cross and High Green, with suitably adjusted feeder bus services. It was comparatively cheap to implement, and coupled with the more frequent service and the cheap fares which applied to the trains, as well as to the buses, additional traffic was won to the railway.

Sheffield-Kiveton Park-Lincolnshire Line

The relatively short section of this line as far as Kiveton Park, that lies within South Yorkshire, carried little local traffic and there was not much scope for development. In the early 1980s the first areas through ticketing system was introduced, enabling people to travel on both buses and trains when a pilot scheme was introduced between Sheffield and coal mining communities around Kiveton Park, and Kiverton Bridge. An experimental bus interchange with a service from Rotherham was tried, together with through fares. But the infrequent rail service and unreliability of bus time-keeping meant that usage was low and the experiment was discontinued.

Sheffield-Dore-Manchester Line/ Chesterfield Line

The South Yorkshire boundary station at Dore lies only some 4 miles south of Sheffield, the station is not ideally placed in relation to the newer residential development, and there are parallel frequent bus services. The occasional train, therefore, had no particular public appeal. Dore is a junction station for the Manchester (via the Hope Valley) and the Chesterfield lines, but the local service to Chesterfield was a casualty of the Beeching cuts. As has been said, the line to Chesterfield was served only by InterCity trains, which ran non-stop from Sheffield. The main line platforms had been out of use since the Beeching cuts and, with PTE approval, were subsequently removed to improve the alignment of the main line. Both the Hope Valley and Dronfield-Chesterfield areas were served by the Executive's buses as part of its Derbyshire network.

There was local pressure for a resumption of the local Chesterfield service and a re-opening of Dronfield station, which was legally possible within the PTE's 25 mile powers. This, however, was resolutely resisted by the PTA as it was outside South Yorkshire, and the County finally

A new station at Goldthorpe was opened on the Swinton & Knottingley line, the train service being supported by both West and South Yorkshire PTEs. *(Author)*

and Conisborough. In the pre-Beeching days there had been a passenger service throughout its length provided on former GC- metals. The route from Barnsley joined the route from Sheffield at Mexborough. On numerous occasions the PTE had looked into re-introducing a passenger service over this route, since the track was still in place and already signalled to passenger standards. However, having regard to all the other pressures and priorities (to which reference has been made in previous chapters) on both the County Council and PTE, neither a financial nor cost-benefit case could be made for a train service – although the line was 'safeguarded' for a long time. (The short-term answer was the introduction by YTC of the X19 service between Barnsley and Doncaster – see Chapter 6.)

refused to support any part of a Chesterfield service. (The special cheap fares did not apply on the PTE buses in Derbyshire, where commercial fares applied and the services were either profitable or supported by Derbyshire County Council.) There was pressure to re-open Dronfield station and eventually Derbyshire County Council produced a package, including a parking provision and a simple bus interchange. It was opened in 1980 by Sir Peter Parker, the then Chairman of British Railways. The feeder buses were provided from SYPTE's Halfway Garage with subsidy arrangements from DCC. These developments tied in with the bus Service Development programme (see Chapter 6).

The Manchester via Hope Valley line, although forming an important trans-Pennine link with Sheffield, lying as it does in Derbyshire, held little interest for the PTA. It could have been a candidate under the 25 mile ruling to link up with Greater Manchester in the west, but neither the PTA nor the Executive felt able to help the like-minded and neighbouring Derbyshire County Council. There was, therefore, little scope for the PTE here but, as has been said in connection with the Doncaster line, BR did undertake its own development with the introduction of more comfortable locomotive-hauled trains and by a series of linkings, instituting a through service between Manchester, Sheffield, Rotherham, Doncaster and on to Humberside.

Dearne Valley Links

The Dearne Valley lay at the heart of the South Yorkshire Coalfield. It ran east-west with Doncaster at the lower (east) end and Barnsley at the west end. Major towns in it were Goldthorpe, Thurnscoe, Swinton, Wath, Mexborough

As referred to previously Swinton had been served by trains on the former Midland line and services were re-introduced with the re-routed Doncaster service. Thurnscoe and Goldthorpe had not had train services since the early 1930's when the trains on the ex-Lancashire & Yorkshire Dearne Valley line had been withdrawn. The Dearne Valley was subject to increasingly high unemployment as the mines and related industries closed. Although quite close to Rotherham, links north and south were poor, particularly by rail, although the S & K line ran right through Thurnscoe, Goldthorpe and Swinton. (The line had been built as an avoiding line for Doncaster for passenger and freight, and thus had few intermediate stations on it. There was in 1974 an infrequent DMU service between York and Sheffield calling at Moorthorpe, Bolton-on-Dearne, Rotherham and stations to Sheffield. It was a poor performing service.

Furthermore, the Dearneways (subsequently X91) route (see Chapter 9) offered a limited stop facility from Thurnscoe to Rotherham and Sheffield. However, with the Doncaster service re-routings and the building of Swinton station, the possibility of building new stations at Goldthorpe and Thurnscoe started to look a possibility. The York service was infrequent and it was difficult to justify much increase in it. However, the possibility of introducing a completely new service in conjunction with West Yorkshire PTE started to be worth investigating. WYPTE were already considering opening stations at

Outwood, Sandal & Agbrigg and Fitzwilliam. After much cross-boundary effort a case was eventually made not only for an hourly Sheffield-Swinton-Moorthorpe-Wakefield (Westgate)-Leeds service but for the building of new stations at Goldthorpe and Thurnscoe. The service was an immediately success and the development of Meadowhall led to even greater success.

The subsequent rationalisation and contraction of the coal mining in that area proved the value of the BR/South Yorkshire PTE agreement, because it has enabled communities, where job losses have been very large, to be connected by fast and relatively frequent train services to alternative main centres of employment, such as Sheffield, Rotherham and Doncaster.

In fact, most of the rail developments were aimed at trying to exploit the value of a rail network to a community on the basis of opening up travel opportunities that were otherwise impossible for people in a low car ownership area. New stations were opened in mining communities such as Thurnscoe and Goldthorpe, which, as in the case of Dodworth and Silkstone Common, enabled marginal cost exploitation of existing but poorly utilised rail services operating these corridors.

It was felt in BR circles at that time that the predominance of transport policy in South Yorkshire was aimed at buses, which was not entirely surprising given the population concentrations and dispersal, and the topography of the area where the railways were naturally confined to the valley bottoms, whilst most of the population resided on the hillsides. There is no doubt that the development of the railway network that has taken place over the last decade has maximised the use of rail but has done so in a way which has been totally compatible with the development of local bus operations.

Clearly the PTE has done much to resuscitate and pump new life into the rail network in South Yorkshire and to take it out of its state of inertia, and possible ultimate closure, to which it was heading in 1974.

Rolling stock

In the late 1970s one of the key issues in South Yorkshire was the reliability and punctuality of the local train service which was beset with difficulties, arising principally from the inadequate rolling stock (ageing DMUs and Pacer units), the latter being the first, and probably last, two-axle vehicles introduced on main line, as opposed to branch line operation. The reliability of these units was badly affected by gearbox and other problems, which many attributed to the two-axle design and the vibration effects. BR came in for heavy criticism on account of these vehicles, as cancellation levels increased and reliability problems 'in service' led to unpunctuality. As ever, however, there is always more than one side to a particular story and it is instructive to recall how it was that this type of unit came to be developed in the first place.

The original DMU fleet, based at Neville Hill in Leeds, covered the whole of the area bounded by South Yorkshire, as well as West Yorkshire PTEs, and by the early 1980s was in need of replacement. Some would argue it was overdue for replacement in terms of customer appeal having been introduced in the period 1955-1964. BR came forward with proposals to develop a second generation of diesel multiple units, based on an advanced technical specification, which involved an above-floor mounted diesel engine and electric transmission – the Class 210 DMU. This was over-specified and too expensive. Initially the PTEs in both West and South Yorkshire favoured the development of a much simpler and cheaper vehicle because obviously they would pick up the cost through Section 20. Also it was the feeling of many in BR at that time that PTEs (not surprisingly and probably justifiably) were in the mood to challenge traditional BR engineering and operating practices.

In some way BR over-reacted to this by a series of railbus developments which culminated in the 20 Class 140 railbuses delivered to West Yorkshire PTE. South Yorkshire PTE declined to have anything to do with such vehicles on the grounds that coaches on motorways and dual-carriageway roads offered a better alternative in passenger comfort at far less cost. Whilst subsequent developments of the 'Pacer' units (as they became known) – Classes 142 and 143 – were improved – their ride was inevitably poor compared to that of a bogie vehicle.

The PTEs had been pressing BR to produce a modern version of the classic underfloor-engined DMU. Their pleas were heard by Metro-Cammell (with whom the PTEs had always had a close and sympathetic relationship). The private initiative of Metro-Cammell led to the building of a modern, second-generation DMU. Although only five cars (a two-car and a three-car) of Class 151 were built, this galvanised BR into producing the Class 150 Sprinter units. Subsequently Metro-Cammell built the Super-Sprinter Class 156 units. Later, in 1990, the Class 158s were introduced.

There were other issues around railways which did not immediately impact on the PTE, but which non-the-less brought BR into contact with local politicians with responsibility for transport. Reference has already been made to the significant issues surrounding freight and the contraction of the old industrial base of South Yorkshire, but there was, in the late 1970s/early 1980s, also the issue of the InterCity service from Sheffield to London. High Speed Trains, the 125s, had recently been introduced onto the ECML via Doncaster, and unfavourable comparisons were rightly drawn between the quality of the train service between Sheffield and London and Leeds, Doncaster and London.

These were very sensitive issues at a time when South Yorkshire and Sheffield in particular, was having to fight very hard for its corner in the face of the contraction of its traditional industry base. Trying to promote itself as a commercial, as well as an industrial centre, it was important that Sheffield's transport links were of the best. There is no doubt that the Eastern Region of British Rail, of which the Sheffield Division was then a part, was totally focused on the maximum development of HSTs on the ECML, and little interested in what it viewed as sub-optimal deployment of sets on the Midland Main Line from Sheffield to St.

Pancras. This was a running sore in Sheffield at the time, not least when offers to pay a contract price for running the Master Cutler as an HST (made by Sheffield City Council, South Yorkshire County Council and the Chamber of Commerce) were rejected.

The BR case at the time was that the solution for Sheffield was electrification and the introduction of the APT. It is a tribute to the development of a more business-led a approach within BR, and in particular the creation of the InterCity business sector in 1982, that virtually the first act of the InterCity Director, Cyril Bleasdale, was to re-deploy HSTs to the Midland Main Line. Journey times previously said to be impossible are now being easily achieved.

A senior BR manager has very fond memories of the people who were deeply involved in the this period of rail development in South Yorkshire, not least the politicians such as Councillors Thwaites and Waugh, who had a grand vision for transport in their county, and alongside similar visionaries within the PTE, were prepared to bulldoze their way towards realising their objectives. They did it in true South Yorkshire style and never seemed to forget the communities whence they came, and which had elected them. He recalls in particular, a fairly fraught meeting of the PTA taking place at the County Hall in Barnsley when at lunchtime the Committee Chairman said "It is time fr'uz dinners" and then sent out for fish and chips, which were brought back by the County Hall staff in large cardboard boxes, unwrapped, and the meeting continued.

Following the loss of bus operating powers both the PTA and PTE took a greater interest in railway services – another irony of de-regulation and privatisation. The long-heralded service linking Sheffield with Leeds, via the Dearne Valley towns and Wakefield, was introduced in 1988, together with new stations at Thurnscoe and Goldthorpe, to complement Rotherham Central opened earlier in 1987. An hourly all-day service was introduced. The PTE opened a massive bus/train/car interchange at Meadowhall in 1990 to complement the adjacent large out-of-town shopping development. A four-platform station was required because of its location at the junction of the Barnsley and Rotherham lines. Supertram also serves this interchange. All these developments had been planned in the days of SYCC and the original SYPTE.

The diagram shown below appeared on the PTE's bus maps issued to the public and is an indication of its commitment to promote integrated public transport. (SYPTE)

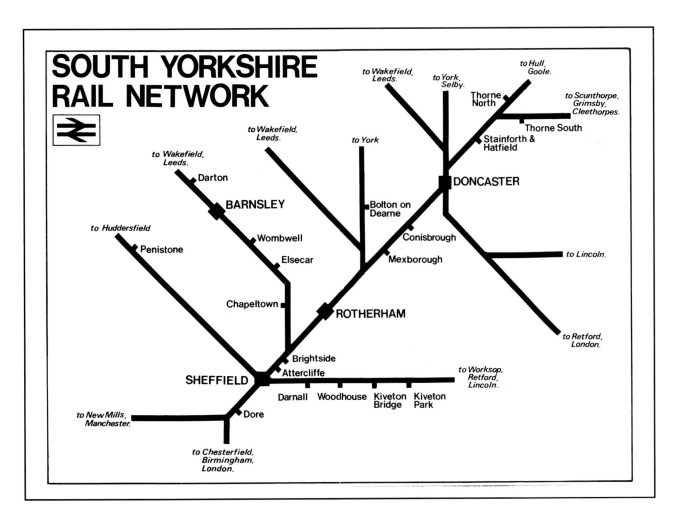

11 THE END OF AN ERA

The change of government at Westminster in March 1979, when Jim Callaghan lost power to Margaret Thatcher following 'The Winter of Discontent', set the scene for major changes. The 'Iron Lady' came to power on a ticket that included de-nationalisation, de-regulation, free rein competition – the market philosophy. She was completely unsympathetic to the public sector either at national or local level. She even once reportedly queried "What was 'society'?". This was the antithesis of 'Each shall strive for the benefit of all'. It became clear over time that neither the Prime Minister nor her government had any understanding of the urban transport problem and certainly no sympathy with public transport.

The first signs of change in the public transport field came in 1980, with a new Transport Act. The licensing of express coaches was eased by the simple expedient of changing the onus for objection. Since the 1930 Transport Act any operator seeking to operate a new express service had to show 'need' for such a service. Invariably the Railways objected, although not automatically so since the 1960s changes (Beeching, et al), and existing operators also objected. Objections were on the grounds that the 'need' identified was already catered for. From 1980 onus was put on the objector to show why a service should not be run. Effectively coach companies were free to provide whatever services they felt were capable of being profitable. The overall benefits of this liberalisation were claimed by the government to be an increase of 60% in services over 3 years[10]. The figure was disputed[27]; coach mileage increase was relatively insignificant; fares had come down and service frequencies had increased on popular routes at the cost of service reductions to smaller towns and communities. A number of major new players came onto the scene, including British Coachways, a federation of operators including Wallace Arnold and Grey Green Coaches; another operator was Trathens of Plymouth. However, these new or expanded operators did not last long before either giving up, or coming into some arrangement with National Express – the NBC Coaching Subsidiary – which had been very effective in expanding its services and benefitting from the newer arrangements. In itself this gave a warning to government to what a large, existing operator could do.

In addition to relaxing coach licensing, the 1980 Act set up the idea of 'Trial Areas'. These were to be locations where the local authority was desirous of having de-regulated bus operation to build on the experience of licensing relaxation in the express coaching field. Little interest was shown by local authorities and virtually none by operators either. However, following some arm-twisting three areas were designated Trial Areas. One was the City of Hereford which soon became notorious for its 'bus wars'. The other two, in Norfolk and Devon, were inconsequential in their effects[27].

The cut-backs in government expenditure, and the knock-on effect on local government, coupled with the continuing high inflation, led to increasing problems in funding public transport in general, but to particular problems in the Metropolitan areas. Operating costs were rising and passenger levels declining further, as unemployment increased, cutting the journey to work levels, and reducing the money people had to spend, thus hitting optional off-peak travel. These problems were felt particularly harshly in South Yorkshire with its predominance of old heavy industries all in public ownership, but also being severely cut-back. Repeatedly each year the SYCC re-assessed its policy and renewed its commitment to cheap fares and service development. Greater London Council (GLC) and the other Metropolitan Councils also continued this line, but to a lesser extent, except for the GLC which faced a different battle.

In the local elections of May 1981, the Labour Party won the GLC from the Conservatives: Ken Livingston became Leader of the Council and Dave Wetzel became Chairman of the Transport Committee. In their election manifesto Labour had promised to cut fares by 25% and thus began, in June 1981, the 'Fares Fair' campaign. When the main changes were introduced in October 1981 the fares were reduced by 32% and a major fares simplification was introduced by extending zonal fares on the whole LT Bus & Underground network. The campaign, arguments and counter-arguments went on for nearly two years, including battles raging in the Courts because of an action initiated by the London Borough of Bromley. By the time of the next general election in June 1983, the government had decided to take over LT from the GLC (a Tory government Nationalisation!) and also to initiate steps for getting rid of the GLC and Metropolitan Councils. The 1983 Transport Act provided the powers to take over LT from the GLC, as well as powers to lay down guidelines for public transport subsidies to GLC and the Metropolitan Counties[25] through the introduction of a three-year planning process.

'Save your Cheap Fares' Campaign

The passage of the 1983 Transport Act, with its implications for the fares policy, created a flurry in the dovecotes in South Yorkshire and provided a foretaste of what was to come. SYCC decided to mount a campaign 'Save your cheap fares', and the redoubtable Councillor Doris Askham became its co-ordinator supported, amongst others, by Councillor Alice Sargent[2]. The campaigners achieved over a million signatures. Coincidentally, the first of the 'Nipper' bus services was introduced at this time, as described in Chapter 6. On a more serious note, when the County Council came to consider the new legislation it calculated that it would mean a 50% increase on fares in June 1983, with a similar increase in October, 1983 together with a 12½% cut in bus services. Following legal advice the County Council felt they were acting within their powers to ignore the guidance on subsidies. Two other things happened at the same time: May 1983 saw a series of lightning strikes taking place on SYPTE's buses and a delegation from the EEC (now EU) arrived to study the County's policy and transportation system. It beggars belief that, in the midst of all their other woes from a very hostile government, that the PTA and PTE had to contend with these lightning strikes by the very people on whose support everyone – Politician and Management – could have expected.

Also during this period the government produced a White Paper – *Rates – proposals for Rates Limitation, etc*. This envisaged the concept of 'rate-capping' which was to be included in the future Rates Bill.

'Streamlining the Cities'

In October 1984 the government published a White Paper entitled *Streamlining the Cities*[25]. This proposed the abolition of the GLC and the six Metropolitan County Councils. This is not the place to debate the pros and cons of Metropolitan government, whether in the provinces or in the capital. But two comments are perhaps relevant to the South Yorkshire story. Firstly, SYCC had never cut fares – it had pegged them and, at the time, held them steady since 1975 – eight years. Had GLC adopted such a subtle approach it is arguable that they would not have been challenged, since there does appear to have been a consensus that the ratio of fares income to subsidy had got out of proportion in London[26]. Secondly, the GLC policy had enabled LT to introduce a zonal fares system across the whole bus and underground network. This was a master stroke by LT and a courageous one; one which SYPTE was never able to achieve, indeed no PTE had, at a stroke, wrought such a change. Experience from the Continent had shown the vital importance of having an integrated fares system which was easily understandable – LT were the only ones to achieve it and the benefits are still being felt to this day.

The Government put forward proposals for further legislation, with the declared aim of ensuring greater stability and certainty for public transport in London and the conurbations. Their stated intention was to clarify the legal position of subsidies, to introduce mechanisms that would limit the level of subsidy, and ensure that it was clear what the subsidies were buying. At a meeting with officers of the Department of Transport the Passenger Transport Executives had been asked for a considered and agreed reply to questions about the forthcoming legislation. A working part had been formed to draft a reply.

The AMA had been invited to consult the Department of Transport on the proposals and had decided not to do so. The PTEs agreed to a request from the AMA not to reply to the Department of Transport without further

As part of the campaign orchestrated by the PTA against the 1985 Transport Bill, members of the public were encouraged to sign a petition against it. Besides the traditional forms for signature, prominent citizens were also invited to actually sign the PTE's mobile information bus, which had been suitably repainted with slogans for the occasion.
(Mike Greenwood)

advice from them. In considering the draft reply the PTEs thought that some of the comments needed to be made without delay to correct some of the Government's views before they were included in legislation. Many points in the draft were not agreed and no decision had been made to send a corrected and approved version to anyone when copies were 'leaked' to the Government and the AMA.

In an already highly charged political scene this did not help anyone except, perhaps, the Department of Transport. Some of the ideas in the PTE draft were sensible. It would have been an advantage to clear up the legal uncertainties, to have policies that were not subject to the possibility of major variation year by year, but covered three years, as recommended by the Monopolies and Mergers Commission, and to have better methods of assessing the value of subsidies. In fact some of the comments on measuring the benefits of policies, or of actual services, were based on work done in South Yorkshire and referred to in reports to the Council by the JPTU. They might have been part of the Council's submission if it had made one. But there were other parts of the draft still far from being agreed, and some of these concerned PTA/PTE relationships: comments that should only have been made if unanimous and if the promise to the AMA had been honoured.

However, before an agreed draft had been completed, the White Paper and the Transport Bill had been published, but as the Bill was unlikely to receive the Royal Assent in time, it would not affect the Budget for 1983/84.

Rates Act 1984

The Rates Act 1984 introduced the concept of 'rate-capping' on to local authorities. Individual local authorities, in this case SYCC and the four Metropolitan Districts, would determine the rate they considered necessary to fund the services they were to provide. The District Rate would include the precept from SYPTE. Under 'rate-capping' the government determined an Expenditure Limit (EL) for each council which was not to be exceeded. Over the winter of 1985/86 the EL for the transitional period was to provide major problems.

Buses White Paper

The *Buses* White Paper[10] was published in July 1984. Its main proposals were:

- the abolition of Road Service Licensing
- no subsidies to be paid for local services, except through a tendering system
- PTEs to lose their operating powers and powers over NBC
- the PTE operations, and those of the municipalities, were to be transferred to Limited Liability Companies under the Companies Acts, prior to sale to the private sector
- NBC & SBG were to be broken up and sold to the private sector
- taxi and hire cars to be allowed to carry passengers at separate fares

The Government invited views on its White Paper and allowed only four months up to the end of October for them. It received over 8,000 submissions. The House of Commons Transport Committee quickly established an Inquiry into the proposals of the *Buses* White Paper. It sat weekly and took tomes of evidence. It even held one session in Hereford where it took evidence, and saw for itself what was happening. Its thorough report came out early in 1985, well after the consultation period and indeed after the publication of the Transport Bill 1985.

The Transport Bill, when published, was a misnomer since it was the *Buses* White Paper written in Bill format. It contained virtually no changes, dealing only with buses, and not the wider transport issues. As had been suspected by those in the industry the consultation had been a complete sham. However, that had not stopped either the Passenger Transport Executive Group (PTEG) or the NBC and SBG from producing a considerable amount of evidence in support of their views. The Bus & Coach Council (BCC), naturally, established a Working Party on the matter and, as with all such things took too long to come up with an answer which was 'all things to all men'. Perhaps the government knew this would happen and thus chose to ignore vested, but knowledgeable, interests.

The timescale proposed by the Government for all these changes was ridiculously tight. The Bill was published in January 1985, it was expected to receive the Royal Assent in July 1985, transitional arrangements would follow from July to March 1986, and full deregulation would be in operation by April 1986. It would have been a tight timescale for any one of the major elements, for example deregulation itself, but to require all measures to be introduced simultaneously was over-facing. The breaking up of the PTEs, the separation of the municipalities, let alone the breaking and sale of NBC and SBG, were major items in themselves. Furthermore, in the case of the PTEs, another White Paper *Streamlining the Cities* (CMND 9063) [25] proposed the abolition or the Metropolitan Counties to a similar timescale.

Because they were so greatly motivated by political reasons it was unlikely that the Government would be deflected from introducing its plans for the bus industry, but the most strenuous efforts would have to be deployed to seek amendments, to make the new legislation as workable and as acceptable as possible. By the end of 1983 it was apparent that with all the proposals for change in the industry, and in local government structures and financing, the Executive organisation would need to be adjusted to enable it to meet the new challenges.

I was redesignated the Controller of Executive Planning and Development with the Planning section, taking over a much wider remit. The main new areas of responsibilities covered corporate planning, embracing defence of the PTEs and PTAs, and the strategic and co-ordination aspects of the 1968 Act which had been so successfully implemented in South Yorkshire. The Operations function came under the control of the Traffic Manager, Bob Rowe, who subsequently became Controller of Operations.

Against a changing background new arrangements for strategic planning of road and rail services, and liaison with highway and general planning, would need to be developed, three-years plans prepared and presented, and on-going studies such as the South Yorkshire Transport Study and Operating Systems Development continued. One era was ending but local public transport would be an important part of the future. Although many successes could be claimed there was lots of scope for improvements, but the Government proposals at that stage did not seem to be the best way to make them. It is much easier to lose passengers than to gain them, in spite of what some of the service elasticity theorists seemed to think.

SYPTE realised that, if implemented, the changes would have a more dramatic effect on their operations than on any other operator because of the policies that the County Council had pursued. From a professional point-of-view, if there were to be changes then it was best for these to be spread over the longest timescale so as to soften the blow to both passengers and staff.

In spite of professional opposition to the proposals both by SYPTE, PTEG and indeed virtually the whole bus and coach industry, it had to be recognised that the Government was barely eighteen months into its life and had an enormous majority. The odds of defeating it were extremely long. However, with the passage of time the County Council – now also fighting for its very own survival – was becoming more and more entrenched in its view on public transport. The Association of Metropolitan Authorities

(AMA) had decided to fight both the Transport and the Abolition legislation. Accordingly it would not countenance in public the professional view that what time was available must be used to ameliorate the damage likely to be done by these two measures.

SYPTE decided that whilst it would 'fight' the Transport Bill through PTEG and the BCC, it would plan its internal actions with a view to being a responsible public transport operator and a good employer. By being fair and objective it was hoped to walk the tightrope between the practical and the political. A key part of its efforts were, therefore, devoted to keeping the SYPTE workforce fully informed of what was going on, what were the alternatives and what were the implications. 'The Strategy for Survival' was produced in this period and was presented to staff through extensive consultations and individual 'surgeries' at garages. It was a daunting challenge to which the PTE rose.

Under the direction of the DG, Ian Smith, a Co-ordinating Group (COG) was established consisting of:

The Commercial Director, Peter Sephton
The Controller of Executive Planning & Development,
   (the Author – D.S. Hellewell)
The Chief Finance Officer, Alex Ritchie
The Controller of Manpower Services, Wilf Kemp
The Chief Planning Officer, Phil Haywood
The Secretary, Ian Hoskisson

The job of this group was to mastermind the transition of the PTE from being an operating and planning organisation to a planning and securing organisation. It was also necessary to lay the foundation for the operating side to be established as a separate company. This had to be done in the context of the demise of the SYCC and the establishment of a 'shadow' PTE. It also had to be done against an externally-imposed timetable which had little regard to the practical and human issues to be considered.

COG co-ordinated the activities of four sub-groups dealing with:

Resource Allocation   Tendering Activities
Commercial Information   Resource Utilisation

Much of the detailed work fell to Wilf Kemp, Phil Haywood, Melvin Johnson, and the Author.

An earlier decision by the Executive – at the suggestion of the Author – was now to show its value. The Executive had commissioned the Consultants MVA to produce a computer-based model of the Sheffield bus network using their VIP's system. This had its origins in a Volvo-produced model and both London Transport and West Midlands PTE had gained experience with it. However, its application to Sheffield was its largest application at the time, since it was designed to cover the whole of the Sheffield District's operations. Because of their smaller scale the Rotherham & Doncaster services could be handled in a conventional manner, with SYT's own Business Model being used to evaluate the options.

The campaign against the Transport Bill also included the use of outdoor poster sites. *(Mike Greenwood)*

Using the VIP's model, alternative networks could be evaluated to determine the most profitable network or the financial performance of different sizes of network, relative to the scale of the existing operation. It will be appreciated that in 1985/86 virtually every mile operated by SYPTE was loss-making – about 75% of the costs were then coming from the SYCC by way of subsidy. The new regime proposed that bus services should be provided commercially, i.e. should be profitable. Those that could not be so provided but were considered to be necessary, were to be put out to tender for operators to bid for.

For the operator – South Yorkshire Transport in due course – the basic objective was to have the most profitable network. But regard had to be paid to two important issues. Firstly, such a network was likely to be substantially smaller than the existing network, which meant that to retain the same total network, post-deregulation, the Executive would have to put out a lot of services to tender. In itself this had two implications. Firstly, the Executive and the new PTA were going to be rate-capped and there was a financial limit to what they could afford to put out to tender. Secondly, the smaller the network the more staff would be made redundant. This was a major social concern, but also had severe financial consequences. The PTE's funds had also to cover the redundancy provisions.

The second main issue related to the levels of competition that could be expected. South Yorkshire was, historically, 'good bus territory' and this was known throughout the industry. SYCC policies had ensured high levels of bus usage and although fares were bound to rise substantially, there was an underlying strength in the market. Accordingly it was considered by the PTE that there was a likelihood of substantial competition. Competition would come in terms of the commercial network and also in tendering for subsidised services. The smaller the commercial network registered for SYT, the larger would be the tendered network, thus attracting competition for these services, and allowing new operators to become established on the basis of tendered work. Once established they would be hard to dislodge, even if they lost tendered work at subsequent 'bidding rounds'.

An event organised as part of the ongoing public awareness campaign against the Transport Bill was a 'behind the scenes' look at Greenland Road garage when an open day was held there on 10th August 1985. One of the attractions was an opportunity to drive a bus, by utilising the training fleet. *(Mike Greenwood)*

Furthermore, the smaller SYT's commercial network the more opportunity it left for other commercial operators to come in.

The VIP's model enabled SYPTE to model these different scenarios and proved itself to be an invaluable tool. It will be readily appreciated that there were numerous, interactive processes which had to be carefully analysed, considered and assessed. Two fundamental issues of major significance related to fares and costs. These and other related issues will be dealt with in the next chapter.

Throughout this period it was necessary to keep the staff as fully informed as possible about the changes and their implications. The PTE's existing consultative structure was used through the period. A number of special, one-day Seminars were held at SYPTE's Sports & Social Club at Meadow Head (not to be confused with Meadowhall!). There were also numerous meetings of individual groups of staff and at individual locations. It was also necessary to keep SYCC informed and, from April 1985, the 'Shadow' PTA. A series of seminars was arranged for both these groups since there was a major case of persuasion for the County Council, who could see all they had worked for being dismantled, and for the shadow PTA to become aware of their onerous responsibilities. It has to be remembered that the four Metropolitan Districts – Barnsley, Doncaster, Rotherham and Sheffield – were also taking over all the previous County functions – planning; highways, including traffic management; and the emergency services. They were also faced with ever-tightening budgetary constraints.

For the professionals a completely new role was to be faced. Nobody still in the industry had been involved in the pre-1930 deregulated scene when, in any case, municipalities were in quite a strong position. All the industry's (considerable) experience had been gained in a regulated world and most of it post World War II. It was, therefore, necessary to run a number of management seminars, to educate senior and middle levels of management, on a whole range of issues including costing, finance, marketing, customer service and other similar skills, that were going to be of even greater importance than hitherto.

These were traumatic days for the County Council and especially for the key members – Roy Thwaites, Alex Waugh, John Cornwell and others. They were fighting on two fronts: first to avoid abolition of the County Council and secondly against bus deregulation. The Executive put a great deal of effort into explaining the implications of deregulation as they saw it. This assisted the County Council in their campaign against deregulation. However, it also showed to the Members why SYPTE was having to take the steps it was, since it appeared inevitable that both abolition and deregulation would occur.

The problem of abolition faced the six Metropolitan

Counties and the GLC, and an anti-Abolition campaign was spearheaded by the AMA. The anti-deregulation campaign involved PTEG, the BCC and the AMA. It was important to try and keep all these organisations more-or-less in step since, in the final analysis, the PTEs were still under Political control of the PTA – SYCC, etc. At this stage the Shadow PTA had little influence, except in the sidelines at the AMA. PTEG decided, in February 1985, to mount a campaign in Parliament to seek revisions to the proposed legislation. (It was not possible to mount a wrecking campaign, even if that was the real intent!) In any case the PTEG had done a great deal of work since the publication of the *Buses* White Paper into the cost-effectiveness of the present arrangement (to be abandoned) and of a number of alternatives. The preferred scenario was to go for a franchising arrangement, as was subsequently adopted for London. This would retain the benefits of a PTE having an overall view of the public transport requirements of the area, including rail services, whilst bringing in competitive bidding for the provision of services themselves. It would also have made it easier to retain through-ticketing and overall network publicity. In shorthand, this was described as 'off-road' competition.

The PTEG campaign in London was headed up by the Author, who established an office at 55 Broadway, where accommodation was rented from LT. Other PTEs seconded staff as and when required, and particular mention should be made of Roger Simpson, Secretary of West Yorkshire PTE and Bill Tyson of GMPTE. A great deal of hard work was put in by the PTE Group, under the direction of James Isaac, who was the then Chairman of PTEG. Some 28 significant changes were brought about and numerous minor points were won. The Transport Bill became law in October. For bus operators changes started to come in immediately. The bus deregulation that came in on 26th October 1986 was little different from the concepts outlined in the *Buses* White Paper of July 1984.

It has been said, and indeed it may be partly true, that the County's success helped to bring about the demise of the Metropolitan Counties. The Conservative Government's policy of seeking to reduce spending on public transport, as part of its overall aim to cut public expenditure, was directly challenged by GLC and the Metropolitan Counties, all Labour Party controlled, and the argument became polarised into a party political issue.

An animated view of the front of Greenland Road Garage on the occasion of the open day in 1985. *(Mike Greenwood)*

12 RE-ORGANISATION – AGAIN

1985-1986 – Dividing the Spoils

Whereas the new organisation introduced on April 1st 1974 was evolved from the previous arrangements within a constant framework of service provision, the re-organisation required by the Transport Act 1985 was revolutionary and wholesale, requiring a complete re-think. It was to be a re-organisation for survival in a very different world from that known to anybody then in the business.

Within SYPTE operations there had been a very strong commitment to the County's policies, particularly those relating to service and vehicle development, and services for those sections and parts of the community with special needs. There was less sympathy with the continuation of 'cheap fares' for two main reasons. Firstly, it was clear that sooner or later SYCC would be forced to give up the policy and central government policy would be imposed, probably overnight, with detrimental effects on the travelling public and staff. Secondly, because insufficient income was being generated and the County could not increase its subsidy (it was already paying 75% of the costs), there were insufficient funds to continue the necessary development programmes passenger growth was requiring. However, and above all, the level of interference from SYCC had got to a ridiculous position.

In conceiving the organisational parameters there was, therefore, a very strong public service element (in the event, as will be seen, possibly too strong an element). The PTE felt a very strong responsibility to its staff. The PTE also felt it had a role to protect its customers, since there was nobody else to speak up for them. Within these parameters of 'social conscience' there was a feeling of release that 'now it was entirely up to us and our own efforts'. The new Company would stand or fall by its own efforts. Every person would have an individual contribution to make, staffing levels would have to be scaled down. Nobody involved had the slightest doubt that everybody would rise to the challenge. The task was daunting, but so were the opportunities. The opportunity that was taken in SELNEC in 1969 and missed in SYPTE in 1973/74 would not be passed up this time.

The proposed 'scheme of reorganisation' had to be approved by the Secretary of State for Transport before it could be implemented. Under section 59 of the Transport Act 1985 he had power to accept, modify, reject or approve the schemes put to him. The 'schemes' themselves had to show that a viable company had been created with a long-term future. The government was paranoiac that there should be absolutely no chance of subsidies creeping back

into bus operation. 'Transparency' was the key-word. The legislation was biased against existing public sector operators, particularly the PTEs and the municipalities. (NBC accounts had been prepared under Companies Act legislation.) Conversely, the legislation tried to make everything easy for the new operators. Indeed, there was a specific Clause in the Act (Cl. 80) placing a duty on a PTA not to inhibit competition – such was the vengeance of the government,.

The proposals had to:

- identify and value property, rights and liabilities to be transferred to the Company
- contain the details of a viable Business Plan
- allow the PTE to receive loan or equity capital in exchange for the assets/liabilities transferred

The Business Plan had to include the results for the previous two years operation (1984/85 and 1985/86) and the pre- and post deregulation forecasts for 1986/87. (It will be remembered that Deregulation Day – D-Day – came on October 26th 1986, ie in the middle of the financial year). The Plan had to include estimated results from commercial and tendered bus routes and an assessment of continuing financial viability. Accounts were to be prepared in compliance with the requirements of the Companies Act and Transport Act, 1985.

The Transport Act, 1985 received the Royal Assent in October 1985 when it was signed by HRH The Princess Royal, in the absence of HM The Queen. (Thus the biggest change in road passenger transport for over half a century was signed by the Honorary President of the Chartered Institute of Transport!) The timescale for implementing the change was to be very tight. The Initial Company (as the new Company was officially known until the Secretary of State had approved the Scheme of Reorganisation) had to be registered by February 20th 1986. The name chosen for the Company was 'South Yorkshire Transport Ltd.', to be known as 'South Yorkshire's Transport'. However, a number of other names were registered to prevent them getting into other people's hands. These included: Sheffield Buses, Rotherham Buses, Doncaster Buses, Hallam Buses and a few others.

The transitional Registration arrangements were covered by Section 139 and Schedule 6 of the 1985 Act and by various guidance notes. To say they were complex was an understatement. They tended to affect new operators more than existing ones, but SYT had to be on its guard and there were regular sorties to the Licensing Authority at Leeds, since fourteen days was a long time to wait before the next edition of Notices & Proceedings. Registrations of commercial services were to be completed by 28th February, ie within four months of the legislation being enacted. In the event the first outline of the prospectus – the kernel of the Business Plan – was produced on 6th March and the First Draft on March 14th, the Second Draft following a week later after the first run of the financial model. The Scheme was submitted to the Secretary of State – the infamous Nicholas Ridley – on 31st March 1986. It is a relevant the quote from part of the Director General's Foreward to SYT's Prospectus[28] (as the Business Plan was called):

'The Prospectus put forward requires the approval of the Secretary of State and this is now sought. The timescale imposed by the Transport Act 1985 is extremely tight. However, in compliance with the legislation the Executive registered 'the Initial Company' (South Yorkshire Transport (No. 2) Limited) by February 20th and registered by February 28th those commercial services which that company will operate from October 26th 1986. If the Initial Company is to be able to operate commercially, as required by the Act, it is necessary that the matters set out in this Prospectus are accepted. The Executive are proceeding on the basis of this assumption, since to do otherwise would prejudice the implementation of the necessary changes to achieve this objective'.

'Stick that in your pipe and smoke it!' – in effect saying 'You brought in the legislation to wreck all that South Yorkshire, in line with Continental and North American policies – had achieved over twelve years. The professionals in the SYPTE have complied with the Legislation to the letter (and won the grudging acceptance of SYCC to do so, when you (the S of S) thought you would have a fight on your hands, as you had done on previous occasions.' It was a major achievement for all concerned, even if it was taking public transport in a direction many were unhappy with.

RESIDUAL PTE

Most of the foregoing relates to bus operation in the deregulated environment that was to exist post 26th October 1985. The PTE had, of course, other responsibilities from the 1968 Act most of which were to continue e.g. responsibility for local railway services. (The two major exceptions were the loss of bus operating powers and the loss of influence over other operators – NBC and the independents.) In addition the PTE was given additional responsibilities to manage the tendering system for non-commercial routes. This was to produce an immediate and on-going workload. Additionally the PTE continued ownership of, and responsibility for, bus stations and interchanges throughout the County (except for Barnsley which was owned by YTC, but for which SYPTE had long-standing plans to develop into a full interchange).

It was the view of the Executive, supported by the County Council and 'shadow' PTA, that every attempt should be made to maintain the existing bus route network and frequency of services, however and whoever operated it. Thus by deducting the commercial registered network from the existing bus network it was possible to determine those routes that would require to be put out to tender. On a similar comparative basis, it was possible to determine where 'service augmentation' was going to be required. 'Service augmentation' related to those services where the frequency of the commercial registered service was considered to be inadequate and thus required augmentation.

The PTE had to bear in mind a number of things with regard to tendered services. First and foremost they only had a certain amount of money available to cover all their responsibilities – concessionary fares, local train services, tendered services and redundancy payments. Secondly, none of their actions must inhibit, prevent or distort competition. Thirdly, tendered routes were to be let individually not in groups or packages – although operators could bid for them in that way. Fourthly, it was expected that tenders would be let for two or three years with the maximum period allowed being five years. Bearing in mind the PTE's workload, and the need to achieve some continuity, there was a desire to let longer life tenders. Conversely, such actions could inhibit commercial room for manoeuvre but, more importantly, it committed PTE finances ahead and thus removed the flexibility that might be required in other sectors.

The route modelling for the Commercial Service was carried out under the direction of the Controller of Executive Planning and Development – from Christmas 1985 he had been appointed as Operations Director (designate) in SYT. The model was then used to evaluate the tendered route network and the service augmentation programme referred to above. After January 1986 this was done under the direction of Phil Haywood, Chief Planning Officer (who became the PTE's Director of Planning in due course). 'Chinese Walls' were built within the Exchange Street Offices so that the Commercial services and the tendered services were kept apart. SYPTE were scrupulous in their attention to detail, and their compliance with both the spirit and letter of the law – although most were very unhappy with it. It was also essential that existing operators registering commercial services, eg NBC subsidiaries, or new operators felt that the PTE was handling this commercially sensitive information in confidence. Physically the staff of the Initial Company (SYT) could not get out of Exchange Street offices until their own Head Office was ready for occupation.

The 'new' Executive was to consist of three full-time directors and five part-time directors. The full-time Directors were as shown below:

Director General	: Ian Smith (no change)
Director of Finance	: Alec Ritchie (previously Chief Finance Officer)
Director of Planning	: Albert Booth (no change)
Secretary	: Ian Hoskisson (no change)

The five part-time directors were to be the Clerk and Chief Financial Officer to the PTA – Bob Johnson, a role he had held since David Chynoweth's departure – and the Chief Executives of the four Metropolitan Districts: Barnsley, Doncaster, Rotherham and Sheffield. A significant change was that the Director of Finance did not become responsible for the Administration function and Ian Hoskisson answered direct to the Executive as previously. It is interesting to note that the joint finance and administration function raised its head again as it had done in 1974! It was decided that SYPTE should remain in the Exchange Street offices.

One of the reasons for having the Chief Executives of the four Metropolitan Districts on the Executive was to give effect to the need for close liaison with the Metropolitan Districts with their changed responsibilities regarding transport. The Metropolitan Districts became the highway authorities responsible for traffic management matters affecting public transport, whilst the PTE continued its responsibilities for bus stations and interchanges. There were also a number of policy matters relating to the provision of tendered bus services such as concessionary fares, education and social services transport.

SOUTH YORKSHIRE TRANSPORT (SYT)

The requirements of the 1985 Transport Act necessitated fundamental changes to meet the demands of a competitive market. The 'Strategy for Survival' depended upon a total change in culture and management style in order to survive within the cost/revenue framework of the 'open market'.

It should be noted that the process of identifying the policies and strategies ultimately adopted by SYT started long before the Company began to trade independently. The identification of new structure and strategy requirements, together with the principal redundancy negotiations, were enacted prior to the formation of the Company and continued as the Company took action in the light of actual trading circumstances.

SYT Culture

Responding to the demands and challenges created by the Transport Act 1985 required an inevitable culture change throughout SYT. Previous political and Trade Union aspirations were overtaken by the need to succeed. Formal fares policy, and service network ideals, had to be abandoned and job security became increasingly dependent upon market forces. All efforts had to be concentrated upon bus operation with a divestment of other activities. Profitability assumed the highest importance and services were required to generate sufficient revenue to cover operating costs and a share of the Company overheads.

Management and workforce needed to react more quickly to market and financial demands, threats and opportunities. To support this requirement substantial changes in structure, resources, communication and management style were implemented.

Re-structuring of the former PTE operations

The changes required by the Transport Act 1985 that brought about deregulation of the bus industry, and the effects of local government re-organisation, following the Local Government Act 1985, meant that the former direct operations of the PTE had to be restructured completely:

– superfluous staff and management roles eliminated
– overmanning in operations and engineering resolved by redundancy programmes
– requisite manpower levels based on maximum attainable efficiency levels for the assessed future work load
– surplus resources reduced
– garage closures
– fleet size reduced to match the new service requirements plus minimum/optimum spares
– unit management approach developed.
– specific objectives established for line management, delegated authority to enable achievement.
– element of salary based on performance
– Company Council introduced involving all representative groups, aimed at better understanding of Company objectives and performance and generating faster reaction times
– improved communication methods involving all employees by establishment of Garage Committees
– labour utilisation improved through revised schedules and working practices
– low labour costs through:
    agreed pay cuts
    adopting market rate pay levels for new platform and engineering staff
– financial information systems revised to provide performance data as a basis on which to take remedial action
– new products introduced and greater emphasis on 'Customer Care' adopted

The Co-ordinating Group (COG) considered four alternative organisations for the new bus operating company (the 'Initial Company'):

- Retention of the existing District Structure
- Divisionalisation
- a Centralised organisation
- a Garage-based organisation

Acknowledging the fact the 'when companies reorganise they bleed'[29] the Prospectus included this comment: 'In considering the alternatives, therefore, it was necessary not only to consider the requirements of the Act and the guidance notes, but also to have regard to the practical problems encountered during any transition'.

It had to be remembered that throughout this period bus services had to continue to be provided safely and efficiently with a staff whose future was surrounded by a considerable amount of uncertainty. Staff motivation was very important. Furthermore, the Executive knew that fares would have to rise substantially and it was their desire that such increases should be introduced as soon as possible and phased over as long a period as possible. Right from the first meeting with staff representatives in October 1985 it had been made clear that:

– every attempt would be made to retain the earnings of individuals, i.e. their take-home pay, but that they would have to work a lot harder for it, i.e. a policy of increasing productivity rather than cutting wage rates.
– it was inevitable that there would have to be a substantial number of redundancies, but it was hoped to obtain these on a voluntary basis, through the most generous redundancy package that the County Council/PTA could afford, having regard to government rate-capping.
– there would be substantial staff consultation with staff representatives, as well as there being individual surgeries at all locations

Retention of Existing District Structure

The retention of the existing arrangements had the benefit of removing uncertainties and retaining a structure that was well tried. However, it had the disadvantage of perpetuating the imbalance between District sizes, with Sheffield representing about 3/5ths of the operation. Also the District was a further tier between the Head Office at Sheffield and the individual garages, thus, to an extent the Management was remote from the workforce. Because of their size this had not posed a particular problem with Bootham Lane at Doncaster or Halfway relative to Rotherham. However, in the case of Sheffield with the four large garages, the continuation of this additional tier was felt to be a disadvantage in a future, competitive situation.

Divisionalisation

Whilst not overcoming the problem of a tier between Head Office and garage, the creation of two divisions had the advantage of overcoming the imbalance that existed within the existing district structure, as referred to previously. There were a number of combinations within a two-division arrangement. One possible scenario was to have a Hallam Division covering the garages of East Bank, Leadmill, Herries Road and Halfway with a Don Division covering the garages of Greenland Road, Rotherham, Doncaster and Bootham Lane. Divisionalisation seemed to offer no advantages over the District structure and thus was pursued no further.

Centralisation

From time-to-time there had been criticisms of SYPTE retaining a de-centralised structure since its size was about 1/3 of the largest PTEs like Greater Manchester or West Midlands. Furthermore, West Yorkshire had replaced its original five District structure with a two-division structure.

Geographically South Yorkshire was a multi-centred conurbation, with the PTE operating in three of the four main centres. The majority of bus passengers were local to their own town or city. Whilst centralisation might have shown some economies, it was felt wrong for two main reasons. Firstly, the geography of the conurbation just referred to. Secondly, despite the Act requiring one Initial Company, there was the clear desire to decentralise. This trend was also seen in many transport organisations at that time. Thus a move towards centralisation would be going in the wrong direction.

Garage-based

The garage is the centre of bus operations, it is where the service is produced, it is 'the ground floor'. Decisions cannot be delegated below garage level. It is also at that level that most of the costs arise and, therefore, can best be controlled. Vehicles and staff are allocated to garages and thus it is possible to establish an 'esprit-de-corps' and a competitive spirit. There were, however, a number of disadvantages about a garage-based organisation. Garages are not necessarily well located or even located relevant to the routes running out of them. A further problem, so far as bus services in Sheffield was concerned, was that services from all four garages inter-twined.

To be successful, decisions must be delegated to the Garage Manager but he, in turn, must be supported by a small team. Clearly, however, care needed to be taken to ensure that there was not more management staff in eight garages than there were in three Districts. An equally important factor was that successful transport had become a business which needed advanced information technology, good marketing techniques and quality professional management. It was not possible to afford these facilities at individual garages but they could be provided by a small central servicing unit and shared by each garage.

The Adopted Scheme

Having carefully weighed and considered the pro's and con's of the above-mentioned four alternatives, the Executive concluded that a garage-based organisation would be the most suitable. Each of the four essential functions: engineering and personnel, finance and administration and operations was to be headed by a Director. These three Directors, together with the Managing Director, formed the new company board.

The Garage Manager was to be solely responsible for the profitable operations of his garage. So far as the commercial services were concerned he would be responsible for ensuring their profitability and taking whatever steps he felt necessary to achieve the profitability targets. Initially registered services would be allocated to individual garages in a manner which combined the opportunity to commence on a profitable basis, with any obvious geographical aspects of route location. Thereafter the development of those services would be a matter for the individual Garage Managers. A Garage Manager would be given financial, operating, engineering and productivity targets which he was expected to achieve. Part of a Garage

Manager's salary was to be performance-related.

SYT was to have a small headquarters team determining Engineering, Personnel, Finance, Marketing and Operational policies. All policy would be implemented by the Garage Managers who were to be answerable to the Operations Director through one of the two Assistant Operations Directors. The small central functions were also to monitor the performance of the individual garages and ensure that qualitative standards were met and financial performance achieved or bettered.

Also assisting the Operations Directors there was to be a Commercial Manager. He would be responsible for four areas of work: marketing, business analysis, customer service and Coachline and Private Hire. For SYT to be successful in the future environment it would be essential to have marketing strategies based on a scientific analysis of the business and its trends. One of the failings of the bus industry was that it had been too 'production orientated'. The customer service team would seek to correct this omission. The profitable expansion of Coachline and productive use of the bus fleet, through private hire, would also be sought by this manager.

The Directors and Chief Officers of South Yorkshire Transport Ltd. were appointed over the December 1985/ January 1986 period and were as follows:

Chairman & Managing Director	:	Peter Sephton, (ex-Commercial Director, SYPTE)
Finance Director & Secretary	:	Michael Pestereff (ex-Financial Controller, SYPTE)
Personnel Director	:	Wilf Kemp (ex-Controller of Manpower Services, SYPTE)
Operations Director	:	Scott Hellewell (ex-Controller of Executive Planning and Development)
Assistant Operations Director (South)	:	Ian Davies (previously District Manager, Sheffield)
Assistant Operations Director (North)	:	Bob Rowe (ex-Controller of Operations)
Commercial Manager	:	Tom Young (new appointment from outside)
Finance Manager	:	Melvin Johnson (ex-Chief Accountant SYPTE)
Engineering Manager	:	Bill Bland (ex-Technical Services Manager, SYPTE)

Dennis Dominator No. 2467 resplendent in the new South Yorkshire Transport Limited livery. The final Dominators ordered by the PTE were in fact delivered in this style. *(Mike Greenwood)*

Personnel Manager	:	Ron Blythe (ex-Manpower Services Manager, SYPTE)

The non-Executive Directors were:

Robert Brook	:	Former Chairman of NBC who was appointed Deputy Chairman & Chairman of the Audit Committee
Roy Thwaites	:	representing the Residuary Body & former Leader of SYCC
Alex Waugh	:	representing Sheffield and former Chairman of the Transport Committee
Graham Kyte	:	representing Barnsley and a former Committee Clerk to the SYCC Transport Committee
Vernon Thornes	:	representing Rotherham and a leading Labour Party official
Brian Key	:	representing Doncaster, and a former MEP
Ted Gleeson	:	representing the workforce being a lifelong T & GWU member and Secretary of the Sheffield Passenger Branch.

Whilst it was relatively easy to identify those activities that were to be left with the 'residual' PTE and those that were to be transferred to the 'Initial Company', there were a number of activities that were shared between the two organisations. These included: computing, training, catering, consultancy, building and property services and central engineering. The first concept was to have four subsidiary companies, the shareholding to reflect the use each made of the subsidiary concerned. It was hoped that, over time, they would have been able to trade profitably in their own right with the majority of work coming from outside SYPTE/SYT after a transitional period. However, the PTE's specialist advisers indicated that there could be problems with this sort of arrangement and the idea was dropped.

In the event the Computer and Training were transferred to SYT. The Training Centre at Meadowhall became the company's headquarters and the Training Section was reduced to be in-line with anticipated future requirements. Catering was an integral part of providing for the needs of the business and this function was also transferred to the Company. However, hours of opening were reduced, some of the less-used canteens were closed and catering became a

cost centre in SYT. Some canteens were equipped with freezers, automatic vending machines and microwave ovens at the PTE's expense prior to vesting. Meals were charged at the price of the food and a £½m pa subsidy was removed.

Central Engineering consisted of the Central Works at Queens Road, and premises at Olive Grove and Rutland Way posed major problems. There were also paint shops at Rotherham and Doncaster and extensive workshops at Doncaster, recently built. Philosophically there has always been much debate in the bus industry as to the pros and cons of a Central Works. In general terms these were carryovers from tramway days and this was true of Queens Road. All PTEs at the time had retained their Central Works as had many municipalities. They were, however, a major overhead cost. Engineers liked central works because it gave them an 'Empire', traffic men thought they took buses off the road unnecessarily since the Works had to be 'fed' buses to keep them happy! In the circumstances of 1985/86 the decision to retain or close Queens Road was bound up with the decision as to how many operating garages were needed. This will be dealt with later.

As has been indicated previously, SYT was the largest bus operator in South Yorkshire carrying 76% (264m passengers) of the passengers and operating 70% (68.7m passengers) of the mileage. It operated 1058 vehicles from eight garages. The Peak Vehicle Requirement (PVR) was 845, giving 30% spare vehicles. It operated in five counties and its passenger per mile figure – 7.09 – was the highest in Britain, even more than LT! On an average day 722,000 passenger were carried which was equivalent to every inhabitant in the county making 200 journeys per year. The 'Initial Company', therefore, had an excellent base from which to start, but it had to get its costs down and its fares up dramatically if it was to survive in the deregulated world.

The former training centre at Amos Road Sheffield became the new Company's head office. It is now the head office of SYPTA Limited. *(Mike Greenwood)*

Role and Objectives of SYT

These were set out in the Business Plan (28). The role of SYT was to:

- Meet the legal requirements of the Transport Act 1985 and the Companies Act 1985.
- Maximise employment within a 'financial viability' framework of operating company and tendering procedures
- Carry on coaching and related activities and expand these where profitable development could be seen
- Operate the maximum framework of local services within the commercial and financial constraints of SYT

The Objectives of the company were seen as being to:

- Maximise the proportion of the network that could be operated profitably, having due regard to likely competitive pressures
- Develop or enter into related activities, e.g. coaching, travel shops
- Secure the maximum number of services put out to tender.

Since all bus services operated in South Yorkshire made a loss, all SYPTE bus services had to be evaluated to assess their future commercial potential. Some of the issues relating to the size of the commercial network and the balance of the tendered network have already been discussed. Within the Commercial routes there were a number of complex inter-relationships which involved fares, service levels, type of service, resources required (staff and vehicles) all of which affect cost. Redundancies had to be taken into account for both financial and social reasons. Questions concerning cross-subsidies within a route, between routes, within networks by time period, etc. also had to considered. Fares, margins, returns and competition were also issues.

SYPTE had developed a Computer Route Evaluation Model which had been used to evaluate options contained in the PTE's Three Year Plan for 1986/7 to 1988/9, as part of the SYCC/SYPTE planning process, and related to TPP funding and application. This model was improved and developed to become SYT's Business Model. This took historic data on patronage, revenue, mileage and costs and produced forecasts of changes to several policy variables. These included: fare and service levels; costs and productivity targets, inflation and Concessionary fares. The model was designed to assess the contribution made by a route over its marginal cost. The model used 5 time-periods for Monday-to-Friday, 3 for Saturday and one for Sundays. Key elements included:

- Costs : the effect of productivity improvements on unit costs, manpower and vehicle requirements
- Patronage: changes in patronage analysed by four categories of passenger
- Revenue : forecasts made for the four passenger categories, including revenue from concessionary fares.

HASTUS Computer Scheduling was used to re-schedule all routes and most of the old Spanish customs were taken out, although initially the four Sheffield garages tried to retain some of them. Wholesale reductions in cost both by elimination of items, as well as by increased productivity, were made. Ranges of fare increases were evaluated. For a pre-determined rate-of-return, and for a fixed cost level, fare levels were determined for a range of route networks. To retain the whole of the former SYPTE network would have required a 400% increase in fares! For a 100% increase in fares the size of network was also determined. This was considered to be far too small and exposing SYT to unnecessary levels of competition.

The optimum level of fare increase was considered to be 250% – an unheard of figure. With off-peak discounts of 5p or 10p, and a monthly SYT TravelCard, the average fare increase was reduced to 225%. With this fare increase and cost assumptions, including 100% OPO, a Commercial Network was determined, as being 61% of the overall average of the former SYPTE network or 21.737m miles per annum. Broken down by time period it was:

Weekdays	am	46%
	am peak	66%
	inter peak	74%
	pm peak	69%
	pm	51%
Saturday	am	30%
	daytime	62%
	pm	47%
Sundays	all day	43%

No schools or works services were registered as commercial. However, the City Clipper (at a fare of 10p), certain Colliery and Sheffield Nightline services were registered as commercial. The peak vehicle equipment (PVR) for commercial services was 514 which, allowing for 15% spares, gave a fleet strength of 592 – a reduction of 466 vehicles (44%). Of course this was before taking account of any tendered services, but gave some idea of the scale of redundancies to be considered, and also the whole question of numbers of operating garages required and the allocation of routes.

As discussed earlier it had been decided to adopt a garage-based management structure. The concept was that each garage retained would have a nucleus of commercial routes on which it could survive. This would then protect the garage and indeed the company from the vagaries of the tendering system. It was not known how tendering would work out in practice, how successful or otherwise SYT would be in winning the work, how much competition there would be for it, and how long central government would continue to provide funds.

As has been indicated earlier, the tendering exercise was a major one for SYPTE. However, it was crucial to all bus operators – not just SYT – to know (a) what routes were being put out to tender, (b) what service augmentation was going to be sought, how it was to be achieved and, most importantly, who had been successful. Answers to these questions were crucial if sensible manpower and resource planning was to be achieved. Also once successful, the tendered services had to be registered in the normal way, 42 days before operation commenced. In turn this meant that all tenders must be known early in September 1986 – but school services which would come in about then would have to be registered by mid July. It was felt by the operators that SYPTE were dilatory in the tendering process and were unaware of the problems facing operators. On the other hand the PTE would point out that the operators had no idea of the bureaucracy that they had to go through to get tendered routes agreed in the first place, before even issuing the tenders. Before the split of SYPTE/SYT it had been pointed out to the 'shadow' PTA that they would have to devise rules and delegate action to the PTE if the tendering process was to work efficiently. It appeared they had not heeded this warning.

Although there was a great deal of competition for tendered routes – there were about 60 operators bidding – SYT was successful in general terms. However, after a good start, success tailed off and a revision to cost per mile and cross-subsidy issues had to be made. Service augmentation caused a great deal of heartache. For example, an existing 15 minute service might have been registered commercially as a 20-minute frequency post deregulation. If the PTE felt this was insufficient it might put out a tender for an hourly service for augmentation purposes. If the commercial operator did not win it the effect was to have a competitor on the route on at least one journey each hour. It would have been preferable for the PTE and operators to have discussed the problem – but the PTE were afeared of talking to operators thinking the OFT might object!

Garages

It was now becoming urgent to determine the number of garages that SYT would retain. Surveys of their condition had already been undertaken, regard had been made to the recent investment and valuations were made for alternative uses. The number of commercial services indicated that only six garages were necessary to achieve the anticipated capacity – commercial registrations plus winning about half the anticipated tendered work. Services could just be provided out of 5 garages but with substantial overloading and associated congestion which led to inefficiencies. The question of Central Works was revisited. A garage closure would mean the re-allocation of work between the other garages, this would cause upset to the staff, revisions to services already registered, upset local feelings because of the effect on local employment and a number of other issues. In the end it was decided to retain all 8 operating garages and to close Central Works. This strategy led to 1580 being made redundant out of a workforce of 5300 – 30%.

As this new structure was formed it was possible to piece together the eventual picture and identify the

component parts of the old SYPTE that would no longer be needed in the brave new world.

Central Works

In many respects the closure of the Central Works was a sad affair. Only a couple of years prior the 'top shop' had been completely refurbished at considerable expense and a new MOT inspection bay had been built at the rear of the works. Inside the works the building was steeped in its tramway history with a meeting room known as the 'Oak Room' that had furniture produced by craftsmen who had manufactured teak framing on the trams. But the tradition was to be lost forever as the works closed and apart from a brief use of part of the premises for a short spell in later years by a new bus company (Yorkshire Terrier), the works were doomed to fall into empty disrepair and eventual demolition – to give way to a modern retail park. Where trams once would glide gracefully into the ornate archway at the Queens Road entrance there is now a Netto supermarket thrusting brash commerciality upon passers by – not unlike the fate of the bus industry.

At the same time the smaller workshop at Olive Grove was also closed down, but these premises, which had only been in use for a couple of years, were taken over by the City Council for maintaining their lorries.

In Sheffield city centre the District Office was closed down and SYT moved its senior staff out to its erstwhile training centre at Meadowhall. Several years later the SY Supertram Company were to take up residence in the old Arundel Gate offices. At Doncaster the unique Dennis Dominator trolleybus, that had been running on an experimental basis adjacent to the race-course, was parked in the workshop at Leicester Avenue and left to gather dust by the PTE – a victim of deregulation. A promising project that was never to be – but who knows, there are very encouraging sounds being heard at Doncaster concerning future plans for trolleybuses – alas not Dominators though!

The transformation of the bus operations into a stand-alone company had been a massive task, but was completed as planned and everyone now had to adapt, for the first time ever, to the competitive world. The newly registered services could not be changed until February 1987 and in the intervening period all operators were carefully scrutinising their networks to see if all was well.

The proportion of commercial services at each garage was as follows:

Leadmill	64%	Greenland	64%
Herries	57%	East Bank	62%
Rotherham	65%	Dunscroft	50%
Doncaster	68%	Halfway	43%

In order to balance the workload and to provide the essential nucleus of commercial services a programme of transfer of work between garages was to be instigated. It had been a feature of Sheffield operation that two garages often shared a route between them, but this was now considered undesirable, since the object was to associate garages and routes in the minds of the staff. Work was transferred from Rotherham to Herries and Greenland and some of Greenland's work transferred to Halfway. There was also to be some transfer from Doncaster to Dunscroft. Whilst there was initially considerable opposition, the logic of the new world came through and most, but not all of the transfers were achieved.

Not all eight garages had the same status and this was reflected in their staffing levels and arrangements. In each large garage the Garage Manager was supported by a Traffic Manager, a Garage Engineer and a Garage Finance and Personnel Manager. These four people formed the 'garage team' at Doncaster (Leicester Avenue), Rotherham (Midland Road), Greenland Road, Herries Road and East Bank Garages. Bootham Lane had a Garage Manager and an Inspector-in-Charge. Halfway Garage had a Garage Manager and an Engineering Foreman. Leadmill Garage, Sheffield, whilst being retained, had a revised role. In addition to retaining some of its registered commercial services it also became the base for Coachline operations in Sheffield, and was intended to be the new base from which to introduce a developing fleet of minibuses. It had a Garage Manager, Traffic Officer and a Vehicle Foreman.

So far as tendered-for services were concerned, Garage Managers were expected to compete with other SYT garages. SYT received, centrally, tenders issued by a tendering authority, and then sent them out to the garages. On receipt of completed tenders SYT submitted the tender considered most likely to be successful. Once a garage had won a tendered-for service it would incorporate its operation in the most cost-effective manner. In terms of performance Garage Managers were expected to ensure that the conditions of the tendered-for services were complied with. All this was monitored by Headquarter's Operations.

Having regard to the difficulties encountered by SYPTE in the days of the County's pro-public transport policy, it is astounding what was achieved and the speed with which it was achieved During the Summer of 1986 there was all the preparatory work for D-Day on 26th October. A major series of surgeries and consultations were held in each garage to explain what was being done. There was also, regrettably, a major programme of redundancies, with virtually all being achieved voluntarily However, a great deal of experienced talent was lost, particularly in the Inspectorate and Foreman grades. The Company decided that it would prepare its own publicity, and the former PTE enquiry offices were changed into Travel Shops, selling also a range of complementary goods. A central telephone enquiry bureau was established at Rotherham Garage – although local phone numbers were used for the public. It was staffed by young people specially selected for their customer friendliness and then trained in public transport matters.

Alternative liveries had been developed earlier in the year. There was neither the time nor the money to repaint the fleet and, in any event, a degree of continuity was required for recognition purposes. It was decided, therefore, to paint the lower half of the buses red and use an SYT South Yorkshire's Transport decal – between decks a brown and red stripe was added. How this transformed the prosaic livery of SYPTE and raised everybody's spirits! By D-Day all the fleet had received its new legal lettering and the SYT decal stuck over the SYPTE logo.

South Yorkshire still had a vast number of crew operated buses working, particularly in the Sheffield area, and a phasing out plan was developed which was to see total OPO by October 1986. As could be imagined this caused a great strain on the industrial relations front which had, to say the least, been volatile during recent years and in the event very large numbers of early retirements took place. The driving school was stepped up and many of the conducting staff were trained up to driving duties with older drivers being offered early retirement in order to make way for the newly trained staff coming through. In the event, whilst this was a very equitable policy and one which found great favour with the staff representatives, it turned out to be an absolute gift to the emerging competing operators who were able to pick up a ready-made, trained driving staff who were more than pleased to work for them at very short notice and supplement their pensions.

To effect the OPO conversions all vehicles had to be fitted with electronic ticket machines and some types were utilised for the first time in this configuration even though they were nearing the end of their normal working lives. Most notably in this respect were the Ailsas which previously had only operated crew duties in Sheffield even though Doncaster staff had happily worked them as OPO for some time. Similarly all the Fleetlines, particularly the ECW batch, were converted, and routes such as 51 and 52 which were extremely busy cross-city services became OPO for the first time. These conversions were not without their problems, of course, and the slower running times on the busy routes certainly did not impress the customers at the time, who were starting to feel the effects of deregulation a little earlier than in most parts of the country.

Interestingly some quite elderly buses appeared in the new livery for a short time before being withdrawn – particularly the DMS type Fleetlines, Alexander Fleetlines, East Lancs Fleetlines and even one of the Ailsas, and a very handsome looking bus it turned out to be. The PTE symbol (normally referred to as the 'flying duck') had to be removed from all the company vehicles and premises, as deregulation drew near, since this was to remain with the PTE for a while – and the separation of SYT and PTE had to be absolute.

As well as sorting out the vehicles' livery there were to be quite a number of withdrawals, since the level of service to be operated at 'D' day was going to be much less than that previously. In the event, whole batches of buses turned up with other operators. Many of the ECW Fleetlines in the 800 series were snapped up by Ribble and could regularly be seen running in Bolton. Ailsas went North to Eastern Scottish and South to Hampshire Bus, in large batches.

In addition to the vast reduction in numbers of platform staff, there also had to be wholesale reduction in the number of supervisory and office staff. Again early retirements and voluntary redundancy packages were offered, and an enormous amount of knowledge and experience was lost – yet not entirely – since some of these people later decided to take up jobs with the newly developing, competing operators and some came back through later acquisitions.

The nivitability that the fares would have to rise considerably if a reasonable level of service was to be registered commercially had already been commented upon. This was necessary if redundancies were to be kept to an acceptable level. Early in 1986 it was clear that a rise of between 250 and 300% was required. The original idea had been to have two fares increases: one around January 1986 and another around September 1986 – certainly not on D-Day itself. There were conflicting arguments internally and no experience of the effect such a dramatic increase would have on the passengers. Several meetings were held with the outgoing County Council but all to no avail. They steadfastly refused to allow a fares increase before their demise on March 31st 1986. Considerable pressure was put on the 'shadow' PTA and they realised that they had no option, but were loathe to agree such a rise as virtually their first action. In the end they were courageous enough to agree and the new fares came in on 6th April 1986. Truly it was the end of the era, but not quite.

The enormous fares increases, amounting in many cases to 300%, were to be the cause, not surprisingly, of a passenger recession and whilst overall numbers had been slowly but surely increasing in previous years under the low fares policy, this came to an abrupt end as the trend was rapidly reversed. Traffic congestion increased in the area as people turned to private transport, and the lack of an extensive road building policy in recent years was soon to take its toll in terms of hold ups that caused buses to run late, and add to the sudden unattractiveness of a once acclaimed bus network.

Whilst 1986 had seen a great slimming down of staff in readiness for deregulation, it was realised that competitive forces would require other measures to be taken, and very quickly improvements to efficiency levels, and lower rates of pay for new-started drivers, were introduced. These were obviously unpalatable measures for the workforce and industrial relations were very strained, but there was a commitment to succeed and strikes or industrial action did not take place.

The era of the minibus was starting to dawn as referred to in Chapter 7. In a short space of time SYPTE became keen to put out tenders for this type of vehicle as they realised that costs per mile were going to be much lower.

Adult Fares				
Distance miles	Existing Fare	Fare from 1.4.86	% Increase	Off Peak Discount Fares*
1	5p	10p	100	110p
2	5p	20p	300	15p
3	10p	30p	200	25p
4	10p	40p	300	35p
5	10p	40p	300	35p
6	10p	40p	300	35p
7	15p	50p	230	45p
8	15p	60p	300	50p
9	15p	60p	300	50p
10	20p Up to a Maximum of 25p	70p	250	60p

* Note: Available to passengers travelling between 0930 and 1530 hours and from 1800 to 2130 hours, Mondays to Fridays, plus all day until 2130 hours on Saturdays and Sundays.

Typical of Sheffield in pre-deregulation days is this view of Commercial Street. The right hand side of the carriageway is now utilised by Supertram. *(Mike Greenwood)*

13 DE-REGULATED OPERATIONS

1986-1995 SYT/MAINLINE OPERATIONS & ACQUISITIONS

October 26th 1986 came and went without all of the razzmatazz which was expected. It was a rather dull, boring day and it rained. The only let down for SYT was the fact that the new publicity was not available (such was the pressure on the printers) until a couple of days later. This put considerable pressure on the Company's Travel

A central telephone response unit was established at Rotherham to deal with travel enquiries following deregulation. *(Mike Greenwood)*

Centres and central phone enquiry facility at Rotherham, with managers taking turns to relieve the hard-pressed staff. The passengers in South Yorkshire did not notice much difference, as was the intention of SYPTE and SYT. Most times remained unaltered, there were some new services and there was a new Company with the blue and white buses. This situation was in marked contrast to that which occurred in Manchester or Leeds, where complete route networks and new numbers had been introduced, along with other changes, which confused passengers and operators alike.

The tender prices were submitted to the PTE, and, after a few worrying weeks, the results were announced. Most of the tenders had been awarded to SYT which had maintained all of its early morning and later night services, schools and works services, and a lot of the normal service work deemed to be non-commercial.

It was at this point that the first surprises of the new regime were felt. Very few operators had envisaged running commercial routes in South Yorkshire against the established operators – in fact only Coachcraft in Doncaster and Groves in Sheffield planned to do so and each only with a handful of vehicles. However, when the results of tender awards became known – and this was as late as September 1986 – it became apparent that an operator from outside the County (West Riding) had been successful in winning several large contracts. It was their intention to use their premises at Charlotte Road from where they were operating their National Travel East subsidiary running coaches on express and tours work.

A three-month freeze on service changes was built into the deregulation process and in this period operators (and prospective operators) were looking around at what commercial opportunities might be available to them. The new SYT had introduced a fleet of minibuses following hard on the heels of its success with the original 'Little Nippers'. This time, however, they were of the new generation van-derived chassis in the form of Dodge S56 a far cry from the old Bristol LHSs which had introduced the concept to South Yorkshire a couple of years earlier. A bright new livery of red, yellow and white looked very attractive on the Reeve Burgess bodywork and on the early deliveries some were fitted with coach style seats which found a ready market for private hire in the 25-seater category. Much experimentation took place with these vehicles, in particular, their usage in penetrating housing estates which had previously not been served directly by the traditional large size bus. It was to be only a short while before this type of vehicle was utilised to operate high frequency services in the competitive battle that was to break out amongst operators in the area before long.

Following the end of the 'freeze' period in January 1987 operators were free to initiate the 42 days registration process and introduce routes at will. As tenders expired and were re-issued, new Companies, able to gain loans based on the guaranteed income of tenders, came into the market. SUT and Excelsior won tenders in Rotherham and Sheffield, whilst other operators, who won school tenders, built up very good commercial operations during the day-time inter-peak periods. Coachcraft (briefly) and Wilfreda

Route branding for the Sixty Shuttle and the Lodge Moor link are seen here on Metrobus 497 and Dodge 133 respectively.

(Mike Greenwood/Bob Rowe)

Beehive operated in Doncaster, Andrews, Groves and Sheafline in Sheffield, and Richardson in all four South Yorkshire towns, but not all at the same time.

In 1988 SYT, faced with financial losses, decided that its operation in Sheffield could be run from three garages instead of four, and in April of that year East Bank garage was closed. Major cost savings ensued but after a short while two new competing bus companies were to start up. One was Sheafline, formed by a group of mainly ex-East Bank drivers, the other, Yorkshire Terrier, was developed by the ex-East Bank management team who decided to leave when their garage was closed down.

Vehicle and route branding had gone through various phases since de-regulation. The introduction of minibuses in early 1987 saw Little Nippers on the streets of Doncaster, Rotherham and Sheffield. In Sheffield service 60, the frequent Hospital and University service, which was subjected to competition from Sheffield and District, was re-launched as the 'Sixty Shuttle'. The fleet of Metrobuses allocated to this service gained between-decks branding and window vinyls. The impression was very effective and

buses on service 60 could be easily identified amongst the streams of buses in Sheffield's High Street. The corresponding Little Nipper Service to Lodge Moor, service M60, was similarly branded and named 'Lodge Moor Link'.

Following the departure of the Author to Metrolink in Manchester, a new Operations Director was appointed. This was Bob Montgomery of minibus 'fame' in Devon and Manchester. The competitive situation became very intense and services such as No. 52 had three operators competing against SYT for business. Bob soon started changing things with minibuses replacing double-deckers. A new structure within SYT centralised marketing and service planning, removed Garage Managers and had garage structure based upon Operations Managers and Engineering Managers. The marketing and network aspects of the Company were developed in the early 1990s, with a massive publicity campaign which was aimed at reducing the passenger recession, which was at an all-time high of around 18% per annum.

By this time the much reported 'bus wars' in Sheffield were well under way and public attention was frequently being drawn to the number of buses passing through city centre streets, such as High Street, and causing their own congestion. Meanwhile in Rotherham and Doncaster comparably little competitive activity was experienced, although Wilfreda Beehive in Doncaster and Gordons in Rotherham had started to run local services. Coachcraft in Doncaster, that had started up at deregulation, quickly pulled out of bus operations, but the long established Leon Motors started to expand beyond their previously restricted services.

Acquisitions

The first acquisition by South Yorkshire Transport Ltd. as successors to SYPTE took place on 27th June 1988, when H. Wilson Ltd, trading as 'Premier' was purchased. This was one of the original companies identified in the early days of the PTE as an acquisition being desirable in the pursuance of the County's policy on integration. Contact with Mr. R. Wilson, the proprietor, had been maintained over the years, and it was no surprise when he decided to sell to SYT despite receiving offers from other groups. In any event, the Premier operation could not be regarded as totally free standing, as all the services to the North East of Doncaster were jointly operated with SYT, and had been since SYPTE acquired the first independent in Doncaster in 1976.

In its fight back campaign against the West Riding incursion in Sheffield, SYT formed a joint company in Wakefield known as Compass Buses in partnership with a Mr P. Bell who had previously operated coaches there. In a very short space of time a substantial fleet of ex-SYT buses including Nationals, Dodges, Leopards and even Dennis Dominos were running in Wakefield in competition with West Riding. This acquisition, on 9th November 1988, of Compass Buses Ltd. was, however, a little different. This company had only been established the previous year to carry out operations in the Wakefield area, with SYT having a minority share in the business. The acquisition represented the purchase of the remaining part of the company, and this preceded a strategy which was to unfold over the next twelve month. Before this happened the business of Richardson Travel Ltd was acquired on 26th June, 1989. Richardson had been a coach operator prior to deregulation, but moved into bus operation after 1986. Interestingly the business brought with it a service to Manchester, a city that had been served by SYPTE up to 1986.

Nineteen-eighty-nine was a momentous year for South Yorkshire Transport. The previous year had seen a veritable explosion of new operators in Sheffield; Yorkshire Terrier had commenced on 1st August (Yorkshire Day!); Sheafline PSV Ltd. had commenced in

Dodges in Eager Beaver livery arrived on the Sheffield scene in February 1989 on service 52; they were later extended to other services such as route 33, where 313 is seen in Haymarket.
(Mike Greenwood)

Competition was not confined to Sheffield; in Doncaster, after an initial foray by Crystals, Wilfreda Beehive (a merger of two previous coach operators) became established. A Leyland National new to Bristol Omnibus is waiting at Lothian Road terminus. *(Mike Greenwood)*

September; and Andrews had commenced on 3rd October. These joined the existing operations of Mike Groves; Sheffield & District, by now a Caldaire Holdings subsidiary; and SUT Ltd., owned by ATL (Holdings) and operating out of the old National Travel (East) (and before that, Sheffield United Tours) garage at Charlotte Road. This had been used by Sheffield & District from 1986 until 1987 during the time that both Sheffield & District and National Travel (East) had been owned by the West Riding Group. Four of these operators were acquired in 1989, leading to about 50% of SYT's operations being converted to Mainline, Eager Beaver or Little Nipper identity. Some Dennis Dominos sported the Little Nipper livery. Sheffield and District was purchased in September 1989 whilst SUT followed in October, Groves in November and Sheafline in December. Such a large number of acquisitions in such a short period raised the interest of the MMC, which was asked in the following March by the Secretary of State to investigate and report.

Both SUT and Sheafline were in serious difficulty with the Traffic Commissioners over vehicle maintenance. SUT negotiated a sale to SYT whilst Sheafline very nearly sold the business to North Western before being acquired by SYT.

The fourth company taken over that became the subject of the MMC investigation was Sheafline. *(Gary Nolan)*

SYT rationalised its acquired businesses onto the Charlotte Road site and the new fleet adopted the Sheafline name and fleet livery, standardising almost entirely on the Leyland National type. The premises of Groves, Richardsons, Sheffield and District, and Sheafline's Tinsley tram shed were closed down and a new management team brought in to run the acquired Sheafline fleet from its Charlotte Road site. In January 1991 a further operator appeared, Basic Hour, trading as Sheffield Omnibus. A twelve vehicle operation started using ex-Preston Atlantean AN68/2s.

An acquisition which did not cause concern within the MMC was that of Don Valley Bus Services (Beenak) from Stevensons of Uttoxeter. This fourteen bus operation runs as a separate Company utilising Mercedes mini and midibuses, along with several cascaded Dodge S56s from the main fleet. The mix of operations between tendered and commercial is about 50/50 within Don Valley, whereas within the main Company the proportion of commercial operation is now above 90%.

Before long another regrouping of the remaining companies was under way. The Andrews fleet was sold to Yorkshire Traction followed by that of South Riding and by 1995 the fleets of Yorkshire Terrier and Sheffield Omnibus similarly were disposed to the Barnsley operator. Traction closed down its acquired premises at Blackburn Road (South Riding), Darnall (Andrews) and Chesterfield (SOC) in its quest to develop the profitability of its Sheffield business and concentrated on only two sites, the Ecclesfield one and that at Halfway. The Yorkshire Terrier fleet retained its livery whilst the other buses at Ecclesfield started to appear in a light blue and cream colour scheme with the fleet name Andrews Sheffield Omnibus on the side.

Vehicles

There have been significant changes on the vehicle front since deregulation. The introduction of 240 Reeve Burgess

and Northern Counties bodied Dodge S56s between 1987 and 1991 ousted all of the remaining Fleetlines, and almost all of the large fleet of Atlanteans in Sheffield. A small batch of coach-seated Alexander-bodied Dennis Dominators introduced in 1987 enhanced the 'Fastline' fleet, several of them being initially allocated to the growing Coachline Fleet for use on popular Coastal Express Services. Dodge MkII and III were the standard vehicle, some with Northern Counties bodies but the rest were all Reeve Burgess. Amongst these acquisitions were four Ivecos that were purchased second-hand to fill a vehicle shortage and although non-standard and smaller than the rest of the minibus fleet these buses have given excellent service mainly in the Doncaster fleet. Later deliveries of Dodge minibuses were fitted with Allison transmissions which extended the gearbox life tremendously when compared with the original Dodge Torqueflite units; these were never really man enough for the hilly terrain around Sheffield.

Following the purchase of Sheafline and SUT, initially the fleet remained more or less as when acquired. Groves and Richardson's vehicles were not acquired. The operation of Leyland Nationals has had its problems. Fortunately, the Mark IIs, those fitted with Gardner engines and the two Greenways, are a little more reliable. The need to reduce the National fleet had led to the new vehicle order mentioned above.

However, by this time SYT was improving the presentation of its fleet by adopting a new livery of red and yellow introducing the Mainline trading name. This move followed great internal activity that saw drivers being specialised on to individual routes and particular efforts being made to improve customer care. In Rotherham a yellow and blue version was used whereas in Doncaster a red, yellow and silver colour scheme was adopted. The Mainline livery was standardised on the red and yellow scheme but with a blue and silver band around the skirt panels. Very quickly this bright livery was applied to the

In comparison with earlier events, the takeover in 1994/5 of the three operators seen above, namely Yorkshire Terrier, Sheffield Omnibus and Andrews, by Yorkshire Traction, did not result in an enquiry. At the rear is a Mainline vehicle in current livery. *(Mike Greenwood)*

whole fleet and the Mainline name replaced the old SYT fleet names overnight.

Probably the most outstanding purchase was of 140 Alexander PS-bodied Volvo B10M saloons from 1991 to 1995. These vehicles were introduced as part of the process of introducing new standards of comfort to customers and drivers and converting services to Mainline branding. In order to test the midibus market a Plaxton Pointer-bodied Volvo B6, and Northern Counties-bodied Dennis Dart, were purchased in 1992. After twelve months of operation there was very little to chose between them, although the B6's air suspension rides a little better on Sheffield's terrible roads. At the time of writing a Volvo B10L low floor bus is on trial. Thirty-five Volvo B6s have also been delivered with Pointer bodies. Forty more Alexander-bodied Volvo B10Ms were delivered from February 1996.

Buyout of Company

Almost since its conception, the employees of SYT had cherished a desire to buy the company but it took almost four years of protracted negotiations before this was achieved. Whilst the owner – the PTA – had always been reluctant to sell, there was increasing pressure from the Government for disposal, with the result that early in 1993 the PTA agreed, with some reluctance, to a sale taking place. However, only the bus operating business was to be sold to the employees, and the assets were to be retained with South Yorkshire Transport which was subsequently somewhat confusingly renamed SYPTA Ltd, now managed by the ubiquitous Bob Rowe.

In order to effect the sale in this manner, therefore, a subsidiary of SYT was formed named Mainline Group Ltd. This name was chosen as it had been decided that

building on the success of the 'Mainline' concept, all the operations should be so branded. Thus from 7th June, 1993 the bus operations of SYT were 'hived down' into Mainline, a company with a new operator's licence and therefore a new set of service registrations. Subsequently Mainline Group Ltd was sold to its employees on 16th November 1993 as an ESOP although all the property remained with the parent company. This was a particularly equitable arrangement whereby all staff (with two years' service) were given shares – the number depending upon length of service not rank or salary levels. Before this was done, the SUT operations at Charlotte Road, which by now were only branded as 'Sheafline' were transferred to Greenland Road and Herries Road with effect from 17th July 1993.

Mainline had subsequently acquired the vacant East Bank garage and utilised the opportunity of re-opening this location and closing down its Leadmill and Herries operating centres. It had already closed down the Charlotte Road site and merged the Sheafline fleet into Greenland Road and Herries Road.

Current operations are run from Olive Grove Garage (re-opened 1994) Greenland, Halfway, Rotherham, Leger Way (formerly Leicester Avenue) and Bootham Lane at Dunscroft. Compared with 1986 the Company is more efficient and more customer orientated. The use of computer systems has grown considerably to such an extent that job losses amongst official staff continue each year. The future for Mainline is rosy, despite the new wave of competition in the form of Andrews, Sheffield Omnibus, Supertram,

The Middlewood corridor was the first to use the Mainline unit concept and branding and here No. 1692 operates in the original Sheffield Mainline livery. *(Mike Greenwood)*

In Doncaster the yellow gave way to battleship grey when the unit was established in 1990. *(Mike Greenwood)*

The Rotherham Mainline version used the traditional blue (as a band) in its version. Number 2429 represents the type. *(Mike Greenwood)*

South Riding and Yorkshire Terrier in Sheffield, and Wilfreda Beehive in Doncaster. Fortunately, Mainline has grown out of a pedigree background, and has survived the change from an operation which was heavily subsidised, to one which is more dependent on a good customer base, which it certainly is aiming to build on.

(Upper) In due course the decision was taken to utilise a standard Mainline livery and the suffixes were dropped. Volvo B10M No. 698 displays the current style, which acknowledges its predecessors by the inclusion of blue and grey bands. *(Mike Greenwood)*

(Lower) In 1990 a trial commenced (shades of 1978!) with the introduction of a Plaxton Pointer bodied Volvo B6 (No 401, seen above) and a Northern Counties Paladin bodied Dennis Dart. Subsequently in 1995 30 Plaxton bodied Volvo B6s entered service, although built to a 9.9m length with 40 seats, rather than the 8.5m length and 34 seats of the original. *(David Cole)*

SUPERTRAM

A map showing the extent of the Supertram system. Terminii are shown as follows: Middlewood – top left; Meadowhall – top right; Halfway – lower right;

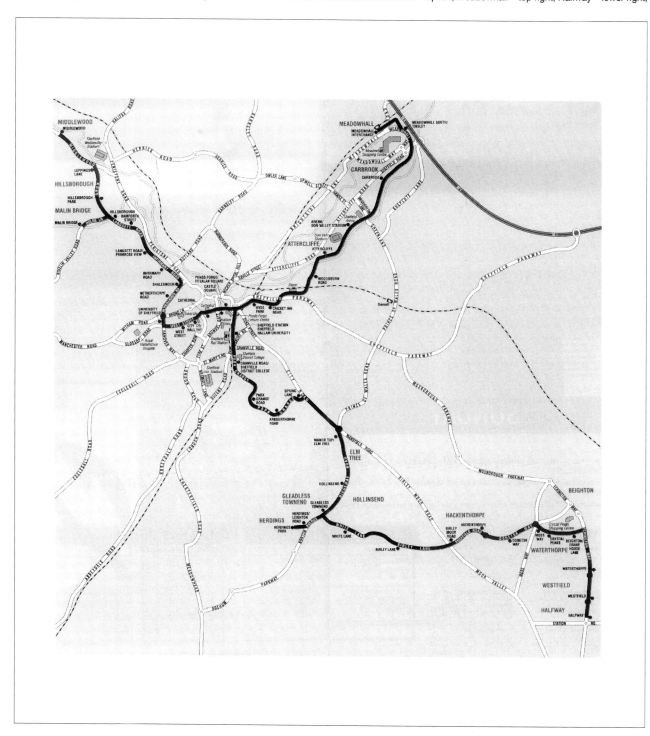

Although Supertram forms the final chapter in this 25 year review of South Yorkshire's Transport, its story predates this period. The subject of 'light rail' or 'segregated passenger transport systems' (SPTS) has been a theme which has run in parallel throughout the period covered by this book, although it only came to fruition in 1994 – hence its position in the book.

In the mid-1960s Tom Constantine, a Senior Lecturer in the Department of Civil Engineering at Sheffield University, and a Junior Research Assistant, A.P. (Tony) Young (later to be very well-known in PTE circles) undertook a preliminary study into the feasibility of re-introducing trams into Sheffield[30]. Shortly afterwards Tom Constantine became Professor of Civil Engineering at Salford University and Tony followed him across the Pennines.

The subject of LRT/SPTS surfaced again in the S/R LUTS Study to which reference has already been made earlier in the book[7]. The PTE's *Transport Development Plan*[17] commented that S/R LUTS 'looked closely at a streetcar system serving the main radial routes as in Sheffield, with an extension to Rotherham .... Further tests showed that a reduced (LRT) network was more cost-effective and recommended it for further examination, and possible introduction after 1986'. From this a basic 7-line radial network was proposed with lines radiating to Middlewood, Stannington, Mosborough, Rotherham, Shiregreen, Jordanthorpe and Totley, with a common gyratory arrangement in the city centre. The Plan[17] made a number of references to LRT in connection with both the medium to longer term operational planning proposals and when dealing with vehicle design and development, new system and energy. It concluded by remarking: 'a segregated transit system could have notable advantages in reliability, cleanliness, quietness, higher acceleration and average speeds and cheapness of operation'.

The high capital cost was a serious drawback and articulated buses were seen as an interim solution on the main routes. It was thought that 'a segregated system would be more successful in acting as an alternative to the private car ....'. Readers will note the use of the euphemism 'segregated transit system' or 'segregated passenger transport system' (SPTS) was slipping into use. The Executive – ever cautious – did not want to nail its colours to the LRT mast. To an extent that was understandable because of the high capital cost of any such scheme and its unproven nature – in British eyes. It has to be remembered that in 1977/78 there were very few people pushing LRT, whilst the Executive was staffed with Directors who had actual experience of trams and, in some cases, had participated in their demise. Nobody would accept a 're-invented tram', 'light rail' was barely understood and 'Supertram' was not even thought of – so SPTS literally became the shorthand. However, the Executive approved the S/R LUTS findings regarding SPTS, and similar approval was given in the County Structure Plan in 1979.

The next step was for the PTE to set up an 'SPTS' Team under the direction of the Controller of Operations & Planning (the Author) and drawing staff from both the Planning Section and the Engineering Department. Key people involved were Roger Pickup, Bernard Pratt, Richard Barlow and John Jordan. This team produced a report *The Future Development of Public Transport in Sheffield – Results of Preliminary Investigation*[31] in January 1980. This proposed that a Feasibility Study should be undertaken. The team was widened to become the SPTS Working Group with the County involved through the JTPU.

The SPTS Working Group reviewed in great detail the options available for improvement of public transport, including bus-based systems such as trolleybuses and guided buses, and also rail-based systems, both totally segregated and street running. In July 1983 a report was published entitled *Segregated Passenger Transport System*[32]. This recommendation to the County Council that a modern tramway system was the preferred option. The Study had shown that '.... if segregation could be justified, giving reduced running times and increased reliability, with attendant benefits to both passenger and operator, the light rail system was the most cost-effective. Trolleybus associated infrastructure costs could not produce the productivity sufficient to finance the investment, because of the limitation on vehicle size.

In June 1982 the Research Section of SYPTE's Engineering Department had produced a major Research Report entitled *A Technology Assessment of a Light Rail System* which provided substantial input to the 1983 Report[32]. Up to now the work had looked at all the corridors in Sheffield previously identified[7] as being candidates for SPTS. Following consideration of the 1983 Report[32], and for reasons outlined below, it was decided to concentrate efforts on the Hillsborough and Mosborough corridors.

It should be appreciated that the Executive was pursuing a multi-strand philosophy:

– improvements to existing operations through improved vehicle maintenance, staff recruitment and bus priorities
– developing a new standard bus to produce further improvement and to reduce costs, with more extensive bus priorities
– operation of articulated buses with maximum priorities possible, short of segregation, on main trunk routes
– evaluation of alternative traction modes and degrees of 'track' segregation

Such an approach yielded spin-off benefits at every stage, it was a process of continuous improvement. "It kept the planners feet on the ground whilst raising the horizons of the operators", as the Author once commented.

The key issue was the degree of segregation. Sheffield had pioneered Urban Clearways. Many of these developed into fully-fledged Bus Only Lanes, but these stopped short of the stop line at traffic lights. The next steps would involve the setting back of kerbs at some junctions, often involving minor land acquisition. It was going to be more awkward and more expensive, unless measurable benefits could be shown. The more powerful buses and the bus priorities had enabled bus times to be retained in periods of substantial car growth.

It is also true to say that it was well nigh impossible to negotiate reduced running times, thus benefits were hard to quantify. It is for these and other reasons that the operation of artic buses did not extend to the 81/84 group of services in the Ecclesall-Middlewood via city centre corridor. However, this earlier work on the Middlewood leg of this corridor was used for a detailed assessment of articulated buses (both trolley and diesel) and light rail. Having regard to the developing nature of Mosborough and the need to safeguard possible segregated routes, this corridor was also selected. It will also be remembered that the Hillsborough and Mosborough corridors were amongst those proposed by S/R LUTS. This corridor was 25 km. long and traversed the city centre.

As the work became more technical, the direction and composition of the SPTS Team changed. Bill Kirkland, as Controller of Engineering and Property Services, joined the Author as co-director of the Study and the JPTU was brought in more fully. The involvement of both the Planning Section and Engineering Department also increased, involving Bill Bland amongst others. With the publication of the 'Buses' White Paper and the subsequent lobbying in London the Author gradually withdrew from the scene. However, detailed work continued throughout 1984 and 1985 on proposals for a light rapid transit system linking Hillsborough with Mosborough via the City Centre. This was incorporated into *The South Yorkshire Light Rail Transit Bill*[33], which was deposited in Parliament in November 1985.

Parliamentary Progress

The Parliamentary Powers sought in this Bill were for an LRT line to run from Middlewood (Winns Gardens) by way of Middlewood Road, Langsett Road, with a junction at Hillsborough Corner for a branch from Holme Lane and Stannington, then along Infirmary Road, Netherthorpe Road, Glossop Road, West Street, Church Street, High Street, Commercial Street, over Park Square, Granville Street, up through the Norfolk Park Estate and Gleadless to Birley and Halfway. There was to be a second branch from Gleadless Town End to Herdings. Before the Bill had reached the opposed Bills Committee in the House of Commons, the PTE agreed to withdraw the line from Malin Bridge to Stannington, at the request of Sheffield City Council.

There were two official objectors to the scheme: a resident's group and National Car Parks Ltd (NCP). However, there were doubts as to how committed Sheffield City Council was to the project, and Parliamentary procedures were adjourned on two occasions before the Bill passed the Commons Stage on 20th April 1988. In order for the City Council to re-assess the proposals and give their unreserved backing to the Bill, then stalled in the Commons, a period of intensive consultations took place. This included an exhibition housed in a mock-up of a Supertram car outside the Cathedral, which took place between 12th and 26th September 1987. The public

response was very encouraging with 65% wanting the project to go ahead. Public meetings were also arranged at various centres affected by the proposals. Comforted by the outcome of these consultations and the re-assessment study, the City Council overwhelmingly endorsed the Supertram Scheme at their meeting in October 1987. The House of Lords Opposed Committee also heard, during July 1988, objections from a group of residents and traders, together with objections from the Sheffield and District Chamber of Trade. However, the Bill finally received the Royal Assent on 27th October 1988, nearly three years after its deposition.

The argument with Sheffield City Council was an interesting one and was to be (or still is) a recurring theme in the Supertram story. It also harks back to the very earliest days of South Yorkshire County Council and SYPTE. When it became clear in the late 1970s and early 1980s that work should be put in hand, with a view to achieving, one day, an SPTS system, it was always the view of the Executive that this was a solution to Sheffield's transport problems; it was to benefit and help the city. Therefore, subject to getting satisfactory consultation arrangements, there should be no problems. The Senior members of the Passenger Transport Committee saw it slightly differently in that they guarded their 'rights', as a transport authority, jealously. There is more than a slight irony here since both Councillor Thwaites, who was a former City Councillor and Alex Waugh, represented a City Ward. The Executive pointed out that without the City's co-operation it would be very difficult to achieve the SPTS project. Such a debate would not have gone on in Grenoble or Karlsruhe or even in Portland or San Diego. The public transport industry is good at falling out with itself – perhaps that is why it consistently loses market share!

During the Bill's passage through Parliament both the Transport Act 1985 and the Local Government Act 1985 were passed, changing the ground rules for the project. Supertram had been conceived as the backbone to an integrated public transport system. It was to largely replace buses in the corridors concerned and bus/tram interchanges were to be developed. However, if the project went ahead Supertram would find itself competing for market share in the deregulated free-for-all. Thus in 1987 the viability of Supertram was re-evaluated. This further study concluded that there was still an economic case for it. (A similar re-evaluation was undertaken in the case of Manchester's Metrolink which added another 2½ years (from 1985 to 1988) to the approval of that scheme.)

Meadowhall Line

The City Council's approval in October 1987 came with certain conditions, however. Firstly, a revised alignment had to be found from Manor Top along City Road to Park Grange Road, because the City was renovating parts of the Manor Estate. Secondly, the City wanted the Supertram system extending to serve the Lower Don Valley to assist with its urban regeneration, following the collapse of the steel industry. There was an added objective of serving the proposed new sports Arena, being built for the World Student Games, due to take place in 1991. There were two further requirements (!) namely: that the depot should be re-sited in the Lower Don Valley and not at Halfway as originally envisaged, and that this new – Don Valley – line should be opened first, originally to serve the Games [34]. Again it is incredible, but typical of Sheffield and South Yorkshire, how such major changes could be injected into a scheme, eleven years after S/R LUTS, the PTE Plan of 1978 and the County Structure Plan of 1979.

In February 1988 the PTA authorised SYPTE to evaluate the route for this second line, which had to connect with the 'original' line from Hillsborough to Mosborough, and had to be capable of extension to Rotherham, in line with earlier proposals. It also had to have regard to the proposals for a future Sheffield Airport then being seriously considered for the Don Valley. Fortunately for the planners the former four track alignment of the GC line from Sheffield to Rotherham, on the east side of the valley, was available. Furthermore, there was plenty of redundant railway land in the Nunnery Area. The Study had to be completed in July 1988 and the Bill for the second (Don Valley) line deposited that November.

The South Yorkshire Light Rapid Transit (No. 2) Bill sought powers for:

- the construction of a delta junction at Park Square
- the construction of Parkway Viaduct to run from Park Square to Bernard Road. It was to lie to the South side of the Sheffield Parkway and cross the former Midland line where it is in a cutting.
- an alignment running parallel to Cricket Inn Road
- a bridge across the Parkway
- land for the Depot itself, laying between the Parkway and the former GC line
- a bridge across the GC line near Woodburn Junction
- an alignment along Woodburn Road, crossing Staniforth Road and the Sheffield and South Yorkshire Canal to join the former GC Rotherham line near the Don Valley Stadium
- an alignment parallel to the BR line and then following the former Smithwood/Chapeltown GC route, now parallel and adjacent to the M1 Tinsley Viaduct, before curving back on itself in a single line to terminate at Meadowhall Interchange.

Line 2 was to be completely segregated from other traffic, except at road crossings, of which there were 6 at Bernard Road, Aston Street, Woodburn Road, Staniforth Road, Shirland Lane and Alsing Road [34]. Thus it was to be very different from Line 1 which was entirely street running, albeit with substantial lengths of segregation. Being a fully segregated line had benefits in introducing light rail into the city in a 'gentle' way, so the public became acclimatised to the concept and appreciated its benefits, before encountering the 'difficulties' of street running, particularly in the City Centre. Furthermore such a phased approach would assist in staff training and vehicle testing.

Not only was the No. 2 Bill unopposed in Parliament, it received support from many quarters, including the Chamber of Trade [34]. (Perhaps all parties had learnt the meaning of consultation!) However all was not over. A furious row developed in Parliament with two Opposition MPs threatening all Parliamentary business unless another Private Bill relating to facilities for coal imports was dropped or amended. In due time common sense prevailed and the No. 2 Bill received the Royal Assent on 21st December 1989 – thirteen years after the original idea.

Funding the Scheme

Of course it is one thing to obtain Parliamentary Powers, it is quite another to obtain the necessary finance. In late 1988 SYPTA/SYPTE made an application to the Government for an Infrastructure Grant, under Section 56 of the Transport Act 1968. (It is amazing how the benefits of this Act, which set in motion this whole story, keep coming back!) This was the approach used for all public transport infrastructure schemes outside London, and had been successfully used for Metrolink. Having made the application, after numerous preparatory discussions with DTp officials, it came as no surprise that the criteria for paying Infrastructure Grant were to be radically altered. It happens to virtually every public transport scheme – WCML electrification, T & W Metro, Metrolink et al – but *never* to road schemes! The new rules meant that benefits to users had to be accounted for by their paying higher fares, and depended upon the scheme being profitable, including contributions from developers. Traditionally user social benefits had been the principal justification for schemes.

A further set-back to funding came in November 1989, when the Government told the local authorities that resources would not available in 1990/91 for those elements of Supertram relating to the World Student Games. It was stated that the Government were already investing many millions of pounds in transport infrastructure referring in great detail to the roads programme! Despite this comment the Sheffield Development Corporation (SDC) secured a further £14m grant at this time to ensure the building of a highway through the Lower Don Valley. Private investors had already shown a willingness to become involved in the scheme. There were urgent meetings with the civil servants, in an attempt to keep the project moving forward and keeping the design team together, but the request for a similar grant was refused in February 1990. It was accepted that the project should be safeguarded and £3.5m was allocated for that purpose and for taking the project forward [34].

On 11th December 1990, the Minister for Public Transport – Roger Freeman MP – announced that resources had been made available to fund the majority of the project's costs of £240m. Contributions were also announced as coming from the Meadowhall Centre, SDC and Sheffield City Council, as well as support from the European Regional Development Fund (ERDF). Unfortunately the 'gilt was taken off the gingerbread' by a political argument over possible council charge-capping (the current equivalent of rate-capping in the mid 1980s) and this brought further delay, only being resolved in April 1991 – sixteen months after Royal Assent![34] Why cannot the obtaining of Powers and public grants run in parallel on a 'without prejudice basis'?

Analysis of Funding	£m
Infrastructure Grant	54
ERDF	13
Developer contribution	8
Loans, including interest	165
	240

It was anticipated that the 25 years operating franchise would be sold for £82m, thus giving a net cost of the scheme of £158m.

In determining future usage it is necessary to make forecasts about what degree of competition there would be with the new Supertram system. Whilst a range of forecasts can be produced, based on different assumptions, and sensitivity analyses can be carried out, it is hard to make a cast-iron case. Supertram patronage is very sensitive to bus competition, in terms of choice of service, frequency, journey time and cost. Experience in Tyne & Wear was that immediately after deregulation there was a high level of competition, but this was replaced in time by a more common sense approach. Metrolink also suffered severe competition in the Bury-Manchester corridor. In addition to there being direct competition from GM Buses (then a shareholder in Metrolink!). Metrolink was also affected by the backwash from bus-bus competition along sections of the route. Price elasticity is also partly affected by the level of bus competition. In modelling increased fares, non-user benefits are reduced. Many passengers could not afford to pay the full user benefits. There were also indications that the decongestion benefits produced by light rail systems have been underestimated[35].

Privatisation

Although the Supertram project was to be built with substantial public grants, a Government requirement of the approval of the scheme was that the operation should be transferred to the private sector in due course. (This was different to the approach taken in Manchester, where the Government had insisted that the construction and operation should be undertaken by the private sector and in one single DBOM (design, build, operate and maintain) contract.)

A wholly-owned subsidiary of SYPTE, South Yorkshire Supertram Ltd. (SYSL 1) had been established in 1989 to take the project forward. However, another company – SYSL 2 – was formed to become the operator (and maintainer) of the system for the concessionary period[34]. The idea was that the assets – infrastructure and rolling stock – should be retained by the PTE, since most were built with public funds. However, once SYSL 2 had built up a track-record of profitable operation, it would be sold to the private sector. Again this was a variation on the approach adopted in Manchester but the Government's objective was the same the privatisation of public transport.

Since in both cases the PTAs were of a socialist persuasion, they were not happy with these ideas. However, they realised that without acceding to the Government's requirements, they would not be able to fund their project. On privatisation SYPTE will be allowed to retain 15% of SYSL shares.

Whilst not wishing to descend into party politics, it must be said that the South Yorkshire arrangements are even more tortuous than those adopted in Manchester – and they were bad enough. Building light rail systems in urban areas is not easy. Pioneering such schemes – or re-inventing the tram in Britain's case – was difficult enough with conventional arrangements and forms of contract. Furthermore, nobody really understands the single entity DBOM or divided entity DB:OM approach including DTp officials, contractors or elected members and their officials.

DESIGN

The Meadowhall line, originally Line 2, was built as Phase 1. It is fully segregated over its 7 km. length. Use was made of 3 km. of existing railway alignment, the formation being shared by a single freight track. Of the remaining 22km. of the Middlewood-Mosborough Section, the line is either fully street running, segregated in central reservations, adjacent to highways on existing verges or on undeveloped land. The object was to provide a high quality public transport system offering reliable, regular services with good accessibility to all, and journey times competitive with the car. The need to integrate the swept path of the tram into the environment through which it was passing, was of crucial importance. £2.5m had been allowed for hard and soft landscaping.

Design Process

A project team involving the key organisations was established and included: SYSL, its project managers and consultants, SYPTE and the City Council (as highway and planning authority). Her Majesty's Railway Inspectorate (HMRI) and the Police were involved as and when required. The swept path alignment was developed from the original Parliamentary preliminary design layout and the tram characteristics, to establish basic on-street clearances. The swept path is wider than the tram because it allows for the end-throw and centre-throw of the vehicle itself. The basic parameters of the vehicle were: length 35m. (in three sections); width 2.65 m; minimum horizontal radius 25m. and maximum vertical curve 165 m.

The development of the swept path established the initial alignment and the tramway, highway, traffic management and accommodation works. In turn this was developed by the highway consultants and those responsible for the major structures, so that the vertical and horizontal alignments of the track and the highway could be determined. Under the design-and-build contract, the detailed design then passed to the infrastructure contractor, Balfour Beatty Power Construction, whose design consultants were Sir Owen Williams and Partners. The design of an alignment is an iterative process and is, invariably, a compromise to suit the requirements of the tramway operator, the highway authority, the townplanners, the interests of road users and pedestrians. 1/500 scale drawings were produced which formed the basis of the final engineering construction drawings.

Consultations on the design

A protocol was agreed between SYPTE – the promoters of the Scheme, and who had the Parliamentary Powers – and the City Council whereby designated officers covering transportation, traffic and urban planning disciplines, joined the project working groups. In addition a formal procedure had been agreed, whereby all the designs were processed through the City Council's committee structure. A three stage process was adopted:

Stage 1.   Approval of draft detailed design as the basis for public consultation
Stage 2   Report back from consultation and agreement in principle
Stage 3   Consideration of and agreement to the final detailed design

Peter Gross of South Yorkshire Supertram commented that – "This procedure is as much political as professional in nature and it has worked remarkably well".

As the draft detailed design became available for each of the eight stages, public exhibitions and meetings were organised, supported by extensive publicity, to ensure local residents and businesses could air their views[36]. This consultation process took some four years to complete and there were some 400 meetings.

Interface with road traffic

A crucial element in any street-running tramway or LRT system is to ensure that it gets the maximum amount of priority at signalled road junctions. This is achieved by having transponders in the track connected to the traffic light control system. The passage of the tram activates the transponder. Transponders are also used in advance of tramway junctions, so that an approaching tram can automatically set the route it requires.

Particular attention has been focussed on minimising the interaction between the tram and other traffic. At both priority and signalised junctions, where there is significant turning traffic, separate lanes have been provided to protect tram movements or minimise delays to through movements from queueing vehicles. Wherever possible, the swept path has been segregated in the central reserve, such as at Netherthorpe Road or Ridgeway Road (inbound) or within a wide highway verge as on Donetsk Way and Eckington Way at Mosborough. All movements on and off highway are under traffic signal control. Significant thought has been given to road signing and lining, especially where the tramway layout is unusual and there is potential for accidents during the formative operation period. Differential surface colour, extensive confirmatory signage and lining, and improved lighting have been adopted to clarify acceptable traffic movement practice. [36]

Pedestrian Facilities

In view of potential road safety problems of cars overtaking trams on single carriageway roads, especially at tramstops, central islands have been constructed to prevent these manoeuvres. In many locations these are integrated with new or replacement pedestrian crossing facilities, especially adjacent to tramstops and major signalised junctions. The project has upgraded pedestrian access on many parts of the alignment[36]. Interim arrangements were provided at temporary terminal locations to allow for the phased opening of the system, for example in Fitzalan Square.

Tramstops

A standard design of tramstop was developed so that the whole system has a unified image. In nearly every case straight, side platforms have been used. These are 480 mm above rail level and this permits level boarding and alighting. The furniture on each platform – lighting standards, fencing, nameboards, litter bins, shelters, etc – form a matching set and the resultant effect is of a very neat appearance. The concrete block platform surfaces are supplemented by special tactile blocks. They indicate both the edge of the platform and the door locations of the tram. Shelters are provided by Abacus. The ticket machines – two issuers and one cancellor – are located in the shelters, except where no shelters are provided. Surprisingly, there are no seats at any of the stops[37].

PROJECT MANAGEMENT

In July 1989 SYPTE appointed Turner & Townsend as Project Managers, rather than having an in-house team, as had been done by GMPTE for Metrolink. Their first job was to appraise the returned tenders for both infrastructure works and rolling stock. Advanced design work was sanctioned during 1990/91 with the release of the £3.5m of development funds. Work began on site on 5th August 1991. In addition to the 29 km. of double track line electrified at 750v DC, there were 45 tramstops and 25 engineering structures – some of these were very impressive:

– the steel-bowstring arch girder bridge in Park Square
– the glued-segmental post-tensioned re-inforced concrete Parkway Viaduct
– the steel and composite Norfolk Park Viaduct and several bridges spanning railways and canals.

The project managers reported directly to the Chief Executive of South Yorkshire Supertram Ltd., John Davies – himself an experienced project manager. SYSL was, of course, a wholly-owned subsidiary of SYPTE who were, de facto, the Client. Turner & Townsend also managed, on behalf of the Client, the team of consultant technical advisers, the infrastructure and rolling stock contractors and other specialists and suppliers.

Design and Building Services (DBS) – the consultant arm of Sheffield City Council – acted as Structural, Civil and Highway engineering consultants. They – or their predecessors – had been involved since South Yorkshire County Council days. Similarly, Kennedy & Donkin Transportation (KDT) acted as mechanical, electrical and railway engineering consultants. They had been involved in the Parliamentary promotion stage. Frank Graham Consulting Engineers handled the public consultation and information matters. Following the closure of Bruntons, the architects and landscape consultants were Race Cottam Associates, Globe Architects and Plan Design [38].

On the design and building side, Balfour Beatty Power Construction Ltd. were appointed on 26th September 1990 to be responsible for all the civil and building work, including the power supply, overhead line system, signal installations, tramstops and depot. On the same date Siemens plc were responsible for the design, manufacture and commissioning of the 25 trams built in Germany by Siemens subsidiary, Duwag of Dusseldorf. Operations and maintenance contacts were dealt with later. The project management team was sixteen-strong and housed in SYSL's office, 11A Arundle Gate – the former District Office of SYPTE, pre 1986. A crucial element in project management is the control of interfaces between the different elements, different disciplines and different interests of all those involved in a project as complex as Supertram. Important external relations involve frontagers – be they domestic residences, shop units or industrial properties – and the public utilities, gas, water, BT, Mercury, etc. A meeting structure was devised feeding information and reports up to the monthly Management Steering Group, Chaired by SYSL's Chief Executive.

Time-Cost-Quality

A project master programme was mounted using Asta Power project software. This detailed each phase of design, consultation, construction, manufacture, commissioning and handover. Within the overall master programme there were numerous sub-programmes [38]. A project budget and cash flow across fourteen budget heads was also established. Client satisfaction is more difficult to achieve in a DBOM or DB contract arrangement, since 'fit for purpose criteria' are not always deemed as sufficient indicators of quality One way to achieve this is through a Performance or Reference Specification (the latter was adopted for Metrolink), but this must go into substantial detail if quality is to be ensured. In the case of Supertram, SYPTE required compliance with detailed technical quality standards, and imposed a comprehensive design approval process on the DB contractors. This process was operated and managed by the Project Managers, assisted by the technical consultants within the team.

CONSTRUCTION

Although construction work actually started on 5th August 1991, the official 'cutting the first sod' ceremony was carried out by Roger Freeman MP at Park Square on 16th September that year. Balfour Beatty were responsible for the detailed design and subsequent construction of the infrastructure. There were seven main elements: civil works, trackwork, overhead contact system, power supply and distribution, signalling system, SCADA system and the depot. Within each system there were many variables [34]. An analysis of the structures shows:

Retaining walls	32
Footbridges	12
Bridges	9
Subways	7
Viaducts	2
Underpasses	1
Culvert	1
	64

An estimated 1750 tonnes of steel, 4000 tonnes of re-inforcement steelwork and 23,000 cubic metres of concrete were used. There was 60 km. of trackbed and 120 tons of rail, over 50% of it being grooved tramway rail (Ri 60) inserted into pre-formed concrete channels and encapsulated in resin. Where ballasted track is used BS 80A rail is used. The overhead line consists of 120 km. of contact wire supported 5 – 6 m above the track (according to location). There are 2300 supports, poles or building fixings. The Supervisory Control and Data Acquisition (SCADA) system is based in the Control Centre at the Nunnery Depot.

Track laying taking place at Bernard Road on 4th March 1992. *(Bob Rowe)*

Amongst other things it controls the 750v DC power supplied through 12, 600kW substations (34). Regeneration is expected to provide about 10% of the power (39).

VEHICLE

In the days when Supertram was still 'SPTS' the vehicle selected had been Duwag's design for Frankfurt – the P8. This was a 3-section, four bogie car, 27.43 m. long and 2.35 m. wide, double-ended and double-sided and with four doors per side. It could load from low or high platforms, although in the former case there were two steps to climb. It could carry 170 passengers: 62 seated and 108 at 4m². A single ended, single sided version, to meet the foreseen Sheffield requirements, was 're-seated' to SYPTE then current bus standards, and would have had a capacity of 128 seated, with an all-up capacity of around 150[17]. It was hoped to purchase an existing design rather than design a vehicle specially for Sheffield.

Since the 1978/1982 period, tramway and light railways vehicle design has come a long way, with great emphasis being placed on low floor or partially low-floor vehicles. These ideas were pioneered by the Geneva transport undertaking in Switzerland in 1984 and then followed by Grenoble in 1987. Because of the gradients involved the Sheffield vehicle required to have all axles motored. To do this with conventional motors requires a high floor over the motor bogies. (Since specifying their vehicle, designs using 4-hub motors or designs with body-mounted motors driving through cardan shafts, have become available – at a price – and with unknown reliability levels.) Accordingly the front and rear sections have a low section (480 m. above rail) over a length of 11.8 m. where there are two doors in each section. The centre section – for longer distance travellers – is all seated and has no doors. It has a floor height of 880 mm. and is approached by three steps.

It remains to be seen how this arrangement works in practice on cross-city operation. The low section only represents 34% of the length and the doors are, of necessity, closely spaced. Passenger movement with the tram is, therefore, reduced. (Shades of the two-door bus problems discussed in Chapter 7!) The Supertram is 34.75 m. long – one of the longest ever built – and is 2.65 m. wide. It is built of Corten B Steel and weighs 44.5 tonnes unladen[39].

Undoubtedly it is a most imposing vehicle with a great performance and very quiet and smooth. The finish is up to the usual high Duwag standards – the seats are the same as in the Stuttgart light rail vehicle – designed to attract people out of their Mercedes cars! Rumour has it that when the initial Supertram was on trial in Dusseldorf on the Rheinischebahn system that it out-accelerated a BMW 500 series up to 30 mph – much to the surprise of the BMW driver!

The Supertram is supported on four Duwag bogies. All eight axles are motored to cope with the gradients of up to 10% (1 in 10). Each 277 kW motor drives 670 mm. diameter wheels. Bochum 84 type resilient wheels are fitted. Internally special care has been taken to provide passengers with sufficient grab handles. The interior lining for the ceiling consists of an aluminium honeycomb design, to which coloured melamine resin panels have been bonded. The lining is attached to suspension points welded to the roof section. The inside walls are made of coloured fibre-glass reinforced plastic. The rear wall of the driving cab is made of laminated wood with a melamine veneer[39]. It has large windows which permit a view forward, although the seats face backwards which reduces the effect. There are two designated wheel-chair spaces and room for others. The whole of the interior gives an airy, pleasant feel. It is sad that an impressive vehicle has such a non-descript livery. How is it no outstanding livery has been produced since the cream and dark blue of STD. One visitor to Sheffield remarked recently "when are they going to paint the Supertrams!" They entered service without destination blinds. The vehicles were delivered by road on a specially constructed trailer which came via Immingham, the first arriving on 26th August 1993.

OPERATION

The system opened in phases, as shown overleaf. Once sections of Lines 1 and 2 had been opened (from 22nd August 1994) the system nevertheless worked as two separate lines with parallel single line working from the Commercial Street terminus to the crossovers beyond the

The first tram to arrive inches its way closer to Nunnery depot on 26th August 1993.
(Bob Rowe)

Supertram No. 23 crossing over from wrong line working above Sheffield Station on 17th February 1995 the last day when the terminus of both lines was still Commercial Street. *(Bob Rowe)*

The completion of the system was marked by three days of free travel in October 1995; tram No. 02 is seen loading on the 25th in the City Centre. *(Bob Rowe)*

delta junction.

21st March 1994 to 21st August 1994
Meadowhall – Commercial Street

22nd August 1994 to 4th December 1994
Meadowhall – Commercial Street
Spring Lane – Commercial Street

5th December 1994 to 17th February 1995
Meadowhall – Commercial Street
Gleadless – Commercial Street

18th February 1995 to 26th February 1995
Meadowhall – Cathedral
Gleadless – Cathedral

27th February 1995 to 26th March 1995
Meadowhall – Cathedral
Halfway – Shalesmoor

3rd April 1995 to 3rd September 1995
Meadowhall – Cathedral

Halfway/Herdings – Shalesmoor

4th September to 22nd October 1995
Meadowhall – Shalesmoor (Yellow) (Monday
Halfway – Cathedral (Blue) (to
Herdings – Cathedral (Green) (Saturday

Halfway – Meadowhall (Purple) (Sundays
Herdings — Shalesmoor (Orange) (only

23rd October 1995
Meadowhall – Middlewood (Yellow) (Monday
Halfway – Malin Bridge (Blue) (to
Herdings – Cathedral (Green) (Saturday

Halfway – Meadowhall (Purple) (Sundays
Herdings – Malin Bridge (Orange) (only

The coloured route number pattern, introduced with effect from 4th September 1995, is shown in the route number box of the trams and all publicity. On weekdays services run from 0600 to midnight, and on the yellow and blue routes trams run every 10 minutes during the day, giving a 5-minute frequency over the common section between Hillsborough and Fitzalan Square. The green route operates every 30 minutes all day. The completion of the system was celebrated in October with three days of free travel over the whole of the network, and typical journey times from the Cathedral at this stage were:–

Meadowhall	18 minutes
Middlewood	21 minutes
Malin Bridge	19 minutes
Crystal Peaks	30 minutes
Halfway	38 minutes
Herdings	24 minutes

This timetable requires 22 trams (8 yellow, 12 blue and 2 green). One difficulty already being experienced in a bus deregulated market is that quicker times by bus can be offered by operators following a more direct route than the tram, albeit omitting most intermediate stops.

All trams are driven on sight and obey road traffic lights where there are signalled junctions. Here they have their own tram signals and often have priority, but not at all junctions. The maximum permitted speed on the system is 80 km/hr (50 mph) but is frequently lower because of curvature-imposed restrictions, eg 20 km/h (12mph) over the Bow String Bridge and round the delta junction When adjacent to, or running in, the highway the maximum speed permitted is that of the highway – usually 30 or 40 mph (48 or 64 km/h).

Driver Training

Driver training commenced on the running line in November 1993, whilst trial running started in the latter half of December 1993. Phase 2 driver training began on 11th July 1994 and trial running commenced on 8th August 1994[40]. All applicants for tram driving must have a valid motor vehicle licence. The training period is nine weeks. On average every Supertram driver received 30 hours of practical training before he or she underwent the qualification process.

Prior to Phase 1 six members of the senior staff went to Tuen Mun Light Rail Transit in Hong Kong – where Wilfred Lau had been in the operating management. They had a five-week intensive course in June 1993, two weeks of which were in driver training. Before going to Hong Kong they had spent a day at the National Tramway Museum, at Crich in Derbyshire, to gain some hands-on experience. They also visited Metrolink for a day to have an appreciation of light rail operation. None of the six had had any previous fixed rail experience and three had no experience of public transport. Three had come from the bus industry[40].

Before the first Supertram was delivered to Sheffield four Senior members of staff went to Dusseldorf for a three-day visit, to gain first-hand driving experience of the Supertram vehicle on the Rheinischebahn system, both in segregated and mixed traffic running conditions. One of these staff was included in the Tuen Mun Group, whilst another two had extensive experience in driving trams and LRVs. All of these earlier appointees had a heavy involvement in the testing and commissioning activities, and thus accumulated even more experience. A Test Driver from the Rheinischebahn came to Sheffield for two weeks to give advice to the commissioning teams, who, in due course, moved to train their colleagues. This cascade approach followed the lines of that adopted so successfully in Metrolink. A senior official of the Rhenischebahn's driver licensing authority came to Sheffield to assess the competence of the Supertram drivers.

During the trial running of Phase 1, Sheffield experienced blizzard conditions lasting several days. On one afternoon the whole city became snarled up with road traffic and Supertram was the only form of transport still running. Unfortunately it was not then open for public service – nevertheless a good omen for the future! [40]

Prior to the commencement of driver training for Phase 2, arrangements were made for four instructional staff to gain on-street town driving experience in British cities. They underwent a two-day driver training course at Blackpool, followed by a five-day driver training programme at Metrolink. This was followed by almost a week of solo driving between Fitzalan Square and Hillcrest before they took up the task of training their colleagues who had been driving on the Meadowhall line[40].

When looking to future phases, including the all-important section through the city centre, Wilfred Lau made an interesting observation in his 1994 paper[40] some parts of which have already been referred to. Lau said "It is hoped that the Supertram will be given absolute signalling priority at road crossings. It is also hoped that the extent of 'Trams Only' lanes will be increased significantly. It is understood that there are difficulties in doing so. However, such facilities could be given to the Supertram during core hours of the day, including peak periods. These will definitely shorten journey times and make them more predictable and reliable and hence make Supertram more attractive to car users....". This seems a strange comment to make so late in the project (November 1994) when priority and traffic management arrangements should have been built into the alignment at the design stage. Perhaps this reflects the lack of operating resources devoted to the project.

Fares and Ticketing

Supertram is a barrier-free system. Passengers are required to have bought their tickets prior to boarding the vehicle. Tickets may be bought from a number of sales outlets or from self-service vending machines on each platform.

Conceptually this pre-purchase follows LRT practice world-wide, and which works in Manchester though the inability to tender notes creates a different problem in the latter city. However, there were two problems apparent in Sheffield. Firstly, the ticket vending machines were, and are still considered by many to be slow in operation. Secondly, tickets had to be validated. In his article "Tram Operation in Sheffield"[37] Peter Fox commented that the fares and the fare collection system was the Achilles heel

The concept of having separate organisations for Operations and Maintenance has already undergone some change with SYSL taking over the maintenance responsibility directly, rather than through contracting it out. Assuming that the infrastructure and vehicles work satisfactorily, the success of Supertram will rest largely on the competitive environment in which it is forced to operate. Clearly it has a quality product and image on its side, but as bus deregulation has shown, a large part of the market makes decisions on the first-come first-served basis, especially if it is considerably cheaper.

of Supertram. Certainly the ticketing system has now been overhauled and tickets bought on the platform no longer require validation, thus speeding up the flow of passengers on to the trams..

The fares were high, having regard to the prevailing bus fares with which Supertram is still having to compete. Initially the fare if bought at a stop was either 50p, the minimum, which will take passengers a maximum of ten stops, or £1 which covers a single journey on the whole of the network. Books of five or ten single journey tickets can be bought from a ticket agent at a discount. Break-of-journey is permitted thus also making possible interchange between Lines, provided the total journey is completed within 90 minutes.

For Phase 1 Customer Service Staff were deployed on the vehicles themselves, assisting passengers to familiarise themselves with the new system, and to perform revenue protection duties. This ceased when Phase 2 was opened, when they were deployed for a similar role on the new section. Random ticket checks were carried out on Phase 1. Approximately 25% of all passengers carried were checked and 3.5% were found not to have a validated ticket; 0.16% had no ticket at all[40].

As with any system there have been minor irritations and teething troubles to sort out. Some could have been avoided by taking note of hard-won experience elsewhere.

Finally, how did the name SUPERTRAM come into being. No doubt there are many versions but the author believes that it was the brainchild of Bernard Pratt. He pressed for a name to be chosen, and certainly during the early '80's, suggested SUPERTRAM. An anecdote of genuine pedigree says that one of the co-directors of the SPTS Study (Bill Kirkland) phoned Bernard at home one evening and Bernard's son answered. He was told who was calling and was asked to tell his father. The child called his father with the words " It's the man to talk to you about SUPERTRAM". When Bernard came on to the phone, Bill said to him "I give up Bernard, you've even got your family plugging the name".

As the book goes to press concerns are being expressed about the low passenger usage and mounting operating losses of Supertram. The four local authorities (Note: not SYPTA) have commissioned an investigation by management consultants as to what should be done with the system. Meanwhile SYPTE has invited expressions of interest from organisations wanting to take over the operating concession. It is unfortunate that such a technically fine system should be marred by its disappointing performance.

APPENDICES

CHRONOLOGY OF SERVICE DEVELOPMENT

9/9/73, 11/11/73, 1/4/74, 8/12/74, 3/2/75, phased introduction of County-wide service numbering system.

3/3/74   Service 68 Sheffield-Huddersfield-Halifax diverted to run via service X68 and retained. YT.

8/12/75   New service 87 Sheffield-Marchwood introduced.

7/3/76   Revised services 381/384 Barnsley-Stocksbridge-Penistone YT.

22/3/76   Increased frequency on service 171 Doncaster-West Bessacarr

3/5/76   New services 15/16 Hillsborough-Walkley-Crookes introduced.

3/5/76   Revised service 66 Stocksbridge local service.

3/5/76   Revised service 166 Doncaster-Broomhouse Lane (Balby), and new service 157 Doncaster-Alverley Lane (Balby) introduced.

7/6/76   Service X23 Rotherham-Todwick withdrawn and replaced by new service 123 Rotherham-Todwick.

14/6/76   Additional journeys introduced on Baddeley Bros (un-numbered) service between Cubley, Penistone and Holmfirth.

14/6/76   Additional journeys introduced on service 261 Sheffield-Mosborough (Westfield).

18/7/76   Services 82 and 83 revised at Greystones and Ecclesall to form new services 83 and 84 (Middlewood-Sheffield-Ecclesall).

9/8/76   Additional journeys introduced on T. Severn (un-numbered) service between Doncaster, Fishlake and Sykehouse and all journeys diverted via South Bramwith.

21/8/76   Certain journeys on service 274 Mexborough-Goldthorpe extended to Ingsfield Lane, Bolton-on-Dearne YT.

5/9/76   Service 1 (Sheffield-Pitsmoor, Roe Lane) extended to Longley. Certain journeys further extended to Sandstone Road. Service 39 (Upwell Street-Sheffield-Millhouses) and certain journeys on service 34 (Upwell Street-Sheffield-Graves Park) extended to Sandstone Road.

5/9/76   Servicd 17 (Hillsborough-Sheffield-Beauchief) diverted at Millhouses to Totley Book. New service 26 Sheffield-Beauchief introduced.

27/9/76   Certain journeys on services 158/159 (Weston Road-Doncaster-Clay Lane) extended to Edenthorpe.

27/9/76   Certain journeys on service 165 (Doncaster-Bentley) diverted to run in loop in opposite direction in Bentley Village and renumbered 195.

27/9/76   Service 170 (Doncaster-Cantley) extended in Cantley to Cantley Lane.

27/9/76   Service 172 (Doncaster-Hexthorpe) route revised in Hexthorpe.

27/9/76   Service 197 Doncaster-Edlington (Howbeck Drive) route revised between Warmsworth and Edlington.

4/10/76   New service X69 Sheffield-Penistone, one journey only, introduced as replacement for cancelled rail service.

19/10/76   Service 403 (Doncaster-Askern) revised on Saturday and introduced on Tuesday and Friday. WRAC.

21/11/76   Additional evening and Sunday journeys introduced on service 261 Sheffield-Mosborough (Westfield).

17/1/77   Additional journeys introduced on service 154 Doncaster-Castle Hills.

24/1/77   Additional journeys introduced on service 254 Sheffield-Dronfield B&F.

30/1/77   Service 261 Sheffield-Mosborough (Westfield) extended to Owdthorpe Greenway and additional journeys introduced.

31/1/77   Additional journeys introduced on service 1 between Sheffield and Longley.

10/4/77   New service 238 Sheffield-Chatsworth Park introduced on Summer Sunday and Bank Holiday Monday.

25/4/77   New service 259 Halfway-Mosborough-Plumbley introduced B&F.

9/5/77   Service 125 Rotherham-Whiston via Moorgate and service 135 Rotherham-Whiston via Broom Valley linked to form circular services 125/135.

2/5/77   Additional journeys introduced on service 197 Doncaster-Edlington (Howbeck Drive).

23/5/77   Additional journeys introduced on T. Severn (un-numbered) services between Doncaster, Fishlake and Sykehouse.

16/8/77   Service 403 Doncaster-Askern diverted via Braithwaite and Kirkhouse Green. WRAC.

29/8/77   New service X7 Sheffield-Matlby introduced (Express service, Monday to Friday, peaks only).

28/8/77   New service X30 Sheffield-Mosborough (Halfway) via Sheffield Parkway introduced.

3/10/77   Certain evening journeys on service 97 (Nether Edge-Sheffield-Southey Green) extended to Wordsworth Avenue until 3/12/77.

11/12/77   New service X8 Sheffield-Dronfield (Gosforth Valley) introduced. B&F.

11/3/78   Additional journeys introduced on service X30 Sheffield-Mosborough (Halfway).

21/5/78   Major service changed affecting many routes on the Barnsley-Dearne Valley-Doncaster corridor. YT.

5/6/78   Certain journeys on service 34 (Graves Park-Sheffield-Upwell Street) extended to Wensley Street and Hindl House Crescent.

1/9/78   Service 259 Halfway-Mosborough-Plumbley withdrawn. B&F.

24/9/78   Further changes to several routes on the Barnsley-Dearne Valley-Doncaster corridor. YT.

2/10/78   Service 180 Doncaster-Kendal Road run Monday to Friday instead of Tuesday and Friday only.

9/10/78   Revised services 55/156 Doncaster-Rossington, routes revised in Rossington and renumbered 155/156 (E. M. journeys unchanged).

9/10/78   S. Morgan (un-numbered) Doncaster-Goole service revised.

5/2/79   Revised services 139/140/141 Rotherham-Kimberworth Circles and new service 142 introduced.

18/3/79   New service X29 Sheffield-Mosborough (Waterthorpe and Halfway) introduced. B&F.

3/6/79   Several services in Thurnscoe revised. YT.

10/6/79   Major service changes affecting many routes in Doncaster-Hemsworth-Pontefract area (joint scheme with WYPTE) YT, WRAC.

10/6/79   Additional journeys introduced on service 123 Rotherham-Todwick.

9/7/79   Increased frequency on service X29 Sheffield-Mosborough (Waterthorpe and Halfway) B&F integrated into PTE operations.

5/8/79   Service 97 Nether Edge-Sheffield-Southley Green extended to Hillsborough.

2/9/79   Service 60 (Sheffield-Crimicar Lane). Extended in city centre from Midland Station to Central Bus Station.

3/9/79   New service 888 Hillsborough-Roscoe Bank (Hall Park Head) introduced.

3/9/79   All service 95 journeys run to Tinker Lane, Walsley instead of South Road (Intake-Sheffield-Walkley).

3/9/79   Articulated buses introduced onto Sheffield City Clipper.

15/10/79   Additional journeys introduced on service 207 Sheffield-Woodsetts.

6/1/80   Service 55 (Doncaster-Rossington, East Midland journeys) renumbered 155 and ran via same route as other service 155 journeys. EM.

28/1/80   Certain journeys on service 297 Mexborough-Conisbrough diverted via Hill Top, Denaby and renumbered 291.

18/2/80   New service 103 Rotherham-Flanderwell introduced.

18/2/80   New services 120/129 Rotherham-Dinnington circles introduced. Service 126 Rotherham-Aston extended to Kiveton Park. Service 123 Rotherham-Todwick withdrawn. Services 256/257 withdrawn between Kiveton Park and Todwick.

9/3/80   Additional journeys and double-deck buses introduced on service X29 Sheffield-Mosborough (Waterthorpe and Halfway).

24/3/80   Service 250 (no longer T. Severn) Doncaster-Goole diverted via Edenthorpe, revised route in Stainforth.

24/3/80   Additional journeys introduced between Conanby and Doncaster on service 278 Sheffield-Rotherham-Doncaster.

30/3/80   Services 47/48 Sheffield-Shiregreen extended in City Centre from Bridge Street to Flat Street.

30/3/80   Increased frequency introduced on service 60 Sheffield-Crimicar Lane.

31/3/80   Additional journeys introduced on service 87 Sheffield-Marchwood.

31/3/80   Additional journeys introduced on service 888 between Sheffield and Roscoe Bank (Hall Park Head) replacing Hillsborough-Roscoe Bank service.

31/3/80   Additional journeys introduced between Sheffield and Chapeltown on service 80 Sheffield-High Green.

31/3/80	Additional journeys introduced on service 36 Sheffield-Batemoor.
24/5/80	New services 209/210 Sheffield-Matlock. Summer Saturday service operated by Trent, Summer Sunday and Bank Holiday service via Chatsworth Park operated by SYPTE.
3/8/80	Major revision to services between Sheffield, Dronfield and Chesterfield, replacing all existing services (joint scheme with Derbyshire County Council, jointly operated with Chesterfield Transport).
4/8/80	New service 200 Sheffield-Chesterfield-Clay Cross.
5/10/80	Service 10 Rotherham-Chesterfield diverted at Beighton via Westfield and Halfway. BM.
8/11/80	SYPTE replaces Ribble on service X48 Sheffield-Manchester. Revised timetable.
6/12/80	Changes to services in Scawsby, Skellow and Sprotbrough. YT.
14/12/80	Services 270/271 Sheffield-Upton withdrawn between Hemsworth and Upton.
14/12/80	Service 273 Barnsley-Mexborough, Sunday only route revised in Thurnscoe. YT.
22/3/81	Service X19 Doncaster-Barnsley-Manchester withdrawn between Barnsley and Manchester.
30/3/81	Service 250 Doncaster-Goole withdrawn between Moorends and Goole.
15/4/81	Service 255 Sheffield-Dronfield withdrawn and replaced by additional service 285 journeys.
19/4/81	Services 209/210 Sheffield-Matlockl re-introduced for summer. Service 210 extended to Crich.
20/4/81	Revised routes in Brinsworth and Catcliffe on services 130/131/132/133 Rotherham-Brinsworth/Catcliffe.
20(?)/4/81	New services 143 Rotherham-Swallownest, 144 Rotherham-Wentworth and 145 Rotherham-Maltby introduced.
20/4/81	New services 266/267 Rotherham-High Green introduced. Service 116 Rotherham-Chapeltown withdrawn.
3/5/81	New service 248 Sheffield-Woodhead-Glossop introduced on Summer Sunday and Bank Holiday.
25/5/81	Service X36 Rotherham-Barnsley-Leeds withdrawn between Barnsley and Leeds.
?/6/81	Major changes to Barnsley Town Services. YT.
9/8/81	Service 410 Doncaster-Pomtefract diverted via Lutterworth Drive, Woodlands. SYRT.
9/12/81	New service 255 Woodall-Worksop introduced, Wednesday and Saturday.
15/2/82	New service 78 Sheffield-Chapeltown introduced.
11/4/82	Services 209/210 reintroduced for Summer, as 1981.
13/4/82	New service 196 Doncaster-Florence Avenue (Balby) introduced.
17/4/82	New services 237/238/239 Sheffield-Huddersfield-Halifax introduced, replacing service X68. Services 237 and 239 via X68 route, 238 via Grenoside. YT.
17/4/82	Major service changes affecting many routes between Barnsley and Huddersfield, including Penistone, Silkstone and Kexborough. Other changes to Barnsley Town Services. YT.
17/4/82	Services 224/225 Doncaster-Kilnhurst diverted via Hill Top Road, Denaby.
19/4/82	Certain journeys on service 182 Doncaster-Armthorpe diverted via Wickett Hern Road.
28/6/82	New service 116 Rotherham-Thorpe Hesley (Chapelfields) introduced. Service 258 Sheffield-Thorpe Hesley extended to Chapelfields.
3/7/82	New service 342 Barnsley-Shafton Green introduced. YT.
11/7/82	New service 851 Sheffield-Wyming Brook introduced on Summer Sunday and Bank Holiday.
18/7/82	New service X25 Sheffield-Bawtry introduced.
3/10/82	Service 88 extended at Roscoe Bank to Hall Park Head. Service 888 withdrawn.
17/10/82	Service 410 Doncaster-Pontefract diverted at Woodlands via Bosworth Road. SYRT.
30/10/82	Additional journeys introduced on services 381, 382 and 384 between Barnsley and Penistone. YT.
6/12/82	Services 15/16 Hillsborough-Crookes circular services extended at Hillsborough and at Crookes, and via Langsett Estate.
6/12/82	Service 39 Sandstone Road-Sheffield-Millhouses diverted at Woodsetts to Chancet Wood instead of Millhouses.
20/2/83	Aditional journeys introduced on service 191 Doncaster-Finningley. LEON
28/2/83	Service X91 Sheffield-Thurnscoe extended in Thurscoe.
7/3/83	Services X33/X34 Sheffield-Bradford revised as services X33.
7(?)/3/83	Network of 'City Nipper' services in Sheffield introduced, occasional services operated by minibuses.
25/4/83	Service 126 Rotherham-Kiverton Park extended to Harthill.
1/5/83	Service 210 reintroduced for Summer (service 209 not operated).
3/7/83	Certain journeys on service 253 Sheffield-High Moor diverted to Rother Valley Country Park on Summer Sunday.
31/7/83	Service 851 reintroduced for Summer (as 1982)
8/8/83	Special network of services for the disabled introduced in Doncaster.
4/9/83	Major revision to services in Stocksbridge area, including direct services from Sheffield to the Estates, and cancellation of local services.
5/9/83	New service 259 Sheffield-Mosborough (Plumbley) introduced.
12/11/83	Further changes to services between Barnsley and Penistone. YT.
14/11/83	Services 158/159 Weston Road-Doncaster-Edenthorpe extended to Edenthorpe District Centre. Service 159 route revised.
14/11/83	Network of 'Nipper in Rotherham' services inbtroduced. Service 113 renumbered N13, as part of network.
15/11/83	New service 417 Cantley-Edenthorpe-Barnby Dun introduced until 31/3/84.
10/12/83	Services 151/163 Doncaster-Skellow-Bughwallis extended from Burghwallis to Askern. YT
?/12/83	Special network of services for the disabled introduced in Barnsley.
8/1/84	New service 280 Sheffield-Edale introduced on Sunday and Bank Holiday.
12/1/84	Increased frequency on service 60 Sheffield-Crimicar Lane.
25/2/84	New service 315 Barnsley-Ward Green introduced.
26/2/84	New service X28 Sheffield-Beighton (Manor Farm Park) introduced.
5/3/84	Services 85 and 99 (Chesterfield journeys) transferred to East Midland.
24/3/84	Certain journeys on service 85 Sheffield-Retford-Gainsborough diverted via Woodseats. Service 220 Sheffield-Aston introduced.
25/3/85	Simplified fares in 5p multiples introduced.
25/3/84	New services 263 Rotherham-Eckington and 264 Rotherham-Worksop introduced. Services 10, 143 and 256 withdrawn.
26/3/84	Service 99 journeys to Gleadless operated by SYPTE renumbered 25. Journeys to Chesterfield renumbered 55/55A.
25/3/84	All service 85 journeys diverted via Woodsetts
26/3/84	New service X15 Sheffield-Aston introduced.
?/4/84	Major revision to services in Mosborough and Beighton areas, service 25 replaced by 254/255. X30 renumbered 252 and linked to 253 as circular service. X51/X52 Sheffield-Harthill/Spinkill replaced 46/251.
27/5/84	New service 5 Sheffield-Strines circular introduced on Summer Sunday and Bank Holiday.
27/5/84	Service 851 reintroduced for Summer (as 1983)
27/5/84	New service 209 Mosborough-Buxton introduced on Summer Sunday and Bank Holiday.
29/7/84	Services from Sheffield, Rotherham and Swallownest to Rother Valley Country Park introduced for Summer.
28/8/84	Services 8/9 Sheffield Inner Circle diverted between Pitsmoor and Norfolk Bridge to City Centre.
28/8/84	New service X4 Sheffield-Dinnington via M1 Motorway introduced.

23/9/84   Changes to services in Mosborough (Halfway) affecting 252, 253, 263, 264.
16/10/84 New service 198 Doncaster-Old Cantley introduced.
26/11/84 Service 207 Sheffield-Woodsetts withdrawn.
2/12/84   Evening and Sunday service intrtoduced between Ecclesall and Millhouses.
3/12/84   Service 39 Doncaster-Stainton withdrawn. Replaced by revised 147 Doncaster-Worksop. 145 Rotherham-Maltby extended to Stainton.
6/1/85   Service 208 Sheffield-Hanley (Trent) curtailed at Buxton. New service X23 Sheffield-Potteries introduced, operated by PMT.
7/1/85   Service 774 (until 17/2/86) Sheffield-Norton diverted via Hanover Way and renumbered 40.
30/3/85   New service X20 Barnsley-Doncaster introduced. YTC.
?/4/85   Services to Rother Valley Country Park reinstated (as 1984)
?/4/85   Improvements to late-night and early morning services in Sheffield.
28/4/85   Service 192 Doncaster-Finingley-Misson extended to Bawtry.
5/5/85   Service 280 Sheffield-Edale withdrawn between Hathersage and Edale.
19/5/85   New service 6, Deepcar-Bolsterstone-Ewden Valley introduced on Sunday and Bank Holiday
20/5/85   Service 197 Doncaster-Edlington (Howbeck Drive) diverted via St. Peter's Road. Service 169 Doncaster-St. Peter's Road withdrawn.
20/5/85   Service 180 Doncaster-Kendal Road extended to Scawthorpe.
27/5/85   Services 5, 851 reintroduced for Summer (as 1984).
27/5/85   Service 400 Barnsley-Castleton introduced on Sunday and Bank Holiday. YT.
3/6/85   Network of 'Nipper' services in Hillsborough introduced, occasional services operated by minibuses. Services 15/16 withdrawn.
3/6/85   Services 237/238/239 renumbered X37/X38/X39
16/7/85   New service 103 Rotherham-Flanderwell introduced. Service 102 Rotherham-Maltby diverted in Maltby.
29/7/85   Services 200/201 renumbered X10/X11. New service X12 Sheffield-Chesterfield-Walton introduced.
4/8/85   Service 7 Sheffield-Stannington renumbered 86. All services terminating at Campo Lane, Sheffield extended to Central Bus Station.
27/8/85   Service 240 Sheffield-Bakewell diverted via Baslow
1/9/85   Service X25 Sheffield-Bawtry extended to Doncaster. New service X24 Sheffield-Doncaster (via Tickhill) introduced.
23/9/85   New service 35 Sheffield-Sandstone Road, via Beacon Way introduced.
28/9/85   Changes to Barnsley town services. YT.
21/10/85 Services 8/9 Sheffield Inner Circle diverted to serve Royal Hallamshire Hospital.
1/11/95   Network of 'Nipper' services in Barnsley introduced, occasional services operated by minibuses.
2/11/85   Service X90 Sheffield-Mexborough revised and co-ordinated with X91. YT.
18/11/85 Service 186 Doncaster-Thorne-Moorends revised to provide additional journeys to HM Prison, Lindholme.
9/12/85   New service X64 Sheffield-High Green introduced.
16/2/86   Major revision to services in Mosborough and Beighton areas. New service X27 Sheffield-Beighton. Services 254/255 Sheffield-Beighton circles replaced by 260/261.
6/4/86   Large increase in fares due to removal of blanket subsidy. 5p fare introduced on Sheffield City Clipper (previously free).
6/4/86   Services to Rother Valley Country Park re-introduced for Summer (as 1985).
6/4/86   Most remaining conductor-operated services converted to one-man operation.
25/5/86   Services 5/400 re-introduced for Summer (as 1985). Service 851 not reintroduced.
31/5/86   Service revisions including some timetable reductions to many Yorkshire Traction services in Barnsley, Wombwell and Doncaster.
29/6/86, 27/7/86, 10/8/86 programme of timetable revisions reducing frequency of many services in Sheffield.
29/7/86   Service revisions including some timetable reductions to many Yorkshire Traction services in Cudworth, Shafton, Penistone.
11/8/86   Special network of services for the disabled introduced in Sheffield.
26/8/86   New service M10 Plumbley-Waterthorpe introduced in Mosborough.

YT – Yorkshire Traction
EM – East Midland
B&F – Booth and Fisher
WRAC – West Riding
SYRT – South Yorkshire Road Transport

COMPARISON OF STATISTICS

		SYPTE 1985/86	SYT 1986/87
EMPLOYEES	Total	4,976	3,213
	Platform	2,805	1,921
	Engineering	1,221	806
	Other	950	486
FLEET		1,053	951
VEHICLE MILES (millions)		35.6	31.6
PASSENGER JOURNEYS (millions)		265.2	190.0

Comparison of 1986/7 with 1985/6		
	SYT	SYPTE
Miles per employee	+ 37.5%	
Revenue per employee	+ 11.0%	

DIRECTORS AND OFFICERS

DIRECTORS GENERAL

Noel McDonald	1974-1976
H. Norman Kay	1976-1984
Ian P. Smith	1984-1988
Jim H. M. Russell	1988-date

SECRETARY

T. D. Ian Hoskisson   1974-date

DIRECTORS OF FINANCE

Dennis Eyres   1974-1978
Alex F. Ritchie[1]   1979-date

COMMERCIAL DIRECTOR

Ian P. Smith   1980-1984
Peter J. Sephton   1984-1986

DIRECTOR OF OPERATIONS AND PLANNING

H. Norman Kay   1974-1976

DIRECTOR OF PLANNING

Albert E. Booth   1986-1988
Phil J. Haywood   1988-date

DIRECTOR OF ENGINEERING

Eric Kay   1974-1980

TECHNICAL DIRECTOR

Eric Kay   1980-1984
Albert E. Booth   1984-1986

DIRECTOR OF INDUSTRIAL RELATIONS

Len J. Trueman   1974-1980

CONTROLLER OF OPERATIONS AND PLANNING

D. Scott Hellewell[2]   1976-86
Bob Rowe[3]   1984-1986

CONTROLLER OF ENGINEERING AND PROPERTY SERVICES

Bill Kirkland   1979-1986

CONTROLLER OF MANPOWER SERVICES

Ian P. Smith   1979-1980
Wilf Kemp   1980-1986

[1]Chief Finance Officer 1977-1986
[2]Controller of Executive Planning and Development 1985-1986
[3]Controller of Operations 1984

BIBLIOGRAPHY

1. *Sheffield Transport* by C. C. Hall

2. *Traffic in Towns* (The Buchanan Report), 1963, HMSO

3. White Paper *Transport Policy* (Cmnd 3057), July 1966, HMSO

4. White Paper *Public Transport & Traffic* (Cmnd 3481), December 1967, HMSO

5. Transport Act 1968

6. Local Government Act 1972

7. Sheffield & Rotherham Lane Use/Transportation Study

8. *The Rise & Fall of the Republic of South Yorkshire* by Alan Clarke, Sheaf Publishing, Sheffield

9. *Tomorrow's Transport for South Yorkshire*, September 1974, SYPTA

10. White Paper *Buses* (Cmnd 9300), July 1984, HMSO

11. White Paper *Streamlining the cities*, (Cmnd 9063), October 1984, HMSO

12. *London Transport & the Politicians*, by Paul E. Garbutt, Ian Allan Ltd 1985

13. *Subsidised Public Transport and the Demand for Travel* by Dr P. B. Goodwin and others, published by Gower, 1983

14. *The Case for the PTE* produced by SYPTE, January 1984

15. South Yorkshire Transport Yearbook, 1986 edition, published by SYPTE

16. New Double Decker for South Yorkshire, 'Buses', Ian Allan, June 1976

17. Transport Development Plan, SYPTE, 1978

18. South Yorkshire Transport Trolleybus Act

19. *Yorkshire Traction, Early Development*, by J. S. Sykes, published by YTC in 1982.

20. South Yorkshire's Transport Prospectus, SYPTE, March 1976

21. *Rail Passenger Concepts for South Yorkshire*, General Manager, British Rail, Eastern Region, York, November 1973.

22. *The Future of Railways in South Yorkshire*, SYPTE January 1977

23. *The long-term future of local rail services in South Yorkshire*, SYPTE, April 1979

24. *Railway Stations in South Yorkshire*, SYPTE, November 1981

25. *Streamlining the Cities* (Cmnd 9063), October 1984, HMSO

26. *A Strategy for Survival*]
    A Hitch-hiker's Guide to SYPTE, Autumn 1985
    the 1985 Transport Bill]

27. *Lessons of the 1980 Transport Act*, R. P. Kilvington, Newcastle Transport Symposium 1985

28. SYT Prospectus]
    SYT Business Plan] SYPTE March 31st 1986

29. *I tried to run a Railway* by Gerard Fiennes, Ian Allan Ltd, 1967

30. *Passenger Transport Integration Pilot Study, Sheffield Area.* Sheffield University Working Group for Yorkshire and Humberside Economic Planning Council, 1966

31. *The Future of Public Transport in Sheffield - Results of Preliminary Investigation*, SYPTE, January 1980

32. Segregated Passenger Transport System, SPTS Working Group, SYPTE, July 1983

33. South Yorkshire Light Rail Transit Bill, SYPTE, November 1985

34. Commemorative Brochure on the Official Opening of South Yorkshire Supertram, May 23rd 1994, SYPTE.

35. *South Yorkshire Supertram - Achieving Government Funding* by Peter Hague, MVA Consultancy, Light Rail '94 Conference, Sheffield November 1994

36. *South Yorkshire Supertram - The detailed design of an on-street tramway, a Client Overview* by Peter J. Gross, SYSL, Light Rail '94 Conference.

37. *South Yorkshire Supertram - Tram Operation in Sheffield* by Peter Fox, Light Rail Review No. 6, Platform 5 Publishing Ltd, November 1994

38. *Managing the Project* by W. K. Woolgar, Light Rail '94 Conference

39. *Designing & Building the Supertram cars* by David Wilson, Siemans/Düwag, Light Rail '94 Conference

40. *Operating the Supertram System: Initial Experience* by Wilfred Lau, SYSL, Light Rail '94 Conference

INDEX